Evolution of the multinational corporation,
centralised management capable of mobilis
resources and production across frontiers,
had a profound effect on the political and
economic life of otherwise sovereign countries.

Although this excellent study has taken for its
theme the British experience of the rapid growth
of such corporations, it provides a mass of
evidence which can be used to evaluate their
impact elsewhere. The problem to be solved is
how governments can avoid being by-passed
not only by the multinational company but by
currency speculators and others who can
condition the environment within which
government has to create and implement its
policy.

The book examines the methods used by the
British Government to control foreign-owned
firms as distinct from purely British firms, and
the development of policy towards foreign
investment using the motor and computer
industries as examples.

Dr Michael Hodges is lecturer in inter-
disciplinary studies at the University of Kent. He
studied law and history at St. John's,
Cambridge and international relations at the
University of Pennsylvania. European integration
is his present preoccupation.

MULTINATIONAL CORPORATIONS

AND NATIONAL GOVERNMENT

For my parents

Multinational Corporations and National Government

A case study of the United Kingdom's experience 1964–1970

MICHAEL HODGES

SAXON HOUSE | LEXINGTON BOOKS

BIP 00

Published by

SAXON HOUSE, D.C. Heath Ltd.,
Westmead, Farnborough, Hants England

Jointly with

LEXINGTON BOOKS, D.C. Heath & Co.
Lexington Mass. U.S.A.

ISBN 0 347 01034 2
Library of Congress Catalog Card Number 73–21195

Printed in Great Britain by
Kingprint Limited, Richmond, Surrey

Contents

List of tables

Acknowledgements

In a study of contemporary policy-making such as this, primary documents are frequently unavailable because of their confidential nature. I am therefore grateful to the many civil servants, politicians, academics and businessmen who gave so freely of their time in order to clarify the many complex issues involved. Because of the sensitive nature of the subject, few of them can be named, but I am indebted to all of them for their information and advice. As every social scientist knows, comment is free but facts are expensive; I am indebted to the Trustees of the University of Pennsylvania for awarding me Thouron and Penfield Fellowships which made my research possible. I am also grateful to Conrad Jameson Associates (London) for allowing me to use their survey data on British élite attitudes.

One of the defects of the British educational system is that it does not require typing as a basic skill; I am therefore especially grateful to my wife Marilyn for transmuting my uncertain had into type (and to our son Adam for allowing her sufficient time to do so) and for her constant support and encouragement during the elephantine gestation period of this study.

This book originated as a Ph.D. dissertation, and I would like to express my appreciation to my supervisor Professor H.V. Perlmutter of the Wharton School of Finance and Commerce, and to Professor John Dunning of Reading University, for their encouragement and advice. Needless to say, any sins of omission or commission are entirely mine.

Michael Hodges,
September 1973.

1 Multinational Corporations and National Government : The Politics of Transnational Relations

1.1 Towards a wider view of international relations

In recent years there has been increasing criticism of the state-centric paradigm of international relations, which assumes that states are the prime actors in world politics and that the behaviour of non-governmental actors merely conditions the environment within which inter-state politics take place.[1] Critics of the state-centric paradigm argue that it has never been a wholly accurate description of historical reality, and that it has led to an artificial separation by scholars of intra—state and inter-state politics, with the concept of sovereignty acting as a methodological barrier between the two:

> To the expert on domestic politics sovereignty is like a screen cutting off the nation-state from the outside world; intrusions from the outside are accidents, exceptions, and when they do occur do so only within fixed parameters. Sovereignty allows the expert in international politics to treat domestic processes as formally independent from international events which he can then analyze as the interaction of states reacting to external stimuli.[2]

The result of this separation has been that both groups of scholars have developed distinct and incompatible theories and methodologies to deal with their chosen level of analysis,[3] and that neither group has paid more than peripheral attention to the linkages between domestic and international politics brought about by transnational interactions — 'the movement of tangible or intangible items across state boundaries when at least one actor is not an agent of a government or an intergovernmental organisation.'[4] Although foreign policy analysis, which seeks 'to explain foreign policy behaviour as the output of subnational organisations following standard operating procedures or engaging in a problem-solving search,'[5]

1

has attempted to surmount the sovereignty barrier, it has done so by examining the internal dynamics of the foreign policy-making bureaucracies and their effect on interactions at the level of the international system. Even so, it has tended to isolate these dynamics from the rest of the domestic political process, paying little attention to transnational interactions at the societal (i.e. non-governmental) level.[6]

While such transnational interactions have long existed in the modern state system — the influence of the Roman Catholic Church in the domestic politics of European states is an example[7] — developments in technology, particularly in transport and communications systems, have reduced the temporal and spatial barriers between nation-states, and have greatly increased the possibility of interactions between one society and another. Indeed, the factors which have enabled national governments to exercise greater control over their respective societies are identical to those which enable societies to interact with one another in ways which bypass and even undermine the control of national governments:

> Paradoxically, perhaps, the power and also the impotence of a community and the state have mounted simultaneously in a single process: these changes in international conditions have proceeded from precisely those technical, social and economic forces which have been producing the highly integrated community and the modern state.[8]

Although transnational interactions involving non-governmental actors do not necessarily affect the primacy of the state in the regulation of society, or its pre-eminent role in international relations (indeed, transnational interactions at the societal level often are only possible because the state permits them to take place), they do alter relationships both within and between states by creating interdependencies — mutual contingencies which affect the behaviour of the parties involved by placing constraints on their freedom of action — which cut across existing state boundaries.

One vivid example of this process can be seen in the field of speculative currency movements caused by non-governmental actors; while the 'massive run' on sterling in August 1947 amounted to under $ 100 million a day, speculation on a revaluation of the mark led to a movement of over $1000 million into Germany in less than an hour in May 1971.[9] The ability of private bodies to make rapid transfers of currency across national frontiers has not only increased dramatically, but also places increasing constraints on the capacity of national governments to plan and control economic development,[10] and induces them to reassess their existing relationships with other national governments; thus in the dollar crisis of summer 1971 the Nixon administration used the monetary forum as an arena in which to achieve objectives in the security field (to reduce the cost of American overseas troop deployment), and in the trade field (to reduce the protectionist stance of the EEC in relation to American exports).[11]

Although analysts of national political systems have recognised that developments within these systems are conditioned by events in the wider environment, and students of international politics admit that changes within states affect the character of the international political system, the scale and intensity of such transnational interactions can no longer justify the tendency of both schools to 'treat linkages as parameters rather than as data.'[12] An alternative approach, which takes account of these transnational interactions and their effects on domestic and international politics, is the 'transnational politics' model suggested by Karl Kaiser.[13] Kaiser argues that 'transnational politics can be loosely defined as those political processes between national governments (and international organizations) that have been set in motion by interaction within a transnational society', and that such politics are a function of 'horizontal interaction' between various states and various societies and 'vertical interaction' between individual societies and their governmental institutions.[14]

The two types of interaction, while analytically distinct, are both prerequisites for the emergence of transnational politics; if a society is isolated from its counterparts, there is little horizontal interaction which might affect the decision-making framework of its governmental institutions; if there is little vertical interaction between state and society, then horizontal interaction will not be considered relevant to the fulfilment of the tasks of government. In recent times, however, both types of interaction have been increasing, particularly in the industrialised democracies of the west: on the one hand, trade, travel and investment overseas has greatly increased, and is perhaps leading to the creation of a 'transnational society', to use Aron's phrase;[15] while on the other, the evolution of industrialised societies from monarchy to democracy, and from *laissez-faire* economic policies to central economic planning and intervention (including the use of public money to achieve desired objectives of increased welfare and full employment), has made governments less willing to tolerate economic disturbance caused by forces beyond their immediate control.[16] At the same time as technological developments permit a greater degree of transnational interaction, the increase in vertical interaction between societies and their governmental institutions, caused by a growing degree of interventionism on the part of governments (and hence a greater sensitivity to environmental disturbances) and by the advent of mass democracy (which

3

obliges governments to deal with such disturbances in order to preserve electoral support), renders the nation-state much more sensitive to transnational activity than was hitherto the case.

Morse has, indeed, suggested that economic interdependencies have become important policy issues for governments, not only because they constrain policy choices at a time when governmental responsibility for economic management is increasing, but also because 'economic affairs present possibilities for manipulation which are less dramatically costly than manipulation in military and security matters.'[17] Thus economic interdependencies have broadened the range of issues involved in the diplomacy of industrialised states, and provided new forms of diplomatic leverage in inter-state relations.

Indeed, it is the increasing *sensitivity* of national governments to transnational interaction which is at the heart of the issue of interdependence; those who argue that interdependence is decreasing in importance, because the ratio of international trade and investment to domestic economic activity is declining,[18] or that 'interdependence' is in reality a euphemism for asymmetric dependency relationships,[19] are unable to explain why national governments have increasingly assumed the existence of such interdependencies in the formulation of their economic policies.[20] The overall ratio of foreign to domestic economic activity may not be a valid measure of interdependency if the sectoral distribution of the two is not identical — one cannot argue that interdependence is decreasing simply because domestic sales of refrigerators and lawn-mowers have outpaced foreign sales of computers and aircraft — in economics as in politics, there are 'high' and 'low' issues. Similarly, interdependence does not necessarily imply mutual vulnerability, but rather the existence of constraints on the freedom of action of the parties involved, however unequally these may be distributed between them.

1.2   Multinational corporations as transnational actors

If transnational interaction is becoming of increasing importance as an influence on both inter-and intra-state politics, who or what are the agents of this process? The Catholic Church, currency speculators, and tourists have already been cited as examples of organised or informal societal groups which bypass national governments and exert an influence on many societies simultaneously, conditioning the environment within which national governments can formulate and execute their policies. Many other examples could be given, but, as the burgeoning literature on the subject demonstrates, perhaps the most important of these non-governmental transnational actors is the multinational corporation. [21] Although the multinational corporation, which Vernon has defined as 'a cluster of corporations of different nationalities that are joined together by a parent company through bonds of common ownership, that respond to a common strategy, and that draw on a common pool of human and financial resources,' [22] is not a new phenomenon (indeed, one can trace its historical antecedents to the East India Company of the eighteenth century, or even the Hanseatic League two centuries earlier), the rapid growth of international direct investment since the end of the Second World War has produced a situation in which international investment has surpassed trade as the major channel of international economic relations between the industrialised countries of the world. [23] According to OECD estimates, the combined exports of the ten leading capital-exporting countries came to over $130 billion in 1967, while the value of production arising from foreign direct investment in that year amounted to $240 billion. [24] Modelski has argued that:

> ... corporations are an important part of present and future international systems and, even though we need not think of them as becoming governmental organisations in their own right, their political functions as structural components of systems of world politics can only be neglected at our peril. [25]

Developments in technology have now made it no more difficult for a corporation based in New York to control production in Europe, four thousand miles to the east, than to operate plants in California, three thousand miles to the west; a typical IBM 360 computer installation sold in Britain might contain components from as many as four or five IBM plants in different countries. [26] Because multinational companies are responsible for mobilising factors of production across national frontiers, allocating resources among their operations in different nation-states in accordance with a centralised management control system, they can be seen as transnational actors *par excellence.* Indeed, the power of multinational corporations *vis-à-vis* nation-states has been the subject of some debate among economists and political scientists; Kindleberger has gone so far as to say that 'the nation-state is just about through as an economic unit', while Gilpin has contended that 'the role of the nation-state in economic as well as in political life is increasing and that the multinational corporation is actually a stimulant to the further extension of state power in the economic realm.'[27]

Despite the proliferation of tables comparing the GNP of nation-states with the turnover of large multinational corporations, the verdict is not yet in on whether General Motors (1966 turnover $20·2 billion) or Belgium (1966 GNP $18·1 billion) has a better chance of survival in the centuries to come. [28] Nevertheless, the source of the tension between multinational corporations and national governments (as the previous section of this chapter indicated) can only be understood if the growth and spread of multinational companies is seen to have taken place at the same time as the growth in the number of sovereign states and the increasing importance of economic development and economic management as the major function of their governments [29] Although multinational companies in manufacturing (as opposed to resource-based companies which had perforce to be multinational in order to bridge the gap between their sources of raw material and their markets) began to develop at the end of the nineteenth century, [30] they did so at a time when national governments attempted only the minimum of economic management. It is therefore not surprising that the transnational activities of these multinational companies were not considered to be relevant to the policy objectives of host governments; F.A. Mackenzie, the Servan–Schreiber of his day, addressed his 1902 warning of the 'American Invaders' not to the British Government but to British manufacturers. [31]

For the reasons given in the preceding section of this chapter, this situation has now changed — as Kaiser has noted:

> ... in the same way the large corporation has become an essential characteristic of advanced industrial societies, the multinational corporation is becoming one of the basic structural elements of the interdependent multinational economy that is emerging from the international economy of the past. ... With the possible exception of monetary relations there is hardly any area in which transnational politics is likely to have such a substantial impact on world politics in the near future. [32]

Multinational corporations, however, are no more homogeneous than national governments, and in elaborating the national government-multinational corporation interface it is as important to distinguish between the various types of multinational corporation as it is to differentiate between the aspirations of various national governments and their attitudes toward foreign investment. The emergence of transnational political relationships between multinational corporations and national governments is a function of the *vertical interaction* between a society and its governmental institutions and the *horizontal interaction* between the parent company and its foreign subsidiary.

Turning first to the question of vertical interaction, it has already been suggested that the greater the scope and intensity of interaction between a society and its governmental institutions, the greater the sensitivity of the nation-state to horizontal interaction. Mass democracy, which increases the number and range of demand-inputs to the national political system, and provides for feedback processes (in the form of elections, public demonstrations, referenda and the like) which affect the formulation of policy, is one important component of this vertical interaction. Industrialisation, coupled with the extension of the franchise, provides the impetus for welfare-state policies aimed at securing full employment and welfare-maximisation, which are other important stimuli for increasing governmental intervention in economic activity (through central economic planning, publicly controlled enterprises, publicly financed welfare programmes, and similar activities). As governmental economic intervention increases, so does the sensitivity of policy formulation and execution to horizontal interaction — the effects on the national economy of transnational interaction brought about by entities which lie outside the government's territorial jurisdiction:

> Most national economic policies rely for their effectiveness on the separation of markets. ... Increased economic interdependence, by joining national markets, erodes the effectiveness of these policies and hence threatens national autonomy in the determination and pursuit of economic objectives. [33]

Nevertheless, it is necessary to distinguish between the autonomy necessary to formulate economic objectives and the feasibility of achieving those objectives in the absence of transnational economic interaction, in this case direct investment by multinational corporations. A balance must be struck between the economic advantages of foreign direct investment (access to capital, technology, managerial skills, and so on) and the actual or potential constraints which such foreign investment places on the economic autonomy of the host country; the benefits of transnational activities may be greater than the costs of reduced autonomy, and Kaiser has suggested that 'the advancement and welfare of industrial societies and the interaction within the transnational societies between them reinforce each other.' [34] An assessment by host government decision-makers of the costs and benefits of foreign investment, however, involves the attitudes of those decision-makers toward foreign investment:

> An *attitude* is the individual's organization of psychological processes, as inferred from his behaviour, with respect to some aspect of the world which he distinguishes from other aspects. It represents the

residue of his previous experience with which he appoaches any sub-sequent situation including that aspect and, together with the con-temporary influences in such a situation, determines his behaviour in it. Attitudes are enduring in the sense that such residues are carried over to new situations, but they change in so far as new residues are acquired through experience in new situations. [35]

A decision-maker will therefore process 'real' events in accordance with the attitudes he has formed on the subject as a result of his past experi-ence; his perception of transnational activities will consequently be shap-ed by his attitudes, which will also determine the response that he makes to a given situation. It is thus important not only to take into account the objective realities of horizontal interaction brought about by foreign in-vestment, but also the way in which government decision-makers process and interpret these realities.

In this respect the attitudinal typology of governmental decision-makers toward multinational companies developed by Perlmutter is partic-ularly useful. [36] Host country governments may display xenophilic, xenophobic, or geocentric attitudes toward foreign multinational compa-nies, while home country governments might exhibit ethnocentric, poly-centric or geocentric attitudes toward the foreign activities of multina-tional companies headquartered within their territorial jurisdiction. Xeno-philic attitudes of host government decision-makers involve a belief that foreign investment is beneficial to the host economy because it brings with it skills and techniques which are superior to domestic ones, that foreign-owned companies are as (if not more) co-operative compared to. domestic firms, and that foreign business methods should be imitated. Translated into policy, the xenophilic host government attitude would de-emphasise loss of domestic economic autonomy, place minimal restric-tions on foreign investment, and frequently make active attempts to out-bid other governments (in terms of investment incentives) in order to attract foreign investment.

Xenophobic host government attitudes, on the other hand, stem from a basic distrust of and hostility to foreign influences, and are manifested in attempts to insulate the host economy from transnational economic activ-ity and pursue a policy of economic autarchy. Foreign investment is there-fore resisted, and the dangers of a loss of economic sovereignty are stress-ed, with foreign firms seen as being tightly controlled by their parent company (or even its home government) and frequently acting in a man-ner inimical to the host country's interests. Xenophobic attitudes would consequently be manifested in policy terms as a restrictive approach to foreign investment, with emphasis on retaining national control of economically or technologically significant industries. By contrast, geocentric attitudes emphasise the inevitability of the internationalisation of business activity, and in policy terms would imply an encouragement of all firms (domestic or foreign) to attain international capabilities; this might be accompanied by attempts at the intergovernmental level to negotiate codes of investment practice which would protect multinational companies from arbitrary discrimination by host governments and ensure maximum welfare on the global level accruing from the activities of multinational firms. International agreements on proration of the tax liabilities of multinational companies, and the renunciation of attempts at extraterritorial regulation of such companies by national governments, would be examples of a geocentric approach. [37]

Turning to home country government attitudes, the ethnocentric orientation is the counterpart of the xenophobic host country orientation; parent companies are expected to identify themselves with the national interests of the home country and if necessary to be disciplined by the extraterritorial application of home country laws to their overseas operations. Attempts by host governments to exert control over home country foreign subsidiaries would be resisted, if necessary by direct home government pressure on offending host governments, and foreign subsidiaries would be required or encouraged to repatriate the maximum amount of profits, and to have home country nationals in key management positions. Polycentric home government attitudes, on the other hand, would stress the sovereignty of nation-states and would adopt a neutral attitude toward attempts by host governments to control subsidiaries of home country parent companies, emphasising the disruptive effect of imposing home country values on other countries. In policy terms, the polycentric orientation would lead to a minimalist, *laissez-faire* approach toward control of multinational companies based in the home country. Geocentric home government attitudes would be broadly similar to those described above in the discussion of host government attitudes.

Similar attitudinal orientations apply to subsidiary-parent company relationships within the multinational corporation itself; [38] executives of the subsidiary may be xenophilic (acceptance of the superiority of headquarters authority and home country procedures), xenophobic (identification with host country interests and efforts to secure maximum subsidiary autonomy), or geocentric (support for optimum allocation of resources on a global basis). Parent company executives may be ethnocentric (insisting on tight central control and advancement of home country values, at the expense of the host country if necessary), polycentric (an assumption that host country cultures are different, and that subsidiaries should have sufficient autonomy to adapt to them and to promote host country objectives), or geocentric (where discrimination on nationalistic grounds is replaced by efforts toward optimal use of resources on a global basis).

The sensitivity of both home and host governments to transnational economic activity by multinational companies is therefore a function not only of intra-state vertical interaction, but also of the perception of governmental decision-makers of the character of the horizontal interaction brought about by multinational companies, and the character of this horizontal interaction is in turn conditioned by the attitudes of the key decision-makers in both the subsidiary and the headquarters of the multinational firm. Stable multinational company-national government relationships consequently depend upon complementary and/or mutually reinforcing attitudes prevailing within the four entities involved — the home country government, the parent company, the subsidiary, and the host country government. Ethnocentric orientations on the part of the home government and parent company might be balanced by xenophilic orientations within the subsidiary and host government; polycentric home/parent orientations by xenophobic host/subsidiary orientations, geocentric by geocentric, and so on. Tension in multinational company-national government relationships would be engendered by incompatible attitudinal orientations, of which the 'neo-imperialist' ethnocentric home government/parent company, xenophilic subsidiary, and xenophobic host government pattern is the most obvious example. [39]

1.3   The United Kingdom case

The model developed in the previous section of this chapter indicated the complex relationship between vertical and horizontal interaction, and the ways in which the attitudes of the parties involved modify this relationship. The major problem in applying the model to multinational company-nation state relationships lies not only in the paucity of information on the operations of multinational companies, [40] but also in the absence of systematic studies of nation-state reactions to their activities. Where the reactions of host governments to foreign investment have been analysed, scholars have had to rely on fragmentary and primarily ancedotal evidence, [41] and even where attempts have been made to distinguish between the policies of different host governments, [42] these have tended to treat the governments concerned as monolithic entities rather than coalitions of competing and conflicting interests. [43]

It would therefore seem necessary to analyse the reactions of individual host governments to foreign investment, in order to assess the validity of some of the generalised statements about host government perceptions of the costs and benefits of foreign investment which have been made in the existing literature.[44] Do host governments perceive foreign investment in their economies as an indispensible means of capital formation, transfer of technology and management skills, promotion of regional development, stimulation of competition, and amelioration of the balance of payments? How seriously do host governments fear foreign industrial dominance, technological dependence, or constraints on decision-making autonomy imposed by foreign investment? Do they, in fact, distinguish between domestic and foreign companies in their policy-making?

There are good reasons for taking the United Kingdom as the subject for a case-study of host government perceptions of, and reactions to, foreign investment. There have been several recent studies on foreign investment in the UK which provide information on the scope and intensity of the horizontal interaction component in the transnational politics model outlined above,[45] and the UK has long played a dual role as a home and host country for foreign investment, largely because it was one of the first countries to develop a modern industrial economy. As will be seen in the next chapter, the value of UK overseas direct investment is almost double that of foreign investment in the UK, and Britain remains (after Canada) the single most important host country for American direct investment. One might therefore expect that the British Government would be familiar with the implications of international investment for the formulation and achievement of policy objectives, and that its methods for controlling the activities of multinational corporations would be more highly developed than those of other host governments which do not have the benefit of this long experience.

Moreover, between 1964 and 1970, the priod covered by this study, the British Government was controlled by the Labour Party, which was committed to a much greater degree of economic intervention than its Conservative predecessors:

> We want full employment; a faster rate of industrial expansion; a sensible distribution of industry throughout the country; an end to the present chaos in traffic and transport; a brake on rising prices and a solution to our balance of payments problems. ... None of these aims will be achieved by leaving the economy to look after itself. They will only be achieved by a deliberate and massive effort to modernise the economy; to change its structure and to develop with

all possible speed the advanced technology and the new science-based industries with which our future lies. In short, they will only be achieved by Socialist planning. [46]

It might therefore be anticipated that the vertical interaction component of the transnational politics model would increase in both scope and intensity under a Labour Government, and therefore make the formulation and execution of economic policy more sensitive to horizontal interaction brought about by multinational companies operating in the UK.

For both these reasons, then a case-study of the United Kingdom as a host country for foreign investment during the 1964–1970 period would seem likely to highlight some of the problems in multinational corporation-national government relationships; it is important, however, that such a case-study be conducted within a general framework of transnational politics which would enable it to be compared with case-studies of other host governments, and thus reveal differences and similarities in multinational corporation-host government relationships. The multiplicity of problems raised by the development of the multinational corporation justifies an academic division of labour, but not a wasteful duplication of effort. This study, which is limited to the experience of the British Government as a *host* government between 1964 and 1970 (although its concomitant position as a *home* government is also an important factor which must be taken into account), will therefore seek to examine the validity of a range of hypotheses set out below, in the hope that similar studies of other host governments might employ the same propositions and that a more general assessment of their validity would then become possible.

1.4 Multinational corporations and the host country government: some preliminary hypotheses

1.4.1 *Salience of foreign investment* [47]

As a previous section of this chapter indicated, the likelihood of a host government becoming sensitive to, and therefore making a policy issue of, transnational interaction brought about by foreign investment will depend on the degree of vertical interaction within the host country, and the degree of horizontal interaction arising from foreign investment, as perceived (and modified) by the parties involved through their attitudinal orientations.

Proposition (a):
Foreign investment will become more salient as a policy issue for host governments as government intervention in the host economy increases.

Proposition (b):
Foreign investment will become more salient as a policy issue for host governments as the level and industrial distribution of foreign investment increases.

Proposition (c):
Foreign investment will become more salient as a policy issue for host governments where foreign subsidiaries in the host country lack autonomy and are subject to the control of their parent company in all important respects, particularly if the values imposed by the parent company differ from those prevailing in the host country.

Proposition (d):
Foreign investment will become more salient as a policy issue for host governments where government decision-makers perceive that foreign-owned subsidiaries in the host country do not behave in the same way as purely domestic firms, particularly if their behaviour is seen to adversely affect the achievement of national economic goals defined by the host government.
Until foreign investment brings about a significant level of horizontal interaction, therefore (and 'significant' will be defined by host governments in terms of actual or potential constraints on their economic decision-making autonomy, which will in turn be defined in terms of the degree of economic intervention desired), one would not expect foreign-owned companies to be differentiated from domestic firms in the formulation and execution of government economic policy — foreign investment would not be a salient policy issue.

1.4.2 Host government reactions to foreign investment

The reaction of host governments to further foreign investment will be conditioned not only by the existing level of foreign investment, but also by their previous experience concerning foreign investment.

Proposition (a):
The greater the level of foreign investment in a given industry, the more likely that the host government will discourage or prevent further foreign investment in that industry.

Proposition (b):
The more economically and politically powerful the country of origin of the foreign investment, the more likely that the host government will discourage or prevent further foreign investment from that country.

Proposition (c):
The greater the extent of co-operation between host and home country governments, the more likely that the host government will not discourage or prevent further foreign investment from that country.

Proposition (d):
The greater the extent of co-operation between the host government and the foreign firm investing, the more likely that the host government will not discourage or prevent further investment by that firm.

Proposition (e):
The greater the actual or potential transfer of capital, technology, and management skills involved in the foreign investment, the more likely that the host government will not discourage or prevent such investment.

Proposition (f):
The greater the actual or potential contribution of foreign investment to exports and/or import substitution, particularly during a period of balance of payments deficit, the more likely that the host government will not discourage or prevent such investment.

Proposition (g):
The greater the level of host country investment abroad in a given country, the more likely that the host government will not prevent or discourage foreign investment originating from that country.

1.4.3   Attitudes of host government decision-makers

In determining the costs and benefits of foreign investment, the attitudes of individual governmental decision-makers are important in processing (and perhaps distorting) the objective realities of the situation. Since attitudes are formed as a result of experience, one might expect that the emphasis on the various types of cost and benefit caused by foreign investment will vary according to the experience of the individual decision-maker, i.e. the character of his functional responsibilities and the amount of contact he has with foreign investors. Decision-makers will distort, or place undue emphasis upon, certain aspects of a multinational corporation's policies and performance, and such perceptual distortions have their origin in the values which the decision-maker operationalises in a specific case.

Proposition (a):
Perceptual distortion by a host government decision-maker of a foreign firm's policy and performance will be positively related to the functional responsibilities of the department in which he operates.

Proposition (b):
Perceptual distortion by a host government decision-maker of a foreign firm's policy and performance will be positively related to his unfamiliarity or lack of contact with that foreign firm.

1.5 The organisation of this study

Having outlined some preliminary hypotheses concerning host government reactions to foreign investment, it is now necessary to explain how they are to be investigated. The next chapter will delineate the scope and level of foreign investment in the UK, in order to determine the significance of horizontal interaction in the case of the British economy; the following chapter (Chapter 3) will examine the salience of foreign investment in terms of the development by the British Government of methods of controlling foreign-owned firms as distinct from purely British firms. Chapter 4 will outline the attitudes of both civil servants and politicians toward foreign investment, while Chapters 5 and 6 will present historical case-studies of the UK motor and computer industries, indicating how the policy of the British Government toward foreign investment in those industries evolved over time. Finally, Chapter 7 will return to the preliminary hypotheses outlined above, attempt to assess their validity in the case of the British Government during the period 1964–1970, and draw on administration theory to suggest the reasons for the evolution of the Labour Government's policies toward multinational corporations.

This study has a limited objective, namely a detailed analysis of the experience of the British Government in dealing with foreign investment during the 1964–1970 period, and such represents only a small (but hopefully positive) step towards understanding the complexities of the multinational corporation-nation state interface. If the inadequacies of the data on which it is based, and the tentative nature of the conclusions which can be drawn from such information raise more doubts than certainties in the reader's mind, then the utility of an in-depth study of one host government will have been justified; it is important to delineate uncertainties lest they be multiplied when proceeding to a higher level of abstraction, and it is particularly important to do so when dealing with a relatively new and unfamiliar phenomenon such as the multinational corporation. Perhaps our current uncertainty, and the reasons for overcoming it, has been most cogently described by a writer who is by no means an advocate of international capitalism:

> We are never completely contemporaneous with our present. History advances in disguise; it appears on stage wearing the mask of the preceding scene, and we tend to lose the meaning of the play. Each time the curtain rises, continuity has to be re-established. The blame, of course, is not history's but lies in our vision, encumbered with memories and images learned in the past, even when the present is a revolution. [48]

Notes

[1] see, for example, K.W. Deutsch 'External influences on the internal behavior of states' in R.B. Farrell (ed.) *Approaches to International and Comparative Politics* Northwestern University Press, Evanston, Ill. 1966, pp. 44–63; J.N. Rosenau (ed.) *Linkage Politics* Free Press, New York 1969; *International Organization* vol. 25, no. 3 (a special issue on 'Transnational relations and world politics')

[2] Kaiser 'Transnational politics: toward a theory of multinational politics' *International Organization* vol. 25, no. 4 (Autumn 1971), p. 792

[3] J.D. Singer 'The level-of-analysis problem' in K. Knorr and S. Verba (eds.) *The International System: Theoretical Essays*, Princeton Univesity Press, Princeton, N.J. 1961, pp. 77–92

[4] J.S. Nye and R.O. Keohane 'Transnational relations and world politics: an introduction', *International Organization* vol. 25, no. 3 (Summer 1971), p. 332

[5] R. Tanter 'International system and foreign policy approaches' in R. Tanter and R.H. Ullman (eds.) *Theory and Policy in International Relations*, Princeton University Press, Princeton, N.J., p. 7

[6] A departure from this approach may be seen in J.N. Rosenau (ed.) *Domestic Sources of Foreign Policy* Free Press, N.Y. 1967

[7] I. Vallier 'The Roman Catholic Church; a transnational actor', *International Organization* vol. 25, no. 3, (Summer 1971), pp. 479–502

[8] F. H. Hinsley *Sovereignty* Watts, London 1966, p. 221

⁹ R.N. Cooper, 'Economic interdependence and foreign policy in the seventies' *World Politics* vol. 24, no. 2 (January 1972), p. 167

¹⁰ The experience of the British Labour Government in the 1964-7 period is a good example of this, see: W. Beckerman (ed.) *The Labour Government's Economic Record: 1964-1970,* Duckworth, London, 1972, *passim.*

¹¹ E.L. Morse 'The confidence problem and international monetary crises' paper delivered to the International Political Economy Conference, Cumberland Lodge, Windsor, July 1972 (mimeo)

¹² J.N. Rosenau 'Political science in a shrinking world' in Rosenau, op. cit., p. 2

¹³ Kaiser, op. cit., pp. 801—17

¹⁴ ibid., pp. 804, 812

¹⁵ R. Aron *Peace and War* Weidenfeld, London 1966, p. 105

¹⁶ A. Shonfield *Modern Capitalism* O.U.P., Oxford 1969, pp. 66—7

¹⁷ E.L. Morse 'Crisis diplomacy, interdependence, and the politics of international economic relations' in Tanter and Ullman, op. cit., p. 147

¹⁸ K.W. Deutsch and A. Eckstein 'National industrialization and the declining share of the international economic sector, 1890—1959 *World Politics* vol. 13, no. 2 (January 1961), pp. 267—99

¹⁹ K.N. Waltz 'The myth of national interdependence' in C.P. Kindleberger (ed.) *The International Corporation* MIT Press, Cambridge, Mass 1970, pp. 205—23

²⁰ E.L. Morse 'Transnational economic processes' *International Organization* vol. 25, no. 3 (Summer 1971), pp. 373—97

²¹ For a recent survey of this literature, see R.L. Heilbroner 'The multinational corporation and the nation-state' *New York Review of Books* vol. 16, no. 2 (11 February 1971), pp. 20—5

²² R. Vernon 'Multinational business and national economic goals' *International Organization* vol. 25, no. 3 (Summer 1971), p. 694

²³ S.B. Rolfe 'The international corporation in perspective' in S.B. Rolfe and W. Damm (ed.) *The Multinational Corporation in the World Economiy*, Praeger, New York 1970, p. 9

²⁴ Quoted in Kaiser, op. cit., p. 808

²⁵ G. Modelski 'The corporation in world society' *Yearbook of World Affairs 1968* Stevens, London 1968, p. 78

²⁶ C. Tugendhat *The Multinationals* Eyre & Spottiswoode, London 1971, p. 108

²⁷ C.P. Kindleberger *American Business Abroad* Yale University Press, New Haven 1969, p. 207; R. Gilpin 'The politics of transnational economic relations' *International Organization* vol. 25, no. 3 (Summer 1971), p. 419

[28]   J.F. Galloway 'Worldwide corporations and international integration: the case of INTELSAT' *International Organization* vol. 24 (1970), p. 511

[29]   E.L. Morse 'Transnational economic processes' *International Organization* vol. 25, no. 3 (Summer 1971), pp. 375–7

[30]   see J.H. Dunning *American Investment in British Manufacturing Industry* Allen & Unwin, London 1958, pp. 17–37

[31]   F.A. Mackenzie *The American Invaders* Grant Richards, London 1902. Unlike *Le défi Américain*, the book was not a best-seller, and owes its notoriety to its rediscovery in recent years by authors of the Servan-Schreiber school: see, for example, J. Macmillan and B. Harris *The American Take-Over of Britain* Leslie Frewin, London 1968

[32]   Kaiser, op. cit. p. 809

[33]   Cooper, op. cit., p. 164

[34]   Kaiser, op. cit., pp. 809–10

[35]   T.M. Newcomb 'On the definition of attitude' in M. Jahoda and N. Warren (eds.) *Attitudes* Penguin Books, Harmondsworth 1966, p. 22

[36]   H.V. Perlmutter 'Attitudinal patterns in joint decision-making in multinational firm-nation state relationships' Division for Research and Development of Worldwide Institutions, Wharton School of Finance and Commerce, Philadelphia 1971 (mimeo), pp. 42–5

[37]   see R. Vernon *Sovereignty at Bay: The Multinational Spread of U.S. Enterprises* Longman, London 1971, pp. 272–84

[38]   Perlmutter, op. cit., pp. 36–42

[39]   see L. Turner *Multinationals and the Developing World* Allen Lane, London 1973. For other configurations, see Perlmutter, op. cit., Fig. 6

[40]   see D. Osterberg and F. Ajami 'The multinational corporation: expanding the frontiers of world politics' *Journal of Conflict Resolution* vol. 15, no. 4 (1971), pp. 457–70

[41]   see, for example, J.N. Behrman *National Interests and the Multinational Enterprise: Tensions Among the North Atlantic Countries* Prentice-Hall, Englewood Cliffs, N.J. 1970

[42]   Perhaps the most comprehensive survey is to be found in I.A. Litvak and C.J. Maule (eds.) *Foreign Investment: The Experience of Host Countries* Praeger, New York 1970

[43]   A. Downs *Inside Bureaucracy* Little Brown, Boston 1967, pp. 167–71

[44]   see, for example, D.F. Vagts 'The multinational enterprise: a new challenge for transnational law' *Harvard Law Review* vol. 83 (1970), pp. 739–92

[45]   see Chap. 2 for references to these studies.

[46] Labour Party: *General Election Manifesto 1964* The Labour Party, London 1964, p. 8

[47] It should be noted that throughout this study the terms 'foreign investment' and 'multinational corporation' are to a certain extent used interchangeably. This semantic imprecision may be partly excused by the absence of data on multinational corporations (as distinct from binational firms), by the lack of an authoritative definition of what constitutes a multinational corporation, and by an intuitive judgement that foreign investment by multinational corporations is more significant than other types of foreign investment in bringing about horizontal interaction, because the geographical decentralisation of the multinational firm's activities is accompanied by a more sophisticated transnational management control network than would be expected in the case of binational firms.

[48] R. Debray *Revolution in the Revolution?* Penguin Books, Harmondsworth 1968, p. 19

2 The Multinational Corporation in the UK Economy

2.1 Introduction

Before examining the Labour Government's methods of controlling the activities of foreign-owned companies in the UK, and its attitudes toward them (described in Chapter 3 and 4 of this study), it is necessary to assess the role which such companies play in the British economy. An assessment of this kind must of necessity be an incomplete one, owing to the paucity of data on the operations of multinational companies in the UK; as Professor John Dunning has noted:

> We have a reasonable idea of the volume and structure of inward direct investment, but only a very hazy idea of its costs and benefits. We need more disclosure of the facts about the operations of foreign-owned companies, partly to enable us properly to evaluate these costs and benefits and partly to make possible a proper surveillance of such companies.[1]

Given the fragmentary nature of the data, it is possible to make only very tentative judgements on the significance of foreign-owned multinational companies for the UK economy, but this chapter will attempt to draw on published and unpublished statistics from Government and private sources in order to assess both the dimensions of foreign investment in the UK and the performance of foreign-owned companies in UK industry.

2.2 The dimensions of foreign investment in the UK

It is important, when assessing the role of foreign investment in the UK to note that the UK itself is a leading creditor nation on direct investment account, being the source of almost 18 per cent of world total accumulated assets of foreign direct investment in 1966, second only to the United States (61 per cent), and well ahead of France, Canada, Germany, Japan and Sweden.[2] As Table 2·1 indicates, the accumulated value of UK direct investment overseas was almost three times greater than the value of

Table 2.1
Book value of UK direct investment overseas
and foreign direct investment in UK, 1960–70

Year	Value of inward investment (£m)	Value of outward investment (£m)
1960	1,040	2,950
1961	1,290	3,190
1962	1,430	3,410
1963	1,610	3,640
1964	1,780	3,910
1965	1,980	4,215
1966	2,279	4,402
1967	2,425	5,187
1968	2,718	5,585
1969	3,037	6,134
1970	3,376	6,642
Percentage increase 1960–70	224·6	125·2

Note: Excluding oil, banking, insurance
Source: *Board of Trade Journal* 26 January 1968, p. i; 23 September 1970, pp. 645, 649. *Trade and Industry* 23 March 1972, pp. 514, 517

foreign direct investment in the UK in 1960, and almost twice as great by 1970; the Table also shows that the rate of increase of foreign investment in the UK over the 1960–70 period was double the rate of UK direct investment overseas, partly as a result of British Government restrictions on outward investment during the recurrent balance of payments crisis of this period.

It can be seen from a comparison of Tables 2.2 and 2.3 that the bulk of UK overseas investment, almost two-thirds of the total, was concentrated in 1968 in countries with which it had colonial ties in the past, whereas the majority of direct investment in the UK in 1968, almost 90 per cent, emanated from industrialised countries which had no such links with Britain. By far the most important source of foreign investment was the US, accounting for over two-thirds of the 1968 total (even more if one includes US investment channelled through holding companies in Canada and Switzerland, the next two most important sources), and three times the value of UK direct investment in the US Between 1960 and 1968 the value of US investment in the UK tripled, an increase exceeded only by West Germany and Norway (which were the source of only just over 1 per

Table 2.2
UK overseas direct investment by area, 1968
(Book value of accumulated assets, £m)

	Value	%
Sterling area developing countries	1,156·3	20·70
Other developing countries	512·0	9·17
North America	(1,286·9)	(23·04)
US	600·0	10·74
Canada	686·9	12·30
West Europe	(788·5)	(14·12)
of which:		
Belgium/Lux.	112·3	2·01
Denmark	27·4	0·49
Finland	5·4	0·10
France	180·5	3·23
W. Germany	179·3	3·21
Italy	60·3	1·08
Netherlands	96·5	1·73
Norway	11·3	0·20
Sweden	25·8	0·46
Switzerland	43·6	0·78
Other developed countries	(1,841·6)	(32·97)
of which:		
Australia	966·4	17·30
Eire	119·0	2·13
New Zealand	139·7	2·50
South Africa	585·6	10·48
Total	5,585·3	100·0

Note: Excluding oil, banking, insurance
Source: *Board of Trade Journal* 23 September 1970

cent of foreign investment in the UK). The UK in 1968 was a net creditor on the direct investment account for all countries except the US, Netherlands, Sweden and Switzerland; with the addition of Canada, these were the most important sources of foreign investment in 1968, accounting for over 96 per cent of the total. In short, there was no geographical symmetry in UK outward and inward investment, but the substantial net credit position of the US led the Labour Government, and its predecessors, to try to limit outward investment while at the same time placing

Table 2.3: Value of foreign direct investment in the UK by country of origin, 1960–68, selected years

Country/Area	1960 £m	1960 %	1964 £m	1964 %	1968 £m	1968 %	Percentage increase 1960–68
North America	(755·1)	(72·6)	(1,367·1)	(76·2)	(2,045·9)	(75·3)	(170·9)
US	613·1	58·9	1,165·6	65·0	1,822·8	67·1	197·3
Canada	142·0	13·7	201·5	11·2	223·0	8·2	57·0
West Europe	(237·5)	(22·8)	(363·5)	(20·3)	(586·8)	(21·6)	(147·1)
Belgium/Lux.	8·6	0·8	12·0	0·7	14·7	0·5	70·9
Denmark	6·3	0·6	7·4	0·4	13·1	0·5	107·9
Finland	2·5	0·2	3·6	0·2	5·2	0·2	108·0
France	19·4	1·9	38·3	2·1	51·0	1·9	162·9
W. Germany	3·8	0·4	11·0	0·6	26·6	1·0	600·0
Italy	14·0	1·3	15·9	0·8	17·7	0·7	26·4
Netherlands	66·7	6·4	86·4	4·8	168·2	6·2	152·2
Norway	0·6	0·1	1·1	0·1	2·5	0·1	316·7
Sweden	22·4	2·2	28·0	1·6	59·7	2·2	166·5
Switzerland	90·9	8·7	154·5	8·6	225·6	8·3	148·2
Others	2·3	0·2	5·3	0·3	2·5	0·1	8·7
Other areas	(47·8)	(4·6)	(62·4)	(3·5)	(85·4)	(3·1)	(78·7)
Australia	7·6	0·7	7·5	0·4	6·0	0·2	−21·1
Eire	2·4	0·2	1·6	0·1	1·2	0·0	−50·0
New Zealand	2·0	0·2	1·2	0·1	4·1	0·2	105·0
South Africa	23·0	2·2	14·9	0·8	36·8	1·4	60·0
Others	12·8	1·2	37·2	2·1	37·3	1·4	191·4
Total	1,040·0	100·0	1,793·0	100·0	2,718·1	100·0	161·4

Note: Excluding oil, banking, insurance   Source: *Board of Trade Journal* 26 January 1968; 23 September 1970

minimal restrictions on inward investment, lest it provoke retaliatory measures against UK overseas investments.[3]

The significance of foreign-owned firms in the UK economy can be seen from Dunning's computation that the foreign capital stake in 1965 amounted to 6·4 per cent of UK GNP (6·2 per cent attributable to US

Table 2.4
Industrial concentration of foreign investment in the UK:
employment in foreign-controlled manufacturing subsidiaries,
by industry, 1963

SIC MLH	Heading	Foreign* percentage of total	UK percentage of total	Concentration quotient
211–229	Food	7·2	7·2	1·00
231–240	Drink and tobacco	0·4	2·3	0·17
261–263	Coke, ovens, mineral oil refining greases, etc.	1·1	0·6	1·83
271	Dyestuffs, fertilisers and other chemicals	2·1	2·3	0·91
272	Pharmaceutical and toilet preparations	5·0	0·9	5·56
273–277	Explosives, soap, polishes etc.	1·9	1·8	1·06
311–313	Iron and steel	2·1	5·5	0·38
320	Non-ferrous metals	2·8	1·7	1·65
331–339	Mechanical machinery	12·7	8·2	1·55
341–349	Industrial plant and other mechanical engineering	3·8	4·6	0·83
351–352	Scientific instrument and watches	4·6	1·7	2·71
361	Electrical machinery	0·7	2·6	0·27
362–363	Insulated wires and telephone apparatus	6·3	1·8	3·50
364	Radio and other electronic apparatus	7·1	3·0	2·37
365–369	Domestic appliances and other electrical goods	4·6	2·2	2·09
370	Shipbuilding and marine engineering	0·2	2·5	0·08
381–389	Vehicles	20·6	10·0	2·06
391–399	Metal goods n.e.s.	4·0	6·4	0·63
411–450	Textiles and clothing	2·9	16·4	0·18
461–479	Bricks, pottery and furniture	1·5	7·2	0·21
481–489	Paper, printing	2·0	7·3	0·27
491	Rubber	5·1	1·5	3·40
492–499	Other manufacturing industries	1·3	2·3	0·57
	All manufacturing industries	100·0	100·0	

*Firms employing 25 persons or more
Source: Census of Production, 1963

investment), 7·7 per cent of the net capital stock of UK companies (7·1 per cent US controlled), and 11·7 per cent of the net profits of UK companies (10·7 per cent US).[4] Some idea of the industrial concentration of foreign investment can be seen in Table 2.4, which utilises data from the 1963 Census of UK Industrial Production (which became available to the Board of Trade in 1968), on the employment of foreign-controlled manufacturing companies. Table 2.4 shows that foreign-owned firms accounted for an above average share of employment in technology-based industries (pharmaceutical products, machinery, scientific instruments, telecommunications, electronics) and industries with a high income-elasticity of demand (vehicles, rubber, domestic electrical appliances). This indicates that foreign investment has been concentrated in the more dynamic sectors of UK industry, and is of little importance in declining UK industries such as textiles and shipbuilding.

The 1968 data on the number of foreign-owned companies and the value of their assets is set out in Table 2.5, which shows that almost 50 per cent of foreign-owned companies (amounting to 67 per cent of total value of foreign investment) originated from the US, and accounted for 83 per cent of foreign investment in mechanical engineering and 82 per cent in motor vehicles. Canada was strongly represented in metal manufacturing (44 per cent of total value of foreign investment in that industry), largely because of its aluminium and nickel companies. Although Board of Trade industrial classifications of foreign investment are rather too broad to point to individual industries with a high foreign-controlled content, Dunning has compiled a list of such industries from private sources for 1966, and this is reproduced in Table 2.6.

What is interesting, particularly in the light of Government policies and attitudes outlined in Chapters 3 and 4 of this study, is that the manufacture of certain products such as carbon black, sewing machines, baby foods, razor blades, foundation garments and vacuum cleaners, is dominated by foreign-owned firms, without any expression of governmental or public disquiet. In some other fields not covered by Board of Trade statistics, such as the oil industry (where British interests control only BP – the Government holding just under half of the shares – and 40 per cent of Shell) or banking (where foreign banks now account for 30 per cent of bank deposits in the UK,[5] the foreign dominance has been accepted as inevitable and/or desirable, and has caused little controversy. It is difficult to define what is meant by a 'key industry' on *a priori* grounds, but it is notable that foreign investment shows an above-average concentration in eleven sectors accounting for 39 per cent of total UK manufacturing employment in 1963.[6] When the strong foreign representation in the tech-

Table 2.5
Cumulative numbers and values of direct investments in UK by industry and selected areas of origin, 1968
(Book value at end 1968)

Industry	Canada		US		EFTA		EEC		All countries	
	No.	£m	No.	£m	No.	£m	No.	£m	No.	£m
Food, drink and tobacco	8	43·9	38	195·7	7	54·5	12	3·0	70	302·8
Chemicals and allied industries	16	10·8	104	206·0	30	49·4	34	50·5	191	330·0
Metal manufacturing	6	76·2	23	78·6	9	16·0	3	3·4	41	174·0
Mechanical engineering	15	9·9	179	392·0	44	55·6	36	13·4	279	471·2
Electrical engineering	3	0·2	61	176·2	21	37·2	13	110·5	99	324·2
Motor vehicles	4	53·6	12	290·4	2	3·1	4	5·1	53	352·4
Textiles, clothing and footwear	3	0·3	20	8·3	6	2·1	13	9·1	46	21·6
Paper and printing	8	9·1	81	38·5	11	8·0	8	4·2	111	60·5
Rubber	–	–	13	43·9	2	22·2	–	–	15	66·1
Other manufacturing	9	1·3	130	126·9	18	17·3	24	9·6	187	160·2
Distribution	35	11·8	216	161·7	151	38·8	201	47·1	688	285·9
Other activities	27	6·1	165	104·7	41	4·4	71	22·5	351	169·2
Total	134	223·0	1,042	1,822·8	342	308·6	419	278·2	2,099	2,718·1

Note: Excluding oil, banking, insurance
Source: *Board of Trade Journal* 23 September 1970, p. 649

Table 2.6

Foreign control of UK industries, 1966

It has been possible to compile a list, from a number of sources, of the approximate share of the total production by all UK enterprises, of various products, accounted for by foreign-financed companies at the end of 1966. In some cases their share of the total goods bought by UK consumers will be less, due to the contribution of imports.

80% or more
Boot and shoe machinery, carbon black, colour films, custard powder and starch, sewing machines, tinned baby foods, typewriters.

60–79%
Agricultural implements, aluminum semi-manufactures, breakfast cereals, calculating machines, cigarette lighters, domestic boilers, electric shavers, instant coffee, potato chips, razor blades and safety razors, refined petroleum products, soaps and detergents, spark plugs, tinned milk.

50–59%
Cake mixes, cosmetics and toilet preparations, electric switches, ethical proprietaries (drugs sold to National Health Service), frozen foods, foundation garments, pens and pencils, motor cars, pet foods, petroleum refinery construction equipment, refrigerators, rubber tyres, tractors, vacuum cleaners.

40–49%
Computers, locks and keys, photographic equipment, printing and typesetting machinery, watches and clocks.

30–39%
Abrasives, commercial vehicles, dental equipment, floor polishers, elevators and escalators, portable electric tools, washing machines.

15–29%
Greeting cards, industrial instruments, materials handling equipment, medical preparations, soft drinks, mining machinery, paperback books, petro-chemicals, synthetic fibres, telephones and telecommunications equipment, toilet tissues.

Source: Dunning *Foreign Investment in the United Kingdom* pp. 247–8

nology-based industries is also taken into account, the concern expressed in several books published in the mid-1960s can be seen to have justification.[7]

As Table 2.7 shows, almost half of the 550 largest US manufacturing and merchandising firms had one or more subsidiaries in the UK in 1966—67, and 57 per cent of these were among the 300 largest UK foreign-owned subsidiaries, with over 16 per cent among the largest 500 UK companies. When the largest 147 non-US (and non-UK) owned firms are included, 42 per cent of the world's largest (non-UK owned) companies had subsidiaries in the UK, 57 per cent of these being among the 300 largest foreign-owned UK subsidiaries, and just over 18 per cent of these being among the 500 largest UK companies. The 1965 figures published

Table 2.7

Size of foreign parent companies and their UK subsidiaries, 1966—67

		US		Non-US		Total	
		Ex. oil	Inc. oil	Ex. oil	Inc. oil	Ex. oil	Inc. oil
(1)	Number of large foreign firms	522	550	134	147	656	697
(2)	Of which, with one or more UK subsidiaries	244	263	34	38	278	301
(3)	Ratio of (1) to (2)	46·7	47·8	25·4	25·9	42·4	43·2
(4)	Number of (2) among 300 largest UK foreign owned subsidiaries	140	N.A.	19	N.A.	159	N.A.
(5)	Ratio of (4) to (2)	57·3	—	55·9	—	57·1	—
(6)	Number of (2) among largest 500 UK companies	40	44	11	13	51	57
(7)	Ratio of (6) to (2)	16·4	16·7	32·4	34·2	18·3	18·9

Notes: Item (1) derived from *Fortune* 1968 lists of top 550 US largest corporations and merchandising firms, and 200 largest non-US companies (excluding 53 UK-owned firms)
Item (2) derived from *Who Owns Whom* (1968)
Item (4) derived from unpublished Board of Trade Analysis of 300 foreign interest companies (excluding oil) with profits of more than £0·1m or losses of more than £0·5m in 1966
Item (6) derived from *The Times 500 Leading Companies in the UK* (1968—69)

by the Board of Trade showed that 69 large foreign-owned firms, with investments over £5 million, controlled 63 per cent of the total value of foreign direct investment in the UK, while the remaining 37 per cent was controlled by 862 firms; in no sector did these large firms control less than 40 per cent of the total foreign assets, and in some sectors it was especially high — 79 per cent in food, drink and tobacco, 74 per cent in metal manufacture, 79 per cent in electrical engineering, 95 per cent in motor vehicles.[8]

The size of these foreign-owned firms, and their share of the market in UK industries which show a high or increasing degree of concentration,[9] would seem to bear out Kindleberger's observation that 'direct investment belongs to the theory of monopolistic competition.'[10] Although foreign investment in the UK may have increased the competitive market behaviour of domestic firms, it has also accelerated concentration in certain sectors where British companies have been forced to merge in order to rationalise their activities and meet foreign competition — the motor and computer industries being good examples of this process.[11] Dunning observed:

> Competition is usually oligopolistic in character, although occasionally a foreign-owned company may occupy a near-monopolistic position. ... Rarely does it seem that foreign firms play an insignificant role in the industries in which they produce; even quite small enterprises tend to supply highly individualistic or specialized products.[12]

One explanation for this may be the 'product cycle' theory propounded by Vernon and others[13] that firms undertake production abroad in order to exploit their technologically-induced oligopolistic advantage before it is eroded by competition; one would therefore expect foreign-owned firms to be concentrated in sectors characterised by oligopolistic competition. Of foreign-owned companies established in the UK prior to 1946, 85 per cent of their total assets were in manufacturing by 1965, with 72 per cent being concentrated in chemicals, motor vehicles and engineering; of companies established since 1946, the proportions were 80 per cent and 73 per cent respectively,[14] showing a continuing tendency toward concentration in the above industries.

Table 2·8 indicates that in 1965 71 per cent of the companies in which there was a foreign stake, accounting for almost 74 per cent of total foreign investment, were wholly-owned subsidiaries, and the number of companies in which there was a foreign minority stake (18 per cent of the total) amounted to less than 8 per cent of total foreign investment. US investors seemed marginally to prefer wholly-owned subsidiaries in com-

Table 2.8

Number and value of cumulative foreign investment in UK, 1965, by percentage of foreign ownership

Foreign stake	US				Other countries			
	Number	%	Value	%	Number	%	Value	%
100%	384	70·9	972·6	75·4	278	71·1	455·9	70·2
75–99%	30	5·5	60·0	4·6	36	9·2	138·7	21·3
50–74%	22	4·1	124·5	9·7	15	3·8	32·4	5·0
Under 50%	105	19·4	132·1	10·2	62	15·9	22·7	3·5
Total	541	100·0	1,289·2	100·0	391	100·0	649·7	100·0

Notes: Excludes oil, banking, insurance or companies with less than £½m assets

Source: *Board of Trade Journal* 26 January 1968

parison with non-US investors (75 per cent and 70 per cent respectively by value), but non-US investors were less likely to hold minority interests than US investors (4 per cent and 10 per cent respectively), preferring a controlling interest. The financial structure of these firms is also of interest, because of the common assumption that foreign direct investment represents a net addition to the host country's capital stock. [15]

Table 2.9 demonstrates that the total assets in 1965 of the 932 large foreign firms (with net assets over £½m) in the UK amounted to

Table 2.9
Structure of financing of large foreign firms in UK, 1965 (£m)

	US firms		Non-US firms	
	Total	UK share	Total	UK share
Total assets	2,243·9	1,109·5	1,108·4	489·9
Equity capital	1,377·2	115·4	570·4	33·9
Long-term debt		255·1		106·6
Short-term debt	866·7	739·0	538·0	349·4

Note: Excluding oil, banking, insurance and companies with net assets of less than £½m
Source: *Board of Trade Journal* 26 January 1968

£3,532 million, of which 52 per cent was owned by foreign investors; of the remainder, short term debt to UK sources (£1,088 million) represented some 32 per cent of total assets, long-term debt to UK sources (£362 million) accounted for 11 per cent of total assets, and equity capital held by non-controlling investors (£149 million) for 5 per cent. It can thus be seen that the UK contribution to the finance of foreign-owned companies is almost equal to the amount contributed by the foreign investors themselves, and the net addition to the UK capital stock provided from overseas is even smaller when it is remembered that part of the foreign investment is composed of unremitted profits earned by the subsidiary in the UK Dunning found that:

> Over the period 1961–1966, foreign subsidiaries in the UK financed, on average, 37·9 per cent of new investment from retained profits, and 43·4 per cent from capital imported from abroad. Retained earnings accounted for a slightly higher proportion (46·0 per cent) of the growth of North American investment. [16]

During the 1961—66 period foreign-owned firms in the UK reinvested an average of 47·4 per cent (47·3 per cent for North American firms) of their total profits, with the percentage showing a perceptible increase (from 31·3 per cent in 1961 tot 50·5 per cent in 1966) over the period.[17]

Although it might be argued that the extensive (and increasing) reliance on UK sources of capital for expansion of foreign investment in the 1961—66 period was a reflection of the weakness of sterling and a consequent unwillingness of parent companies to inject capital from overseas lest the pound be devalued, this does not explain why such a large percentage of new investment was financed from unremitted profits. Brooke and Remmers found that such internal finance accounted for 88 per cent of investment in fixed assets by 115 foreign subsidiaries in the UK, compared to 78 per cent for British quoted companies in the 1961—67 period, and that internal finance supplied over 100 per cent of total investment needs of foreign subsidiaries in one out of every three years. [18] One explanation might be the higher growth rates of foreign-owned firms compared with UK firms (the average growth rate of US firms in the period 1955—66 was 44 per cent greater than their UK competitors), and their higher profitability 16·5 per cent return on assets for US firms in 1965, compared to 12·3 per cent for UK firms), [19] leading to a larger cash flow coupled with an incentive for expanded investment.

2.3 The performance of foreign investors in the UK

It has been seen in the preceding section that foreign investment in the UK grew at double the rate of UK investment overseas in the decade 1960—1970, that it tended to be concentrated in technology-based industries or those where the economies of scale were greatest, and that almost half of its expansion in the 1961—66 period was provided from UK sources. Having established some of the dimensions of foreign investment, it is necessary to assess its contribution to the UK economy, in terms of productivity, balance of payments, diffusion of technology, regional development, control over subsidiaries by parent companies, taxation and currency policy, personnel policy and labour relations.

2.3.1 *Productivity and profitability*

Kindleberger has contended that:

> ... the international corporation which scanned a world horizon

would be more likely to improve the efficiency of goods and factor markets that function less than optimally because of distance, ignorance, and local monopoly. [20]

Indeed, one of the major arguments which has been advanced concerning the advantages of foreign investment to the host economy has been that it offers a package of new products, financial capital, technological and managerial expertise, access to new markets, and an increase in competition in the host economy. A.E. Safarian, in his study of foreign investment in Canada, emphasised that:

> Access to the parent's stake of knowledge, as embodied in everything from its research and management skills to its production techniques and the products themselves, is at the heart of the process of direct investment. The emphasis so often given to the transfer of monetary capital ... frequently pales by comparison. [21]

One would therefore expect foreign-owned firms in the UK to be both more efficient and more profitable than their British competitors; as Table 2.10 shows, foreign manufacturing firms in 1963 were both more capital intensive (in terms of capital expenditure per employee) and more productive (in terms of net output per employee) than UK-owned firms. Swiss firms were the most capital-intensive and productive, followed by American firms; the average net output per employee for foreign-owned firms was £1,970 (38 per cent higher than for UK firms), and capital expenditure per employee by foreign-owned firms was £234 (105 per cent higher than for UK firms).

This result may be partly explained by noting the concentration of foreign investment in the most dynamic and profitable sectors of industry, such as electronics and pharmaceuticals. However, Dunning and Rowan's study of US-owned firms and their UK competitors found that the main reason why US firms recorded higher profits than UK firms had little to do with their industrial choice, but that wherever they competed with British firms they performed better, without important size or market advantages. [22] Although US-owned firms, as Table 2.11 indicates, consistently achieved higher rates of profit on 1965 figures, [23] it is also evident that non-US owned foreign firms in general had lower rates of profitability than their British counterparts. This underlines the difficulty of using the rate of return on assets employed as an index of the efficiency of multinational companies, since, as Vernon has noted:

Table 2.10

Analysis of manufacturing industries by nationality of enterprise, 1963
Private sector enterprises with industrial activities in the United Kingdom

Nationality of enterprise	Enterprises No.	Establishments No.	Employment '000's	Net output £m	Net output per head £	Capital expenditure less disposals £m	Capital expenditure per head £
All manufacturing Industries	64,367	83,774	7,695	10,470	1,361	983	128
United Kingdom	63,788	82,056	6,842	8,787	1,430	783	114
Australia	5	15	3·0	3·8	1,271	0·5	152
Canada	19	69	33·3	70·5	2,118	5·0	149
Denmark	6	10	0·7	1·3	1,911	0·1	193
Western Germany	7	44	13·4	23·5	1,756	2·2	167
France	20	39	9·9	17·1	1,718	1·0	100
Irish Republic	7	7	0·8	0·7	932	0·1	96
Netherlands	17	52	27·6	44·3	1,604	5·1	186
Sweden	16	27	12·3	18·4	1,496	1·2	94
Switzerland	28	188	138	320	2,326	48·3	351
U.S.A.	434	1,219	595	1,153	1,937	133	224
Other countries	20	48	19·1	29·9	1,564	4·0	212

Source: Board of Trade *Census of Industrial Production 1963* HMSO, London 1969, vol. 132, p. 86

Because of the interrelated character of the operations of the subsidiaries of many multinational enterprises, the division of the profits of such enterprises among different national jurisdictions almost always involves unavoidably arbitrary allocations. [24]

Table 2.11
Profitability of leading foreign-owned firms
and UK public companies, 1965
(Net income divided by net assets, %)

Industry	UK firms	US firms	Non-US
Food and drink	14·0	19·0	5·7
Chemicals	12·8	14·7	12·4
Metal manufacturing	10·4	18·9	22·4
Non-electrical engineering	13·1	19·6	11·5
Electrical engineering	13·8	19·3	4·5
Vehicles	14·9	9·2	11·0
Metal goods	16·0	21·9	14·0
Textiles and clothing	13·7	20·0	15·4
Bricks, pottery, glass	15·5	23·0	—
Paper, printing, publishing	13·0	14·6	6·1
Other manufacturing	13·1	16·6	11·7
Total manufacturing	11·9	15·5	11·0
All industry	12·3	16·5	10·4

Source: J.H. Dunning 'Foreign investment in the United Kingdom' in Litvak and Maule, op. cit., p. 227

One motive for allocating low profits to UK subsidiaries is to minimise taxation (not a strong motive for US companies, because of minimal differences in corporation tax, but a much more plausible explanation of the low profitability of e.g. the Swiss-owned pharmaceutical companies); another explanation may be differences in accounting procedures, and a third the possibility that intra-company transactions may not always be charged on an arm's-length basis. There may be a link between this third factor and the narrowing gap between the profitability of US-owned and British firms: in 1960 US manufacturing firms achieved a 13·3 per cent return on capital (compared to 8·9 per cent for UK companies), while in 1966 the figures were 9·7 per cent and 7·2 per cent respectively; meanwhile, royalty and service fee payments by US-owned manufacturing firms in the UK rose from £14 million in 1960 to £44 million in 1966.[25] Thus the declining profit differential may be due partly to US subsidiaries being charged more realistic prices for the benefits conferred on them by their parent companies, and also the increasing competition from British firms and imports as the technological lead of US firms was eroded. The fact that a profitability gap remains is probably due to the large size of the US firms, and their ability to devote more resources for developing new products and managerial techniques (which are transmitted to their subsidiaries) than is possible for UK firms.[26] Even so, Dunning has argued:

> ... the margin of unavoidable efficiency of UK firms has probably been exaggerated in the past, and is no longer sufficiently large to ensure a net beneficial effect from foreign investment.[27]

2.3.2 Contribution to the balance of payments

The factors which must be taken into account when assessing the contribution of foreign-owned companies to the UK balance of payments are too complex for a full discussion of them in this brief survey, but they may be categorised under four headings:

1   The 'export effect' − that is, the contribution of foreign investment to UK exports.
2   The 'import substitution effect' -- the degree to which production by foreign firms in the UK reduces otherwise unavoidable imports.
3   The 'import effect' − the extent to which production by foreign firms in the UK increases imports of components, raw materials, etc.
4   The 'repatriation effect' − the proportion of income accruing to foreign-owned firms which is taken out of the UK and consequently represents a drain on foreign exchange reserves.[28]

Unfortunately the Board of Trade has only collected data on the export performance of foreign firms, not on their import performance, but Dunning calculated on 1965 figures that the initial balance of payments impact of new US investment in 1965 (in the form of inward investment less the import of capital goods) was £73 million, and the recurrent impact of US investment for 1965 (exports less imports, remitted and reinvested earnings, and royalties and service fees) to be £284 million. If one deducts from this an estimate of the difference between the actual exports of US firms and what they would have exported if they had exported the same percentage of sales as their British competitors, producing a balance of

37

payments opportunity cost of £272 million for 1965, then the net contribution of US firms to the balance of payments was £12 million (plus the £73 million of net investment), equivalent to 6·5 per cent of the assets controlled by US firms in 1965. [29] Such a calculation excludes the external or spill-over effects of foreign investment on the growth of the UK economy, in terms of more efficient use of resources, increased competition, tax revenue and the like, but Steuer has estimated that foreign investment is responsible for a favourable effect on the UK balance of payments, on the order of 10 per cent of the foreign output in the UK.[30]

Board of Trade data on the exports of foreign companies, set out in Table 2.12, indicates that in 1966 foreign firms accounted for almost 23 per cent of total UK exports – a much larger proportion than their share of UK manufacturing assets (about 12 per cent) would lead one to expect. Moreover, almost half of these exports were made to related concerns overseas, compared to 15 per cent of the exports of British firms. Even if one increases this latter figure to discount for small UK exporters with no need for overseas affiliates, it is apparent that British multinational firms do not have such well-developed group overseas marketing arrangements as those of the foreign-owned companies.

The impressive export performance of foreign-owned firms is partly a result of their concentration in high-export industries, (such as motor

Table 2.12
Contribution of foreign and UK-owned firms to UK exports, 1965

		Value £m	%
1	Total UK exports of which:	5,182·0	100·0
2	By UK firms	4,003·7	77·26
	To related concerns	*609·6*	*11·76*
3	By all foreign firms	1,178·3	22·74
	To related concerns	*523·2*	*10·10*
of which:			
(a)	By US-owned firms	700·8	13·52
	By US-owned firms to related concerns	*391·8*	*7·56*
(b)	By non-US owned firms	298·8	5·77
	By non-US owned firms to related concerns	*109·1*	*2·11*

Source: *Board of Trade Journal* 16 August, 1968, pp. 470–2

vehicles, tyres and engineering) and also of their size, which tends to be greater than that of the average UK firm. When size is taken into account, the performance is less impressive; Dunning has estimated that 72 per cent of all exports of foreign firms in 1966 was accounted for by firms exporting £5 million or more — the corresponding figure for British firms was 67 per cent. [31] Even so, it is clear that the overseas marketing facilities of the foreign multinational firms give their UK subsidiaries an advantage over domestic British exporters, although the high level of intra-company exports by foreign firms does give some substance to fears that British exports might be adversely affected by marketing decisions taken by the foreign parent company, and that foreign firms might minimise their UK tax liability by manipulating transfer-prices on intra-company goods transaction.

In conclusion, it must be stressed that it is impossible to give an accurate assessment of the balance of payments contribution of foreign-owned firms, since the Board of Trade never collected data on imports by such firms which would enable their balance of trade to be calculated. On the estimates of Dunning and Steuer quoted above, all that can be said is that the net effect of foreign investment on the UK balance of payments has been positive, but not great.

2.3.3   Diffusion of technology

It has already been shown that foreign investment in the UK is concentrated in industries such as chemicals, electronics and mechanical engineering, where technology plays an important role. Indeed, H.G. Johnson has argued that 'the transference of knowledge ... is the crux of the direct investment process', [32] and many writers have stressed the role of foreign investment in bringing with it technology, new products and management skills.[33] It is not possible to discuss all the issues involved in this brief survey, [34] but in essence the debate about the role of foreign (and particularly American) investment in the development of British technology may be characterised in terms of the benefits of direct investment as a vehicle for technology transfer, and the obstacles created by direct investment to the creation of independent British technological capabilities.

The argument that foreign investment is beneficial to British technology asserts firstly that the foreign subsidiaries introduce new and improved products which improve welfare when they are sold; Dunning found that American companies were largely responsible for increasing the mechanisation of British farming eightfold between 1938 and 1955, and found similar benefits accruing to UK productivity from American-controlled production of office machinery and scientific instruments. [35] Secondly, that foreign subsidiaries introduce new production processes into the UK, employing advanced techniques developed by the parent companies, thus utilising British factor inputs more efficiently than they otherwise would be, particularly if these techniques are imitated by domestic firms as well. [36] Thirdly, that foreign subsidiaries are able to draw on the research and development programmes of their parents, which in the case of US companies are frequently larger than the total UK input into R & D in those industries, often at a reduced or minimal cost, thus greatly expanding the flow of new ideas and knowledge available to the UK. [37]

The counter argument, that foreign investment is a hindrance to British technological development, consists of three main points: firstly, that a major incentive for foreign take-overs of British firms is to gain control over a stock of unexploited ideas, causing the benefits from them to accrue to the parent company abroad rather than the Britsh economy. [38] Secondly, a desire on the part of multinational companies to centralise R & D programmes may mean that the research departments of acquired UK firms are reduced or eliminated (as happened with the take-over of Cossor by Raytheon in 1962) and in the case of new establishments little or no local research may be undertaken; a Stanford Research Institute report indicated that only half of the 200 American firms surveyed undertook R & D in Europe, and that most spent less than 4 per cent of their R & D budget there, using European research primarily as a monitoring activity. [39] Thirdly, the 'product cycle' theory holds that when local production is undertaken, it is usually based on production techniques developed by the parent company at an earlier stage, and that (while the parent company introduces a new generation of products and processes in its home country), the subsidiaries are always using outdated methods. [40]

Taking the 'beneficial' arguments first, it must be said that even if there was no direct investment, new products could be obtained through trade, although direct investment may accelerate product diffusion through better servicing, adapting the product for the UK market, and perhaps reduced cost brought about by local production. There may also be spill-over benefits to the UK economy through taxes on the subsidiary's profits, higher payments to domestic inputs, and effects through imitation — what Quinn has called the 'technology multiplier effect'. [41] The argument that foreign subsidiaries employ factor inputs more efficiently because of the advanced production processes and managerial techniques they import from the parent company and which are then copied by domestic competitors, is supported by Dunning's finding that nearly 80 per cent of US investment in the UK is concentrated in industries whose productivity had risen above the average in the 1955—1965 period. [42] The suggestion that foreign subsidiaries can draw on the R & D programmes of their parent companies, often at little or no cost, depends on the relevance of the parent company's research to the subsidiary's range of products and production processes; Dunning found that in the opinion of research directors of foreign pharmaceutical subsidiaries, between 75 and 100 per cent of the research findings of the parent companies were relevant to the operations of large UK subsidiaries, but for some of the smaller firms it was as low as 10 per cent; in the electronics industry, it was generally between 25 and 50 per cent.[43] There is evidence that many parent companies look on royalties as marginal income, having recouped R & D costs in domestic sales of the product, and consequently the subsidiaries do not bear their full share of research costs. [44]

The first of the negative arguments, that foreign investors take over British firms in order to reap the advantages of a stock of unexploited ideas, raises the question of why the companies concerned were not taken over by other British firms. It may be that, because foreign investors tend to be large companies, they can absorb the risk that the unexploited ideas will be fruitless, while smaller British companies could not take such a risk; certainly it is improbable that the price paid by the acquiring foreign company, in the face of competition from other potential British and foreign purchasers, will be inequitable. As Steuer has noted:

> ... buying at less than the firm is worth to [the foreign company] is still a gain to Britain. There is little point in retaining a claim on innovations in Britain that cannot be profitably exploited in the country. ... The only point it might raise is whether there is some tendency for British research to be directed to activities which cannot be very profitably exploited in Britain. [45]

The second negative argument, that multinational companies tend to centralise R & D programmes and therefore not carry on much research in the UK, is not borne out by the facts; Dunning and Steuer found that where UK and US affiliates compete side by side the latter spend at least as much on R & D as the former, and frequently foreign-owned firms contract-out research to other British firms. [46] However, even if this is the case, it is questionable whether, in view of the serious shortage of technically trained personnel in the UK, [47] it is desirable for foreign companies to carry out research in the UK, since products of that research accrue to the foreign company and the research personnel (usually British) will be

41

taken away from domestic industry where there is already a shortage of such personnel:

> The view that there is danger to British technology when foreign subsidiaries fail to initiate or maintain research efforts appears to be misconceived. The direct opposite view seems to make more sense. [48]

The third negative argument, that foreign subsidiaries market products and use techniques which are one step behind those of the parent company, is linked with the argument that foreign investment leads to a situation of technological dependence. However, assuming that foreign innovations are protected by patents, they could not be duplicated by British firms, which would (in the absence of direct investment) have to import the goods or else manufacture in the UK under licence; this would be to substitute one form of dependence for another. It is usually accepted that the growth rate of an advanced industrial economy like the UK is closely linked to its pace of innovation,[49] but the crucial point is the efficiency of R & D activities, not the national origin of the company undertaking them, particularly since the ideas produced and their diffusion throughout the economy may stimulate further innovation. It may be that the dominance of foreign-owned companies in certain industries prevents British companies from undertaking the necessary amount of R & D to remain competitive, and that this would increase the opportunity of foreign firms to market obsolescent products in the UK,[50] but then the decision has to be made as to whether the UK should retain an independent capability in those industries.[51]

National autonomy in the technological sphere would be extremely costly for the UK, and indeed there is room for scepticism with respect to the economic pay-off of research; Peck pointed out that a very large proportion of US research activity is Government-supported, which would cast doubt on the profitability of much research.[52] Although it may be that foreign firms exploit their monopoly position arising from the innovations they produce, whether such innovations are generated by them in the UK or overseas is irrelevent, and, indeed, if they are generated by British personnel in the UK this may further inhibit British firms from producing rival innovations, given the shortage of trained research personnel. As for the argument that foreign firms use the product cycle to employ out-dated techniques, it must be said that there is no evidence to suggest that domestic factors are used less productively compared to their alternative employment within the UK; the more integrated the multinational firm, the more factor combinations will be influenced by factor costs in the countries in which it operates, and the superior growth rates of foreign-owned firms in the UK suggests that the best techniques are being employed. [53] Further evidence of this may be seen in the export performance of foreign firms (in the section on balance of payments above), which indicated the close association between the growth of US investment in technology-based industries and their share of UK exports in those industries.

In conclusion it must be said that neither the positive nor the negative arguments on the technological contribution of foreign firms to the UK economy are very strong, and in certain cases mutually contradictory (such as the arguments opposing technological dependence but welcoming foreign-controlled R & D programmes in the UK). Indeed, Dunning and Steuer conclude that in relation to technology:

> ... the kind of detailed information required to discriminate between desirable and undesirable inward investment is not likely to be obtained. Nor is the ability to forecast which sensible discrimination would imply. [54]

In so far as multinational companies possess certain technological advantages, the logical objective for UK industry would be to develop similar international capabilities in order to broaden their market base and gain access to more R & D funds, rather than to restrict inward investment, which, although it is only one means of gaining access to technology, does improve productivity and (if in fact it does generate monopoly profits) increase taxation revenue.

2.3.4   Regional development

It is frequently asserted that foreign investment has played an important part in developing the less prosperous regions of the UK, because the Government offers better financial incentives and facilitates the issue of Industrial Development Certificates for foreign investment in the Development Areas. [55] One reason for the willingness of foreign companies to set up in the Development Areas may be that they frequently have no existing plant in the UK and therefore no particular preference for a location close to existing industrial centres; another may be that many foreign companies have more experience of managing geographically decentralised operations than UK domestic firms. Moreover, much of the foreign investment in the less prosperous regions is in light manufacturing or science-based industries where raw materials and transport costs are not very crucial. Dunning has estimated that at the end of 1966 there were about 100,000 people employed by American firms in the less prosperous regions of the UK, providing employment which might otherwise not have been available and a net gain to UK output of between £100 and £200 million (0·3 to 0·6 per cent of GNP), depending on whether the local multiplier effects of the investment are included or not. [56]

However, although much of the foreign investment in the less prosperous regions has been non-competitive with British investment (because it has been concentrated in 'new' industries such as electronics, and because of the high level of unemployment in these regions), and may therefore be seen as a net gain to the national output, it is dubious whether foreign investors have played such a large role in regional development as has commonly been supposed. Much of the foreign investment in the less prosperous regions (as for the UK overall) has been in capital-intensive science-based industries, such as computers and scientific instruments, and therefore does not create a large amount of employment; the Government's investment incentives (as will be seen in the next chapter) encouraged such capital-intensive investment.

Moreover, although foreign firms accounted for almost half the new employment in Scotland in the 1945–65 period, in the less prosperous regions as a whole they accounted for only 18 per cent in the same period (and only 13 per cent in 1960–65). In contrast, foreign firms created 33 per cent of new employment in the industrially congested areas of the South-East and Midlands in 1945–65, and in particular 53 per cent of new employment in the South-East during that period, when British firms found it much more difficult to obtain Government permission to expand in those areas. Indeed it is notable that in Scotland, the main beneficiary of foreign investment in the less prosperous regions, the foreign share of new employment dropped from 66 per cent in the 1945–51 period to 19 per cent in the 1960–65 period. [57] Thus while foreign firms did contribute to new employment in the less prosperous regions (18 per cent 1945–65), their share of new employment in those areas was slightly lower than their contribution to new employment in the UK as a whole (19 per cent 1945–65), which was concentrated in the more prosperous regions. [58]

Even where foreign investment provided employment in the less prosperous UK regions, there is some evidence to suggest that they did so by recruiting workers already in employment rather than from the pool of unemployed (although some of the latter may have been able to fill the jobs in existing industries thus vacated). Steuer found that in Greenock, a Scottish town with 7 per cent unemployment due to its declining textile and shipbuilding industries, three American firms (IBM, Jay Manufacturing and Playtex) employed about 8 per cent of the work force, but recruited

44

them from the employed rather than the unemployed, and by division of labour eliminated the need for advanced training and minimised the raising of skill levels. [59] It is, of course, impossible on such fragmentary evidence to draw any firm conclusions, but it does seem that the contribution of foreign firms to regional development in the UK may have been exaggerated.

2.3.5 Control over subsidiaries by parent companies

It has been seen that the majority of foreign investment in the UK (just over 70 per cent by number of establishments and by value of assets) has been in the form of wholly-owned subsidiaries, with only a minority with a less than 50 per cent foreign stake (18 per cent by number and 8 per cent by value). [60] However, it is important to distinguish between the concept of formal ownership and that of the degree of control exercised by the parent company over its subsidiary, even where it is wholly-owned by the parent company. Dunning found that there was a wide variation in the degree of supervision exercised by US parent companies over their UK subsidiaries, and Perlmutter has suggested that the parent company's orientation toward its subsidiaries (ethnocentric, polycentric or geocentric) has important effects on the limitations it imposes on the decision-making autonomy in areas affecting the overall performance of the multinational group. [61]

In a multinational company the classical economic rationality, that of profit maximisation irrespective of where the power of decision-making is located, does not apply — optimal behaviour of the multinational company as a whole may not necessarily entail optimal behaviour of the subsidiary considered in isolation, because allocation of profits will be determined by such considerations as comparative rates of taxation. The degree of control exercised over the subsidiary (that is, the degree of autonomous decision-making permitted by the parent company), may well affect the subsidiary's contribution to the UK economy, although there is not necessarily a correlation between the degree of autonomy of the subsidiary and the extent to which it makes a positive economic contribution. As was suggested above, an autonomous R & D programme might represent a sub-optimal use of resources from both the parent company's and the UK's point of view, and a high degree of subsidiary autonomy might indicate that the parent company considered the subsidiary to be of marginal importance and not worthy of significant source allocation.

The most recent and comprehensive data on the decision-making autonomy of foreign subsidiaries in the UK comes from a postal survey con-

45

ducted by Steuer in 1968 of 6000 foreign companies, which achieved a somewhat disappointing 10 per cent response. [62] Two-thirds of the companies reporting were wholly-owned subsidiaries, and 65 per cent were American-owned; the majority (62 per cent) were new establishments rather than take-overs of existing UK companies (24 per cent), which were preferred only when there was an existing UK company with special expertise (technical, managerial, or UK marketing). Steuer found that the pattern of ownership remained very stable over time, with no tendency to reduce ownership, and increases in ownership (where ownership was not total) only occurring when the company was in difficulties and tighter control was necessary. [63]

The survey found that overall financial control by the parent company was not tight; where financial targets were set, these were usually by consultation, even for wholly-owned subsidiaries. Perhaps because of the instability of sterling in 1966—67 (the years covered by the survey), there was much tighter control over repatriation of profits. [64] These findings are somewhat at variance with Brooke and Remmers' conclusion that 'finance tends to be the most highly integrated of the functional departments', [65] but it might be that non-financial methods of control were being substituted as the subsidiary won its spurs by successful performance. Such non-financial controls, such as production planning, were found by Steuer to be more extensive in subsidiaries of multinational companies with integrated production than they were for subsidiaries whose product line was different from their parent companies. [66] In pricing policy, Steuer found that 70 per cent set prices independently, 10 per cent in consultation with the parent company, and 8 per cent in accordance with the parent's instructions. [67]

In the determination of export policy, 37 per cent of the firms in the Steuer survey reported no interference by the parent, 22 per cent claimed some geographical restrictions, 9 per cent direct parental co-ordination or control, 14 per cent parental guidance, and 18 per cent made no exports at all. Most subsidiaries were restricted from marketing in the home country of the parent, and US companies from marketing in Communist countries. There was a general tendency for parent companies with large international networks to co-ordinate export policies and (as the data in Table 2.14 above confirms) for much of the subsidiaries' exports to be channelled through affiliates in other markets, partly because of a developed export intelligence network. [68] The greatest autonomy appeared to be in the field of personnel policy, where usually only the most senior appointments were made by the parent company and only few foreign nationals were employed; this confirms Dunning's findings in his case studies of American firms in the electronics and pharmaceuticals industries. [69]

In general, it would appear that the foreign subsidiaries covered by the Steuer survey fall within Perlmutter's 'polycentric' classification, with a relatively low decision-making authority being retained by the parent company; this accords with Vernon's observation that 'as a rule, discipline and co-ordination are maintained much more by common training and conditioning than by a stream of commands from the center'. [70] Steuer found that subsidiaries of centralised multinational firms were less amenable to governmental directive (in this case the pay freeze of 1966) than bi-national firms and joint ventures, but that most firms stressed their anxiety to co-operate with the UK Government. [71] In particular, he found a moderate tendency for subsidiaries controlled by the parent in exporting policy (itself an indicator of the geographical spread of the parent company's interests) to be less amenable to governmental directive. [72] One might hypothesise that the movement from an ethnocentric to a polycentric orientation by the parent companies with regard to their UK subsidiaries has been the result of the impressive performance of such companies (in terms of growth and profitability), compared to their UK competitors, but that there is some indication that some parent companies are showing an increased awareness of their global responsibilities and are therefore less willing to defer to UK interests if they are incompatible. Vernon has noted such an awareness in US companies' attitudes to exchange risks:

> During 1967, at the height of the crisis that preceded the devaluation of sterling, all but three of twenty-five large US-controlled enterprises with subsidiaries in Britain were hedged in some degree against devaluation. It would be surprising if British-owned enterprises were found hedging to the same degree. [73]

However, there is little evidence to suggest that this trend is widespread or that it heralds the development of a geocentric orientation on the part of these companies.

2.3.6 *Taxation and currency policy*

The quotation from Vernon above brings us to the important but shadowy area of the extent to which multinational companies operating in the UK seek to minimise their UK tax liabilities and weaken the position of sterling by manipulating their foreign exchange transactions. A multinational company may minimise its tax burden by artificial transfer-pricing in intra-company transactions, adjustments in royalties and service fees, and arbitrary allocations of administratives costs, so that its profits in high-tax countries are shifted to low-tax countries. As Table 2.12 indicated, 22 per cent of all UK exports in 1966 were sold to related concerns, and in the case of US firms well over half their exports were destined for affiliates overseas, which would create considerable opportunities for transfer-pricing. J.S. Shulman has found that in a study of eight multinational companies, artificial transfer-pricing to minimise taxation produced 'gains [which] have been markedly worthwhile', [74] primarily because tax authorities have great difficulty in determining any norm on which prices should be based, since multinational companies can justly claim that the international integration of production makes it difficult to establish the cost of capital, for example, and the way in which it is amortised, and that (as Steuer's survey indicated above) the setting of prices in transactions between affiliates is often delegated to local management.

Possibly because US and UK corporation tax rates are broadly similar, artificial transfer-pricing on sales of goods between the US parent and its UK subsidiary does not seem to be widely used; in 1965 40 per cent of UK subsidiaries made no purchases at all from their US parent companies, and 60 per cent made no purchases of goods for further processing or assembly. [75] Other foreign subsidiaries in the UK may make some use of artificial transfer-pricing: as Table 2.11 indicated, the average profitability of non-US owned subsidiaries was below that of UK firms and well below that of US-owned firms. The 1967 Sainsbury Commission Report on the UK pharmaceutical industry showed that between 1961 and 1965 the five Swiss subsidiaries showed an average rate of profitability less than half that of US-owned subsidiaries, and at least 30 per cent lower than similar British and other foreign companies:

> Foreign firms reported a much higher cost of materials as a percentage of total cost of manufacture than did British firms ... The highest percentage for manufacture costs is shown by companies owned in Switzerland, but a large part of these costs represents materials at an advanced stage of manufacture, supplied by their parent companies at prices which are not on an open market basis. [76]

The tax differential between the UK and Switzerland provided a greater incentive for a Swiss company to repatriate earnings as interest and royalties (which were not under the Anglo-Swiss tax treaty subject to UK witholding tax), [77] than for an American company, because all remittances to US parent companies are ultimately taxed in the US at the same rate, whatever their form. Nine Swiss companies in Brooke and Remmer's study were notable for their high proportion of intra-company capital

48

debts, ranging between 23 per cent of total capital in 1959 to 37 per cent in 1967, which enabled them to remit as much as possible of their earnings in the form of interest. [78] Such tax avoidance is not confined to foreign-owned companies, however — Rio Tinto Zinc pays only 2 per cent of its tax bill to the British exchequer, and British Petroleum (in which the British Government is the largest shareholder) pays none at all, even though 37 per cent of its employees are located in the UK. [79]

Although it is doubtful whether multinational companies can be held responsible for the devaluation of sterling in 1967, there is evidence that they sought to minimise losses from the impending devaluation by increasing their stocks of imports into the UK, holding up exports, speeding up import payments and profit and fee remittances, and slowing down export payments. [80] Such leading and lagging payments played a considerable role in the pre-devaluation instability which the Labour Government had to face in the 1964–67 period, as can be seen by the swings in the balancing item in periods characterised by uncertainties about exchange rates. [81] Indeed, Turner has claimed that:

> The amount of trade which [multinational companies] are now carrying out across national boundaries has risen so much that they have enough resources to practically bring about a currency devaluation once they have made up their minds that this is going to happen. [82]

It is difficult to see how the companies could avoid taking such preventive action without being accused of negligence by their stockholders, and in any case not all companies were able to protect themselves fully against the 1967 devaluation of sterling: Hoover lost $6·9 million (equivalent to 55 cents per Hoover share, in a year when earnings were worth $2·09 per share), Kodak lost $9·5 million, and ITT $3·2 million, despite vigorous attempts to cover itself in the forward-exchange market. [83] Vernon quotes a study of 25 US subsidiaries in the UK at the time of the 1967 devaluation which indicated that:

> ... the mature and experienced firms took very limited and restrained action to protect their sterling positions against devaluation. Their asserted reasons for that restraint were various. One was a desire not to add to Great Britain's difficulties and to their own public relations problems by conspicuously burdening the British currency with their hedges. But another was the view that even the best of guesses regarding prospects of a currency devaluation was prone to major error and was therefore not worth the internal organizational effort. [84]

49

In the absence of adequate data on transfer-pricing and currency hedging, one must conclude that multinational companies operating in the UK had undoubtedly the *capability* to make full use of the international spread of their activities, but that there are few examples of blatant tax avoidance or currency speculation, and that opportunities for such stratagems are an inevitable result of the increase in foreign direct investment. As the value of UK overseas investment is double that of foreign investment in the UK, it must be said that British companies are even more likely to have an effect on UK tax revenue or sterling stability, since the same opportunities are open to them as to foreign-owned companies; it seems probable that, where tax and currency liabilities are concerned, patriotism is not enough.

2.3.7 Personnel and labour relations

There is no comprehensive information on the number of foreign nationals employed in foreign subsidiaries operating in the UK, but a survey carried out by the American Chamber of Commerce (United Kingdom) indicated that in 1970, over 60 per cent of the 260 American-owned firms reporting had no American citizens on their payrolls, while 104 companies employed 737 Americans out of a total work force of 481,268. Of these American employees, all were in relatively senior positions – 413 in management, 196 in production, and 128 in sales, and the bulk of Americans employed were in the more technical industries such as oil, motor vehicles, and electrical engineering. [85] In a survey carried out in 1961, Dunning found that three-quarters of the US firms in his sample were headed by a British managing director, and that in more than half there were a majority of British nationals on the board of directors. He also found that a much higher percentage of executives in US firms possessed university degrees or similar qualifications than was the case for British firms. [86] Several American firms have stressed their employment of British nationals in senior management positions; Esso (UK) employs no American nationals in top management, and IBM (UK) had only one non-British plant manager in 1970, who was there at the request of the British managing director. [87] Comparable information on the nationality of management of other foreign subsidiaries is not available, but the evidence would suggest that they follow a similar polycentric orientation, with the majority employing British nationals in senior management positions.

As far as labour relations of foreign-owned companies in the UK are concerned, there is little evidence to suggest that they are worse than for UK industry as a whole. In 90 per cent of the American firms covered by Dunning's 1961 survey, labour relations were thought to be good or very good, [88] and Steuer and Gennard found that foreign-owned firms general-ly placed much more emphasis on personnel management, and pioneered the use of productivity agreements in the UK. [89] Some foreign firms have been the subject of criticism for their failure to recognise trade unions — IBM and Kodak are prominent examples — but frequently such firms have avoided labour unrest by higher wages and fringe benefits than their UK competitors. [90] However, despite well-publicised examples of battles for union recognition, such as the Roberts—Arundel affair, [91] the Trades Union Congress found that foreign firms were no more anti-union than British-owned firms, although the foreign firms concerned tended to be larger. [92]

In general the trade union movement in the UK has paid little attention to the problems of foreign-owned firms operating in the UK, apart from two motions at the 1965 and 1968 TUC Congresses deploring non-recog-nition of unions by foreign firms, [93] a section in a 1970 economic review calling for governments to collect more information on international com-panies, [94] and a one-day conference on international companies held in October 1970, which called for the adoption by the UK Government of guidelines for acceptable behaviour by international companies. [95] TUC officials have discounted the possibility of British union participation in collective industrial action against international companies, considering that the exchange of information between the unions of various countries, for use in bargaining at the national level, is more fruitful. [96] The explana-tion for this muted response to foreign firms may well be that most foreign firms have adapted well to the UK industrial relations system (with its high degree of unionisation, covering 40 per cent of the labour force, compared to 22 per cent in the US), [97] and that few foreign firms have switched production from plants in the UK to affiliates overseas. Where such switching has occurred, such as the Roberts—Arundel case mentioned above or the closure of Remington plants in Scotland in 1966, [98] the redundancies caused have been small, and have attracted more press coverage than far more extensive rationalisations by British firms, like the 34,000 workers made redundant by the General Electric Company between 1968 and 1970. [99]

Indeed, there is evidence that industrial relations in foreign-owned firms are better than in their British counterparts; Steuer and Gennard found in their analysis of 1963 and 1968 strike figures that the contribution of foreign-owned firms to total stoppages, whether measured by number of stoppages, number of workers involved, or working days lost, is less than their contribution to total output (see Table 2.13). [100] They found that the causes of disputes in both British and foreign firms were broadly

51

Table 2.13

Comparison of industrial stoppages in foreign-owned and UK firms,
1963 and 1968

		No. of stoppages	Workers involved	Working days lost
1963				
1	Foreign-owned	70	21,046	58,077
2	Domestic	1,998	434,154	1,938,923
3	Total	2,068	455,200	1,997,000
4	Percentage foreign-owned	3·8	4·6	2·9
5	Percentage foreign share of output	10·4	10·4	10·4
1968				
6	Foreign-owned	208	75,532	454,437
7	Domestic	2,170	1,998,468	4,264,563
8	Total	2,378	2,074,000	4,719,000
9	Percentage foreign-owned	8·7	3·6	9·6

Source: Steuer and Gennard, op. cit., p. 121

similar, but that foreign firms were much more successful than their British counterparts in avoiding both small 'wildcat' strikes and long-drawn disputes. [101] The explanation for this better industrial relations record might include a more extensive and better management input into personnel problems, a generally high wage and high productivity policy, and the preference of foreign firms for bargaining on a plant rather than an industry-wide basis. [102]

In conclusion, it can be said that foreign-owned firms have tended to be quite sensitive to the problems of personnel management, preferring to employ British nationals (of above average educational attainment) in senior management positions, and placing more stress on innovative industrial relations practices, such as productivity bargaining, than their British competitors. The result of this emphasis on the importance of personnel management has been that foreign firms have a much better record of industrial relations than UK firms, [103] and in general have not aroused trade union hostility toward their activities, even though disputes involving foreign firms have received wide publicity. In their emphasis on employing British nationals in senior management, and their flexibility in adjusting to the conditions of British industrial relations, foreign firms seem to have adopted a polycentric orientation toward their activities in the UK, with some apparent success.

2.4   Conclusion

It has been seen that foreign investment in the UK has been increasing at twice the rate of UK investment overseas, although the value of UK overseas investment is still double that of foreign investment in the UK. By 1963 about 13 per cent of the output of UK manufacturing industry was controlled by foreign firms, the majority US-owned, and this share is steadily increasing; Dunning estimates that by 1981 US firms alone will control at least 20 per cent of UK manufacturing output on present trends. [104] The rate of increase in foreign investment in the UK, and its concentration in the fastest-growing sectors of the UK economy, might suggest that there is cause for concern at the growing influence of foreign firms in the UK, even though the extent of foreign penetration is not as great as in the Canadian, Australian, and some of the less developed economies; in Canada, for example, foreign companies owned over half the assets of Canadian manufacturing by 1964, and about a third of Australian manufacturing production was controlled by foreign companies in 1962. [105] It should also be remembered that the UK is, after the US, the most important source of overseas direct investment (and is a net creditor on the direct investment account for all countries with the exception of the US, Netherlands, Sweden and Switzerland) and would therefore be a prime target for retaliation if it restricted inward investment unduly. Moreover, inward investment played a crucial role in preventing a marked deterioration in the UK balance of payments during the 1963−70 period; it made the largest positive contribution to the long-term capital account, and (while not equalling outward investment flows), was greater than the deficit on current balance in every year except 1964. [106]

Foreign investment in the UK has been mainly carried out by large foreign companies (much of it in the form of wholly-owned subsidiaries), in industries which display a marked degree of concentration, and this has in itself increased the degree of concentration by forcing British firms to merge in order to remain competitive. Much of the expansion of foreign investment has been financed from retained profits and, in the case of working capital, from UK sources, making the capital contribution of foreign firms to the UK economy rather less impressive than it might at first appear. However, foreign investment must be seen as a package of capital, new products, and technological and managerial expertise, and the performance of foreign-owned firms is markedly better (both in terms of productivity and profitability) than their British counterparts.

It seems from the fragmentary evidence available that foreign-owned companies make a small positive contribution to the UK balance of payments, but (particularly since data on their imports is lacking) no definite conclusions are possible; certainly foreign firms export more of their output than their UK competitors, but because they tend to be part of a multinational integrated production network, they would also be likely to have a higher level of imports. It is important, as in the question of technological transfer, to remember in this context that in the absence of foreign production in the UK, more products would have to be imported or manufactured under licence. While the conventional wisdom that foreign investment brings about technological transfer is hard to evaluate, the common assumption that foreign investment has especially benefited the less prosperous regions of the UK is shown to be mistaken — if anything, foreign investors have been able to exploit their potential mobility by forcing the Government to allow them to set up plants in the industrially congested areas.

Although control over subsidiaries by foreign parent companies does not seem to be highly centralised, and falls within the polycentric orientation, there is evidence that foreign-owned companies do seek to minimise their tax burden by transfer-pricing and their exchange losses by currency hedging and leading and lagging payments. Such practices are difficult to detect, and are an inevitable consequence of the internationalisation of production, but foreign companies do not seem to have been blatant offenders in this respect, and have (as their superior record in labour relations and their preference for British nationals in senior management positions demonstrate) generally gone out of their way not to offend British sensibilities. Very few examples of transfer of production out of the UK by foreign firms seem to have occurred, and no incidents which would suggest that foreign subsidiaries have acted against the interests of the UK under pressure from their home government.

Thus far foreign investment in the UK has caused few serious problems, and has had either a neutral or even a mildly beneficial effect on the British economy. Foreign investment dominates some industries, such as the production of typewriters or of carbon black, but it does not yet exercise a dominant role in the economy as a whole. It might be, at some time in the future, that multinational companies will exercise control over the most dynamic sectors of the UK economy, and the British Government will find its range of policy options severely restricted by the strategies of companies controlling production and marketing of goods on a global basis. However, the multinational corporation is only one manifestation of the economic interdependence which has limited the British Government's decision-making autonomy for many years — Prime Minister Wilson was apt to blame not IBM but the 'gnomes of Zurich' for Britain's economic ills — and there *is* a limit to the autonomy which a small, densely populated island, with few natural resources can expect to enjoy. The important question is whether the British Government appreciated the significance of multinational companies when it formulated its industrial policies, and possessed adequate means of overseeing and controlling their activities; a question which the next two chapters will attempt to answer.

Notes

[1]   J.H. Dunning *The Role of American Investment in the British Economy* (PEP Broadsheet 507) PEP, London 1969, p. 169
[2]   S.E. Rolfe and W. Damm (eds.) *The Multinational Company in the World Economy* Praeger, N.Y. 1970, p. 8
[3]   see Chap. 3 *passim*
[4]   J.H. Dunning 'Foreign investment in the United Kingdom' in J.A. Litvak and C.J. Maule (eds.) *Foreign Investment: The Experience of Host Counstries* Praeger, N.Y. 1970, pp. 208–9
[5]   ibid., p. 214
[6]   see Table 2.4
[7]   J. Macmillan and B. Harris *The American Take-Over of Britain* Leslie Frewin, London 1968; F. Williams *The American Invasion,* Blond, London 1962; P. Millard *British Made?,* Kenneth Mason, Havant 1969
[8]   *Board of Trade Journal* 26 January 1968, p. vii
[9]   Dunning, op. cit., pp. 232–4, found that 80 per cent of US investment was in industries where the three largest firms accounted for more than one-third of the total output
[10]   C.P. Kindleberger *American Business Abroad* Yale University Press, New Haven 1969, pp. 31–2
[11]   see Chaps. 5 and 6
[12]   Dunning, op. cit., p. 216
[13]   R. Vernon 'International investment and international trade in the product cycle' *Quarterly Journal of Economics* vol. 80 (1966), pp. 190–207; S.H. Hymer 'The impact of the multinational firm' in

M. Byé (ed.) *La politique industrielle de l'Europe integrée* Presses Universitaires de France, Paris 1963, pp. 167—85

[14] Dunning, op. cit., p. 211

[15] J.N. Behrman *National Interests and the Multinational Enterprise: Tensions Among the North Atlantic Countries* Prentice-Hall, Englewood Cliffs, N.J. 1970, pp. 14—15

[16] Dunning, op. cit., p. 224

[17] *Board of Trade Journal* 16 July 1968, p. 359

[18] M.Z. Brooke and H.L. Remmers *The Strategy of Multinational Enterprise* Longman, London 1970, pp. 157—8

[19] J.H. Dunning *The Role of American Investment in the British Economy* (see note[1]), pp. 138, 132

[20] Kindleberger, op. cit., p. 189

[21] A.E. Safarian *Foreign Ownership of Canadian Industry* McGraw-Hill, N.Y. 1966, p. 188

[22] J.H. Dunning and D.C. Rowan 'Inter-firm efficiency comparisons: US and UK manufacturing enterprises in Britain' in J.H. Dunning *Studies in International Investment* Allen & Unwin, London 1970, pp. 346—7

[23] The one exception is the motor industry, where Ford suffered prolonged labour disputes in 1965

[24] R. Vernon *Sovereignty at Bay: The Multinational Spread of U.S. Enterprises*, Longman, London 1971, p. 275

[25] Dunning *The Role of American Investment*, p. 131; US Department of Commerce unpublished data on royalty and service fee payments

[26] see Chap. 6

[27] Dunning *Foreign Investment in the United Kingdom* p. 229

[28] see G.C. Moffat 'The foreign ownership and balance of payments effects of direct investment abroad' *Australian Economic Papers* (June 1967), pp. 1—24

[29] Dunning *The Role of American Investment* pp. 146—50

[30] M.D. Steuer *et al The Impact of Foreign Direct Investment on the United Kingdom* HMSO, London 1973, pp. 6—8

[31] Dunning *Foreign Investment in the United Kingdom* p. 230

[32] H.G. Johnson 'The efficiency and welfare implications of the international corporation' in C.P. Kindleberger (ed.) *The International Corporation* MIT Press, Cambridge, Mass. 1970, p. 35

[33] see, for example, Behrman, op. cit., pp. 16—19

[34] see J.B. Quinn 'Technology transfer by multinational companies' *Harvard Business Review* (November—December 1969), pp. 147—61; M. Shanks *The Innovators* Penguin, Harmondsworth 1967; C. Layton *European Advanced Technology* Allen & Unwin, London 1969

[35] J.H. Dunning *American Investment in British Manufacturing Industry* Allen & Unwin, London 1958, pp. 66, 73

[36] J.H. Dunning and M.D. Steuer 'The effects of United States direct investment on British technology' in Dunning *Studies in International Investment* p. 323

[37] Dunning *The Role of American Investment in the British Economy* p. 151

[38] ibid., p. 154

[39] B. Williams *Technology, Investment and Growth* Chapman & Hall, London 1967, p. 21

[40] Vernon, op. cit., p. 71

[41] Quinn, op. cit., pp. 148–9

[42] J.H. Dunning 'Technology, United States investment, and European economic growth' in Kindleberger, op. cit., p. 151

[43] Dunning *The Role of American Investment in the British Economy* pp. 186, 194

[44] Brooke and Remmers, op. cit., pp. 161–2. See also the Monopolies Commission's investigations of Kodak and Champion, described in the next chapter

[45] M.D. Steuer *American Capital and Free Trade* Trade Policy Research Centre, London 1969, p. 36. A similar point is made in the Report of the Central Advisory Council for Science and Technology *Technological Innovation in Britain* HMSO, London 1968, p. 12

[46] Dunning and Steuer, op. cit., p. 330

[47] M.J. Peck 'Science and technology' in R.E. Caves (ed.) *Britain's Economic Prospects* Allen & Unwin, London 1968, pp. 449–62

[48] Steuer, op. cit., p. 38

[49] Central Advisory Council for Science and Technology, op. cit., p. 2

[50] This was one of the arguments used by the Labour Government to sponsor the formation of International Computers Limited, and to provide it with research funds: see Chap. 6

[51] It is interesting to note that, since the abandonment of the Blue Streak missile in 1960, the British Government has been content to remain dependent on the US for supply of its missile systems; apparently the principle of comparative advantage applies even to such key issues as national defence, with no apparent ill effects so far

[52] Peck, op. cit., p. 449

[53] Steuer, op. cit., p. 39

[54] Dunning and Steuer, op. cit., p. 341

[55] see, for example, G. McCrone *Regional Policy in Britain* Allen & Unwin, London 1969, p. 151

[56] Dunning *The Role of American Investment in the British Economy*, p. 143

[57] see Table 3.2

[58] , Table 3.2

[59] M.D. Steuer *et al The Impact of Foreign Direct Investment on the United Kingdom* pp. 108–16

[60] see Table 2.8

[61] J.H. Dunning *American Investment in British Manufacturing Industry* p. 112; H.V. Perlmutter 'The tortuous evolution of the multinational corporation' *Columbia Journal of World Business* vol. 4, no. 1 (January–February 1969), Table 1

[62] Steuer, *et al,* op. cit., pp. 128–60

[63] ibid., p. 134

[64] ibid., p. 147

[65] Brooke and Remmers, op. cit., p. 283

[66] Steuer, op. cit., p. 158

[67] ibid., p. 153

[68] ibid., p. 151

[69] Dunning *The Role of American Investment in the British Economy* pp. 185, 193

[70] Vernon, op. cit., p. 134

[71] Steuer, op. cit., p. 174. This confirms the hypothesis advanced in I.A. Litvak and C.J. Maule 'The multinational firm and conflicting national interests: a general systems approach' *Journal of World Trade Law* vol. 3, no. 3 (1969) pp. 309–18

[72] Steuer, op. cit., pp. 172–3

[73] Vernon, op. cit., pp. 168–9

[74] Quoted in C. Tugendhat *The Multinationals* Eyre & Spottiswoode, London 1971, p. 149

[75] M. Bradshaw 'US exports to foreign affiliates of US firms' *Survey of Current Business* (May 1969) p. 43

[76] *The Relationship of the Pharmaceutical Industry with the National Health Service* (Cmnd. 3410) HMSO, London 1967, p. 118

[77] This loophole was partially closed by an amendment to the treaty in 1966 which extended the UK withholding tax to the payment of licence and royalty fees See *The Financial Times,* 20 September 1966, p. 6

[78] Brooke and Remmers, op. cit., p. 223

[79] W. Kennet, L. Whitty and S. Holland *Sovereignty and Multinational Companies* (Fabian Tract 409) Fabian Society, London 1971, p. 1

[80] Brooke and Remmers, op. cit., pp. 200–3

[81] G.A. Renton and M. Duffy *An Analysis of the UK Balancing Item* (London Business School Econometric Forecasting Unit Discussion Paper no. 6) London Business School, London 1968

[82] L. Turner *Politics and the Multinational Company* (Fabian research series 279) Fabian Society, London 1969, p. 15

[83] *Fortune* 15 September 1968

[84] Vernon, op. cit., p. 133

[85] *American Manufacturers in the United Kingdom* American Chamber of Commerce, London 1971, p. 2

[86] J.H. Dunning 'US subsidiaries in Britain and their UK competitors' *Business Ratios* No. 1 (Autumn 1966), pp. 16–17

[87] Interview with Dr A. Pearce, managing director Esso (UK), 1 June 1970; interview with Mr J. Hargreaves, director of public affairs, IBM (UK), 15 July 1970

[88] Dunning, op. cit., p. 16

[89] M. Steuer and J. Gennard 'Industrial relations, labour disputes and labour utilization in foreign-owned firms in the United Kingdom' in J.H. Dunning (ed.) *The Multinational Enterprise* Allen and Unwin, London 1971, pp. 111–13

[90] *The Sunday Times* 3 October 1971, p. 65

[91] Roberts–Arundel had taken over a British textile firm in 1967 and withdrew union recognition, dismissing union members and replacing them by non-union workers. A strike lasting a year began in November 1967, and the company conceded recognition and reinstatement of union members, but in January 1969 closed down the factory and withdrew its capital to the US. See *The Financial Times* 18 December 1967, p. 1

[92] Trades Union Congress *Annual Report 1967*, TUC, London 1967, pp. 129–32

[93] see *TUC Annual Reports* 1965, p. 405, and 1968, p. 429

[94] *Economic Review 1970* Trades Union Congress, London 1970, p. 39

[95] *The Times* 22 October 1970, p. 24

[96] *International Companies* Trades Union Congress, London 1971; J. Gennard *Multinational Corporations and British Labour: A Review of Attitudes and Responses* British–North American Committee, London 1972, pp. 18–19

[97] *The Economist* 3 September 1966, p. 927

[98] Dunning *The Role of American Investment in the British Economy* p. 164

[99] *The Sunday Times* 11 July 1971, p. 43

[100] Steuer and Gennard, op. cit., pp. 121–3

[101] ibid., p. 130

[102] ibid., p. 143

[103] A notable exception to this is Ford's poor strike record in the motor industry; see Chap. 5, note 117

[104] Dunning *Foreign Investment in the United Kingdom* p. 243

[105] S.E. Rolfe *The International Corporation*, International Chamber of Commerce, Paris 1969, p. 131; D.T. Brash *American Investment in Australian Industry* Harvard University Press, Cambridge, Mass. 1966, p. 30

[106] Central Statistical Office *United Kingdom Balance of Payments 1971* HMSO, London 1971, p. 6

3 Governmental Control over Multinational Companies operating in the UK

'Our investigations ... have made it evident to us that there is much overlapping and consequent obscurity and confusion in the functions of the Departments of executive Government. This is largely due to the fact that many of these Departments have been gradually evolved in compliance with current needs and that the purposes for which they were thus called into being have gradually so altered that the later stages of the process have not accorded in principle with those that were reached earlier. In other instances Departments appear to have been rapidly established without preliminary insistence on definition of function and precise assignment of responsibility. Even where Departments are most free from these defects, we find that there are important features in which the organization falls short of a standard which is becoming progressively recognized as the foundation of efficient action.'

- The Haldane Committee Report on the Machinery of Government, 1918.[1]

3.1 Introduction

As the previous chapter indicated, it was not until the late 1950s that the rate of foreign investment in the UK began to increase markedly, and even during the 1964—70 period there were few industries which were dominated by foreign-owned companies. It is therefore not surprising that the responsibility for overseeing and controlling the activities of multinational companies in the UK was diffused throughout the general governmental machinery for economic management, and that multinational companies were not generally seen as presenting problems different from those caused by the activities of purely national enterprise. As will be seen in the next chapter, the diffusion of responsibility was accompanied by a generally favourable attitude toward inward investment, and in a sense this attitude and the fragmentation of governmental control over foreign-owned companies were reinforced by the lack of co-ordination and communication between the relevant government departments and the general paucity of information on the activities of multinational companies *per se*. This chapter will outline the structure of governmental control over multinational companies operating in the UK, and the ways in which it was implemented, but it should be borne in mind that for most purposes multinational companies were not distinguished from domestic companies by the Labour Government, which continued the policy of 'qualified welcome' for foreign investors which had characterised its predecessors.

There were, however, two factors which are important in understanding the Labour Government's management of the British economy, and in particular its relations with multinational companies operating in the UK; the first was the recurring sterling and balance of payments crises which placed the emphasis on short-term crisis management at the expense of long-term economic planning; and the second was the commitment by the Labour Government to industrial modernisation and economic growth. The 1964 Labour Election Manifesto set out the Party's aims:

> We want full employment; a faster rate of industrial expansion; a sensible distribution of industry throughout the country; an end to the present chaos in traffic and transport; a brake on rising prices and a solution to our balance of payments problems. ... None of these aims will be achieved by leaving the economy to look after itself. They will only be achieved by a deliberate and massive effort to modernize the economy; to change its structure and to develop with all possible speed the advanced technology and the new science-based industries with which our future lies.[2]

The Labour Party therefore advocated a much greater degree of government intervention in the economy, and in particular more centralised economic planning than their Conservative opponents. It might therefore have been anticipated that the Labour Government which came to power in October 1964 would come into conflict with foreign-owned companies whose decision-making centres lay outside the UK, and who would not necessarily be expected to conform to the policies of the British Government. In fact most foreign investment in the UK conformed to the economic objectives contained in the Labour Election Manifesto: it used capital and labour more efficiently, it frequently carried with it technological and managerial expertise, and its export performance was often better than that of purely domestic companies. If there were drawbacks to foreign investment, they were not readily apparent, particularly since there existed no machinery for giving special scrutiny to the activities of multinational companies, and in most areas there was inadequate information on which to base a co-ordinated policy toward them. The result of this lack of co-ordination was a continuation of the policy of treating the problems arising from foreign investment on an *ad hoc* basis, with no clearly defined guidelines of acceptable multinational corporate behaviour.

3.2   The structure of governmental control

When the Labour Government came to power in October 1964, the departments of government with prime responsibility for regulating economic activity were the Treasury and the Board of Trade. Other departments had functional economic responsibilities (the Ministry of Labour dealt with employment, and various other Ministries such as Power, Agriculture, Health, Aviation and Transport sponsored industries in their respective fields), but these two departments had the most effect on the activities of multinational companies in the UK.

The Treasury occupies a central position in the British Government's economic planning and regulation machinery; its control over taxation and exchange control affect companies directly, while its control of public expenditure and general short-term regulation of the economy significantly affect the economic environment. During the early 1960s there was considerable criticism of the pre-eminent position of the Treasury and the unfamiliarity of many Treasury officials with the problems of the private sector, leading a former Permanent Secretary of the Treasury, Lord Bridges, to insist that the Treasury would need

> ... a much better understanding than ever before with the world of business, industry, and commerce; more effective methods of communication in both directions. ... This closer relationship is essential if the Treasury is to discharge its duties of economic co-ordination.[3]

The Plowden Committee, whose report on the Treasury was published in 1961[4] found that too many decisions were taken on an *ad hoc* basis because there was no adequate machinery for bringing the competing demands of different departments together in a single coherent picture which would enable decisions on priorities to be taken.

The Treasury was therefore reorganised in 1962 on the basis of four functional groups, including the Finance Group, which brought together for the first time all questions affecting home and overseas finance, and in particular the movement of capital for private investment.[5] Even after this reorganisation, the Treasury remained one of the smallest government departments, with a total staff in 1968 of 1000 (including secretaries, typists and messengers), with only 124 administrative grade civil servants and a scant two dozen economists – ten fewer than the Ministry of Transport.[6] The small size of the Treasury was due to its central policy-making functions and its relative lack of responsibility for detailed administration and casework, but the consequence of this lack of day to day responsibility has been that 'it normally deals with the outside world through other departments, which act as its eyes, ears, and arms. ... Most Treasury officials see very little of industry or the City in the course of their professional duties.'[7] In 1962 the Conservative Government had taken the first step toward long-range economic planning by creating the National Economic Development Council (NEDC), which formed a meeting ground for Treasury and other officials with representatives of industry and the trade unions, but the creation of the Department of Economic Affairs and the Ministry of Technology in October 1964 reflected the desire of Prime Minister Wilson and his colleagues for much greater emphasis on industrial planning to augment the Treasury's more abstract policy-making. These changes represented a shift away from the priorities with which the Treasury was traditionally associated, namely the maintenance of sterling as a reserve currency and the achievement of a satisfactory balance of payments position – preoccupations which can be seen most clearly in its administration of exchange control (see below) – toward an emphasis on economic growth and full employment, which had usually taken second place in Treasury thinking.[8]

The Board of Trade, the other major component in traditional governmental control over the economy, was a large (17,500 staff in 1968) and in many ways old-fashioned department which had a general resposibility in respect of the UK's commerce, industry and overseas trade. It never enjoyed a glamorous reputation – Edmund Burke described it as 'a compost heap of incompetents'[9] – and its industrial responsibilities formed no coherent whole. An official guide to the Board of Trade indicated this:

> The Government's interest in commerce and industry is handled by the Board of Trade unless there is some special advantage in its being handled elsewhere. [10]

Because much of the work of the Board of Trade has been in the field of international commercial relations, it has been associated with a *laissez-faire* attitude, and Douglas Jay, President of the Board of Trade in 1966,

64

indicated that this was not satisfactory in the context of the Labour Government's more interventionist economic policy: 'We don't want to do what the Board of Trade has traditionally done, that's to say, just sit back and see what happens.'[11] Nevertheless, the variety of its responsibilities in the industrial sphere made the task of co-ordination especially difficult, and the creation of the Department of Economic Affairs and the Ministry of Technology was due to the opinion of the Labour Cabinet that the Board of Trade could not be made into an effective department with comprehensive responsibility for industrial policy. [12]

By 1969 the Board of Trade had ceded responsibility for distribution of industry policy and sponsorship of manufacturing industry to the Minstry of Technology, but it retained certain responsibilities which affected multinational companies operating in the UK. The collection of company financial reports, the administration of monopolies and mergers legislation, and the publication of statistical data on trade and industrial production were the most important of these responsibilities. As with the Treasury, however, there was no specific section of the Board of Trade with special responsibility for overseeing the activities of foreign-owned companies.

The Department of Economic Affairs was created by the Labour Government within days of assuming office in October 1964. The original idea for a long-term planning ministry to act as the promotor of growth and stimulant for change had been hatched by Harold Wilson and George Brown (who presided over the DEA at its inception) in a taxi on the way to the House of Commons before the election campaign, [13] and its subsequent development retained an improvisatory character. Its major task was to produce a National Plan, containing general regional and industry-by-industry analyses of the ways in which an overall growth in the national product of 25 per cent was to be achieved in the period 1964–70. [14] Accordingly a staff of 500 were rapidly recruited, drawing on planning staff from the NEDC, the civil service, the universities and industry. The National Plan was produced in September 1965, as part of the Labour Government's run-up to the 1966 election, and despite its length of over 500 pages, clearly demonstrated the haste with which it had been prepared. Unlike the French Plans, the National Plan gave no guiding figures to enable each branch of industry to place its own growth in relation to the overall rate of 25 per cent, or of the possible sources of the investment which would be necessary to reach that target. [15] The role of foreign investment was touched on only briefly, and in very vague terms:

New productive investment by foreign companies, especially in under-employed areas of the United Kingdom will continue to play an important part in the creation of new industrial capacity. A special effort will be made to attract those companies whose exports to Britain have already secured them a firm basis in the British market, to start local production. There will continue, of course, to be regulation of the acquisition of control of existing British companies. [16]

The primary role of the DEA was co-ordination, and although it had contacts with industry through the NEDC and its various Economic Development Committees (which were expanded to cover most of the important sectors of industry), it had no executive responsibility for implementing the Plan. Its failure to secure necessary executive powers from the Treasury and other departments compounded the difficulty of implementing policies for long-term growth at a time when the British economy was beset with short-term problems, and with the advent of a fresh sterling crisis and a sharp deflationary policy in the summer of 1966, the objectives of the National Plan had to be abandoned. At no time did the DEA attempt to set up guidelines for attracting and controlling foreign investment in the UK, [17] although it was responsible for creating two bodies, the Prices and Incomes Board and the Industrial Reorganisation Corporation, which did add to the Government's control over multinational companies.

The Prices and Incomes Board was established in April 1965 as part of the Labour Government's voluntary prices and incomes policy, providing a means whereby the Government could refer wage and price increases for impartial scrutiny by a body which occupied a semi-autonomous position. The Board was to include a trade unionist, a businessman and independent members, supported by appropriate specialist advice, and its impartiality was underlined in the appointment as its chairman of Mr Aubrey Jones, a former Conservative Cabinet Minister. Nevertheless, the DEA, which had responsibility for referring price and wage increases to the Board, refused to agree to Mr Jones' suggestion that the chairman of an American company should be appointed as a member of the Board. [18] The advent of a statutory prices and incomes policy in 1966 gave the Board an even more important role, since the Prices and Incomes Act 1966 gave the Government power to forbid increases only if the Board concurred. [19]

Nevertheless, the Board had no substantive powers of its own; its recommendations never had the force of law, and depended on acceptance by the Government and the parties concerned; and it could only initiate investigations into matters referred to it by the DEA (or the Department of Employment and Productivity, which assumed control over it in April 1968).[20] Since the DEA had no specific responsibility for monitoring the activities of multinational companies in the UK, it is not surprising that of the 170 reports published by the Board between 1965 and 1970, only five affected foreign-owned companies, and in every case the increase in prices was approved (with minor modifications in three cases).[21] Because the Board's permanent staff was composed of personnel with economic, managerial and civil service experience, its reports were unusually perceptive and authoritative, particularly since most of them were produced within four months of the initial reference and most of the data had to be collected for the first time, due to gaps in the data collected by government departments.[22] The rarity of references to the Board concerning multinational companies (no references on pay increases or productivity agreements, for example) may have been due to the desire of most foreign-owned companies to avoid a confrontation with the DEA, but is more likely to have been due to the lack of data available to the DEA — the IBM Rental Charges reference, for example, was made as a result of pressure from the Ministry of Technology.[23]

The Industrial Reorganisation Corporation was the concrete result of the National Plan's emphasis on the need for more concentration and rationalisation in industry as a means of promoting greater efficiency and international competitiveness. In January 1966 the Secretary of State for Economic Affairs, Mr George Brown, issued a White Paper containing proposals for the establishment of an Industrial Reorganisation Corporation with the task of speeding up re-groupings and mergers aimed at producing bigger and more efficient industrial units.[24] The changes which had so far taken place in this direction, the White Paper indicated, did not yet match the economy's requirements, and the IRC would meet a national need which was not being fulfilled by existing institutions in the public and private sectors. Due to the 1966 General Election, the IRC Act did not come into force until December 1966, but by that time thirty full-time staff had been recruited from banking, industry and the universities, under the chairmanship of Lord Kearton (Chairman of Courtaulds), with Mr Ronald Grierson, a merchant banker, as its full-time Managing Director.[25] Under the terms of the IRC Act, the IRC could draw on up to £150 million of public funds in order to promote or assist the development of any industry or enterprise by loans or the subscription of equity 'when a commercially sound project would be impossible or unduly delayed without IRC funds.'[26]

The IRC had two major functions: firstly, to establish an order of priorities for industrial reorganisation by means of industrial studies so that effort could be concentrated on those industries where IRC action could have the biggest impact in terms of improving economic efficiency and international competitiveness; secondly, to engage in a dialogue with businessmen to explore the ways in which key structural problems could be solved by mergers and rationalisation. Although under Section 2(1) of the IRC Act the Secretary of State for Economic Affairs could request the IRC to take action in any field, the IRC was independent of the Government, and there were few cases of Government interference with IRC projects. In some cases, such as the GEC–AEI merger in the electrical engineering industry in 1967, the IRC was able to push through mergers in the face of opposition from a government department – in this case, the Board of Trade. [27] The IRC Act had guaranteed the independence of the IRC, subject to Treasury approval of expenditure from its initial £150 million allocation, to the extent that mergers carried out under IRC sponsorship would be exempt from examination by the Monopolies Commission. [28]

The creation of the IRC can be seen as the result of the Labour Government's conviction that, as the main problems of the British economy were structural, a direct 'physical' attack could succeed where traditional Keynesian methods of managing demand and the balance of payments had failed, and where market forces had not produced the changes desired. The creation of larger firms would eliminate wasteful duplication of resources, improve the application of technology, and enable economies of scale to be attained. The IRC's role was to bring companies together, and if necessary provide medium-term finance to accelerate the achievement of the opportunities which the merger offered. This would enable British firms to cope with foreign competition and also bring about a fundamental improvement in the balance of payments situation. [29] The emphasis on international competitiveness led the IRC to take an interest in multinational companies, both in terms of creating indigenous British companies which could compete with them, and in terms of seeking trans-national mergers where no viable British alternative existed:

> The IRC recognises the potential importance of mergers across national boundaries and the growing role played by 'multinational' companies in the principal markets of the world. An improvement in the structure of British industry is, at the present time, the IRC's primary task, but there is no doubt that the IRC will increasingly have to consider supporting schemes designed to create industrial groupings on an international scale. [30]

The IRC therefore concentrated on three areas of inquiry in this field:

comparative performance of industries overseas; the position of foreign controlled companies in the UK economy; and the question of trans-national mergers. The IRC's preoccupation with industrial efficiency led it to pay far more attention to these questions than any of the government departments, and its autonomous position enabled it to engage in confidential discussions with multinational companies which produced far more detailed information on their operations than was available to the Government. [31]

Although the IRC stressed that 'it is by no means committed to purely British solutions', and that from 1968 it was empowered to 'borrow in currencies other than sterling which could be used *inter alia* to promote European industrial ventures' [32] it did not develop this side of its activities before it was dissolved by the Conservative Government in 1970, and was not responsible for the Dunlop—Pirelli merger in 1970, which was handled directly by the Treasury. [33] The autonomy of the IRC, together with its informal, selective and highly personalised approach, incurred the criticism of the Conservative Opposition in Parliament and accusations that it usurped the functions of merchant banks and modelled itself on Mussolini's Istituto per la Ricostruzione Industriale. [34] It was therefore not surprising that the Conservative Government dissolved the IRC when it came to power in June 1970, [35] and the IRC executives began the process of destroying their files in order to preserve the confidentiality of their contacts with business. [36]

The Ministry of Technology was, together with the DEA, the major institutional reform introduced by the Labour Government when it came to power in October 1964. Prime Minister Wilson, who had laid much stress in the election campaign on harnessing 'the white heat of the scientific revolution' to the modernisation of British industry, [37] told the House of Commons:

> The Minister of Technology has the general responsibility of guiding and stimulating a major national effort to bring advanced technology and new processes into British industry. The methods employed will include ... studies to identify particular industries or parts of industries suitable for action. ... The Ministry of Technology will in future be the sponsor department for the machine tools, electronics, telecommunications and computer industries. [38]

It was soon evident that the Ministry could not make a wide enough impact or rapid progress with its task of promoting industrial technology from such a limited industrial base, and in February 1966 it was made responsible for the Government's relationship with the rest of the engineering industry, followed in November 1966 by merchant shipbuilding. In February 1967 it also took over the functions of the Ministry of Aviation, which was the main Government link with the aerospace industry and the largest purchaser of electronics equipment. [39] By October 1969 Mintech, as it was popularly known, took over responsibility for the remainder of private industry by absorbing the functions of the Ministry of Power (coal, electricity, gas, oil and steel) and the Board of Trade's sponsorship of most of the remaining manufacturing industries. In addition, it took over from the Board of Trade and the DEA responsibility for the distribution of industry policy, regional planning, the IRC, and investment grants. [40] Thus by the end of 1969 it had become the major government department for the formulation of industrial policy, and in October 1970 the Conservative Government carried this process further by merging it with the Board of Trade to create the Department of Trade and Industry.[41]

The Ministry of Technology's functions linked together scientific and technological research and innovation (government-sponsored research projects came under its supervision), the problems of industrial structure, and the role of public procurement in strengthening the high-technology industries:

> The essence of the Ministry's industrial work is to establish and maintain effective communication and mutual confidence between the Minstry and industry. This is not easy, and repeated changes in the machinery of government such as have taken place in the past make it much more difficult. The benefits from change and regrouping, like those of from all mergers, take time to secure and are slow to accrue. [42]

Although its initial remit included the electronics and computer industries, which brough Mintech into contact with the problems caused by multinational companies, it was not until 1968, after the creation of British Leyland and International Computers as viable indigenous companies in the automotive and computer industries, that the Industry Group of Mintech began to study the more general aspects of multinational corporate activity. [43] The Minister of Technology from July 1966, Mr Anthony Wedgwood Benn, became concerned that the imposition of rigid conditions on foreign firms investing in the UK was not an effective way of dealing with them, and from 1968 onwards initiated a series of dialogues between himself and the chief executives of multinational companies:

We are beginning to establish a direct dialogue with international and multinational corporations that operate within the engineering industry in Britain. These represent a growing part of the world industrial pattern today, and it is through the large firms, operating world-wide, that a great deal of modern technological knowledge, and access to world markets, will ultimately come. ... Though there is a common interest here too, the potential conflicts between the commercial interests of trans-national corporations and British national interests cannot be overlooked. We have to see that, through a continuing dialogue, the British national interest is kept in the forefront and that consultation takes place over a whole range of issues that are of concern to us as well as to them. [44]

Although these 'dialogues' had not developed to any great extent by the time the Labour Government lost office in the summer of 1970 (only eight had taken place in 1969–70),[45] they did represent an important development in Mintech's policy toward multinational companies, toward a continued surveillance of multinational companies beyond the initial scrutiny given by the Treasury's Foreign Exchange Committee of initial investment applications. Although Mintech's major powers lay in stimulating British companies in industries where foreign-owned companies presented formidable competition (its 'Buy British' computer procurement policy is discussed in Chapter 6 of this study), by offering research and development finance and by sponsoring mergers, it did not have any direct powers over the operations of multinational companies, and until 1969 had very little data on which to base its policies. The dialogues, however, did begin to produce some information: 'So few, if any, governments do ask for information that it is usually provided without demur.'[46] Nevertheless, as both an international Mintech working paper and a submission by Mintech to the OECD indicate,[47] the formulation of policy had not gone beyond a tentative initial stage. By 1970 there were no lists of key industries in which further incursions by multinational companies should be closely scrutinised, and there was considerable opposition within Mintech to the idea of guidelines of acceptable corporate behaviour similar to those suggested for Canada by the Watkins Report:

The Government of the recipient country must accept that the multinational company must lay out its resources as it thinks right; and that if the performance of the local subsidiary is bad, nothing can stop the multinational company from drawing its own conclusion. ... If Governments get sensitive about this, they might be put in a quandary if they put pressure on a multinational company and that

71

company refuses to co-operate. ... The basic question is: do we want foreign investment? If we do, we must accept the consequences. [48]

In the main, therefore, Mintech exercised influence over multinational companies indirectly — through representation on the Cabinet Sub-committees on Foreign Investment and Mergers (the existence of which has never been formally acknowledged), by submitting memoranda at the invitation of the Treasury's Foreign Exchange Committee, by moral suasion in the 'dialogue', and by encouraging through mergers, public procurement, and R and D contracts, countervailing British competition in fields where foreign-owned companies were dominant.

Other government departments also had some responsibilities which affected the activities of multinational companies operating in the UK. The Ministry of Power, until 1969, had the responsibility for overseeing the oil industry, and because of the strategic importance of the industry, refused to divulge data on the industry's investment and balance of payments to other government departments; one of the reasons why the oil industry is excluded from the inward and outward investment data compiled by the Board of Trade. [49] The Ministry of Labour (which became the Department of Employment and Productivity in 1968) provided advisory services on industrial relations and manpower use, took over control of the Prices and Incomes Board from the DEA and the Monopolies Commission from the Board of Trade in 1969, and had prime responsibility for mediating in industrial disputes and providing employment statistics. The most important industrial sponsorship functions not assumed by the Ministry of Technology or the Board of Trade were those of the Ministry of Agriculture (food manufacturing) and the Ministry of Health, whose responsibility for the pharmaceutical industry will now be briefly outined.

The Ministry of Health has responsibility for overseeing the pharmaceutical industry, and is in the unique position, due to its control over the National Health Service, of being the only major purchaser of ethical pharmaceutical preparations. As the 1967 Sainsbury Report on the UK pharmaceutical industry indicated, foreign penetration of the pharmaceutical industry is high, and the industry as a whole is dominated by multinational companies; in 1966 American companies controlled 49 per cent of the UK prescription market, Swiss companies 14 per cent, other European companies 10 per cent, and UK companies 27 per cent. [50] In order to control prices of patented drugs, the Ministry of Health introduced in 1957 a Voluntary Price Regulation Scheme, under which UK selling prices were to conform to prices in export markets, but in addition the Minister of Health in 1961 invoked his powers under Section 46 of the Patents Act 1949 to enable all patent rights to be overridden in obtaining supplies of certain drugs for NHS hospitals — the result was that the prices of certain drugs produced by non-patentee firms were as much as ten times cheaper than the prices hitherto charged by the patentee. [51] Despite the Voluntary Price Regulation Scheme and the Minister's power under the Patent Act (which was extended to cover the NHS as a whole in 1968), the Sainsbury Committee found that:

> ... that actual level of profits ... is in some cases much higher than can be considered reasonable. ... We have concluded that the existing conditions under which medicines are supplied to the National Health Service are not such as always to secure that prices and profits are reasonable. [52]

In addition, the Committee drew the attention of the British tax authorities to the use of transfer pricing by foreign-owned drug companies to reduce their UK profits and thus justify price levels to the Ministry of Health, and pointed out that foreign-owned companies exported less (and in most cases ran a balance of payments deficit) than their British counterparts. [53] In general the foreign pharmaceutical companies spent less (as a percentage of sales) on research in the UK, and more on advertising, than their British competitors. [54] The Committee noted:

> We have, however, been very much surprised to discover that the position of the pharmaceutical industry in the United Kingdom economy, the desirability of encouraging its expansion, and the appropriate role of foreign firms in it, have apparently not been explicitly considered in any section or at any level of the Government. ... We therefore recommend that ... particular attention should be paid to the question of whether it is desirable, from the point of view of the economy as a whole, to encourage the introduction or further expansion of firms owned abroad. [55]

The reason for this lack of analysis of the pharmaceutical industry was that the Ministry of Health was preoccupied with its function as principal purchaser of drugs, and did not devote much attention to the economic effects of the pharmaceutical industry as a whole. Provided companies could demonstrate to the Ministry that their UK selling prices were comparable to world market prices, the Ministry was unconcerned with the profitability or balance of payments position of the industry; where the Patent Act powers had been invoked in 1961, this was due to the Ministry's knowledge of much lower prices (particularly of antibiotics) being charged by non-patentee firms in Italy, where no patent protections existed, rather than to any analysis of the profitability of patentee firms.[56] Although the Ministry of Health financed the cost of drugs prescribed by general practitioners under the NHS, it had no powers (such as exist in France) to forbid doctors to prescribe expensive branded drugs; in extreme cases, where an individual doctor exceeded average prescribing costs by 25 per cent, the local Medical Committees were empowered to withold part of the doctor's remuneration, but this was not a particularly effective form of control.[57] The degree to which foreign companies dominate the UK market can be seen from the following table, based on unpublished Ministry of Health figures. The table indicates that only five of the top twenty NHS suppliers were British in 1969, and accounted for just over 13 per cent of total sales to the NHS; eight were US companies controlling over 20 per cent of the NHS market; Swiss companies numbered three, with almost 11 per cent market share; while French and German

Table 3.1
Share of the top twenty pharmaceutical companies
in the NHS market, 1969

Company		Nationality	Sales (£000)	Percentage share of market
1	Merck Sharp & Dohme	US	8,180	7·6
2	Roche Products	Swiss	6,360	5·9
3	Beecham Group	UK	4,340	4·0
4	Glaxo Group	UK	3,010	2·8
5	Bayer	German	2,960	2·7
6	Geigy	Swiss	2,950	2·7
7	ICI	UK	2,880	2·7
8	Wyeth	US	2,760	2·6
9	Hoechst	German	2,760	2·6
10	May & Baker	French	2,470	2·3
11	Smith Kline & French	US	2,360	2·2
12	Wellcome	UK	2,240	2·1
13	CIBA	Swiss	2,110	2·0
14	Pfizer	US	1,900	1·8
15	Roussel	France	1,780	1·6
16	Fisons	UK	1,760	1·6
17	Upjohn	US	1,760	1·6
18	Parke–Davis	US	1,730	1·6
19	Lilly Industries	US	1,660	1·5
20	Riker Laboratories	US	1,640	1·5
Total for top 20 companies			57,610	53·4
Total for all firms			107,950	100·0

companies had just over 9 per cent. Certainly there is no evidence of discrimination against foreign-owned companies in NHS purchasing, although from 1969 onwards the Ministry of Health has included as part of the Voluntary Price Regulation Scheme a requiremnet that each NHS supplier must submit annual financial returns.

In May 1970 the Minister of Health used his statutory powers to force a Swiss company, Hoffman—La Roche, to do so. Subsequently the company's supply of tranquillisers to the NHS market was investigated by the Monopolies Commission, which found that it was making a return on capital of over 70 per cent and was charging its UK subsidiary over forty times the production cost for the supply of the necessary ingredients, in order to finance its future R and D by artificial transfer-pricing. The Commission recommended that Roche should reduce its prices of Librium by 60 per cent and Valium by 75 per cent of its 1970 prices, and that Roche should repay excess profits (estimated at over £11 million) made from sales to the NHS. This decision prompted government authorities in Germany, the Netherlands, Sweden, South Africa and Australia to begin investigations of Roche operations in those countries, and Roche began a protracted lawsuit in the British courts to get the decision overturned. [58]

In general the Ministry of Health seems satisfied that its unique position as the major purchaser of drugs, together with statutory powers to compel companies to submit financial returns and, in extremis, to be deprived of patent protection, gives it sufficient control over the drug companies. In the field of information, however, the Minister has no means of analysing much of the data it gathers (the last computations of royalty payments, for example, were made for the Sainsbury Committee in 1967), and has had to seek help from outside bodies, such as the Chemical Industry Economic Development Committee, for the preparation of industrial studies. [59] Perhaps more seriously, much of the data on exports, capital utilisation and research and development on an industry-wide basis are produced for the Ministry by the Association of the British Pharmaceutical Industry, the industry's leading pressure-group. [60]

The Ministry of Health, therefore, has exercised its control as the major purchaser of drugs to keep prices down (between 1963 and 1969 the wholesale price index for pharmaceutical products dropped 5 per cent, compared to a rise of 21 per cent for all manufactured products in the same period), [61] it made no attempt, through research grants or the sponsoring of mergers, to improve the competitive position of British drug companies. An NEDC study indicated that the Ministry's consumer-oriented approach meant that the export earnings of British drug companies were adversely affected, since overseas drug purchasers were in-

creasingly linking prices to the cost of drugs pertaining in the manufacturing country, and the wholesale prices in the British market were
considerably lower than in eight other countries examined. The effectiveness of the VPRS procedure in putting downward pressure on prices
meant that British companies had less to spend on research and development (the US company Merck Sharp & Dohme's £20 million annual research budget equalled that of the entire British pharmaceutical industry)
and that Britain was also less likely to attract foreign subsidiaries and the
access to the latest medical products which they made possible. [62]

3.3 Government control over initial investment

Foreign companies seeking to invest in the UK are subject to government
control in four main areas: exchange control, under which the permission
of the Treasury is required for the import or export of capital; company
registration, whereby the subsidiaries of foreign companies acquire legal
status in Britain, and must provide financial information on their activities
to the Board of Trade; location of investment, which is controlled by the
Board of Trade's distribution of industry division (absorbed by the Ministry of Technology in October 1969, but substantially unchanged in procedures and policies); and the regulations concerning monopolies and
mergers which will be dealt with in section 4 of this chapter.

3.3.1 Exchange control

The traditional preoccupation of the Treasury with sterling and the balance of payments can be seen most clearly in its administration of the
Exchange Control Act, 1947, which remains the only significant legislation affecting multinational companies as distinct from purely domestic
business enterprises. The provisions of the Exchange Control Act, which
was introduced by the previous Labour Government as an attempt to
control the external monetary crises of the post–1945 period, reflect the
needs of crisis mangement rather than any long-term investment planning
objectives. The Exchange Control Act prohibits, unless the consent of the
Treasury is obtained, virtually all financial transactions between UK residents and persons resident outside the Scheduled Territories (Sterling
Area), and also transactions involving non-residents which take place within the UK. [63] Sections 1 and 2 prohibit persons in or resident in the UK
from buying, borrowing, selling, lending or holding foreign currency; sections 5(c) and 6(i) prohibit persons in or resident in the UK from placing

76

sums to the credit of non-residents; sections 8 and 9 prohibit the issue or transfer of securities to non-residents; and section 30(2) prohibits 'any act whereby a body corporate which is controlled by United Kingdom Residents ceases to be so controlled.' This provision has one important exception, namely that it does not apply to control gained by dealings in the ordinary course of business on a stock exchange, but a Board of Trade report concluded:

> Though this exception in principle permits control to be gained through the purchase of shares on the stock market, it is generally believed that this would be such a slow and expensive way of gaining control of a company that it is thought unlikely to present a serious loophole. [64]

In fact this loophole was used by Philips in January 1967 to take over Pye Telecommunications, which has important defence business, and in 1971 a Ministry of Aviation spokesman admitted that if any foreign bidders attempted to buy the bankrupt Rolls-Royce company, the government's only recourse would be to outbid them for the shares. [65]

The Exchange Control Act is therefore the only British legislation which specifically affects foreign investors *per se*, both in the initial establishment of a subsidiary and the subsequent control of its financial affairs. In essence the Act is a blanket prohibition of any transaction involving non-residents, and the import of capital to set up a new firm or to take over an existing one requires specific permission from the Treasury. Although such Treasury permission, if given, applies to all purposes of the Act, there may be certain conditions attached, which will be discussed below. Two sets of criteria are applied to applications for exchange control permission: firstly, the effect of the investment on foreign exchange reserves; and secondly, the effects of the investment on broader economic interests. The exchange control administration procedure is remarkable for its informal and discreet character — the criteria referred to above have never been made public, but are made known from time to time to the merchant banks of the City, who act as intermediaries between the prospective investors and the Treasury's Exchange Control Committee. [66]

The first criterion, concerning the effect of investment on foreign exchange reserves, is designed to ensure that foreign companies will be largely self-financing in their development. The proposed investment must make an 'appropriate' contribution to the reserves, in so far as the foreign currency inflow is proportionate to the degree of control being taken by the foreign company, so that a 100 per cent controlled subsidiary's controlled fixed assets must be 100 per cent financed by the parent company from external sources. [67] One exception to this rule is where the proposed subsidiary's activities 'promise special advantage' to the British economy, such as establishing a plant in an area of high unemployment, in which case the foreign parent company is permitted to raise fixed interest loans in the UK up to an amount equal to 30 per cent of its stake in the subsidiary. [68] Where the foreign company is taking over an existing British company, the purchase price must be fair in relation to the market value of the assets taken over, including patented inventions and unexploited research. As far as working capital is concerned, there must be no 'excessive reliance' on UK sources for any further finance necessary, and therefore the parent company must provide a percentage of the further capital equal to the percentage of the subsidiary's assets which it controls. In short, the rationale for the foreign exchange criterion is that the foreign exchange reserves should benefit as a compensation for the loss of economic control which results from a foreign investment, and these conditions offer few (if any) obstacles to most potential foreign investors. In those cases where the financing proposals of prospective investors are unacceptable, the Treasury and the Bank of England do their utmost to suggest more acceptable alternatives. [69]

The second criterion, that of general desirability of the investment from the point of view of the British economy, is of much more recent origin, being imposed as a result of representations to the Treasury by the Ministry of Technology in 1967. [70] This deals with matters beyond the scope of the foreign exchange criterion, and the terms of it are considered confidential. It provides for 'special scrutiny' to be given to an investment proposal where the investment might: (a) lead to an 'important sector' of British industry becoming dominated by one or more foreign subsidiaries; (b) 'do damage' to the development of British technology; (c) frustrate an officially-sponsored scheme for rationalising an important sector of British industry. It is important to note that the exact definition of such words as 'important sector' and 'damage' has never been attempted, since, as a Minister of Technology official remarked, 'It is hard to define an elephant, but I know one when I see it.'[71]

The actual procedure for granting exchange control permission is straightforward and remarkably fast; the prospective investor contacts a British commercial or merchant bank, which is aware of the current criteria through formal and informal contacts with Bank of England or Treasury officials. An appropriate financial structure is devised, and the bank applies on behalf of its client to the Bank of England for exemption from the Exchange Control Act provisions; where an appropriate financial structure cannot be devised, the prospective investor usually drops the proposal before a formal application is made to the Bank of England, and this pre-screening carried out by the City banks helps to explain why very few applications for exchange control permission have been refused. Since 1945 there have been less than half a dozen refusals: one concerning a proposed take-over of a defence-related industry where the foreign investor could not give guarantees of continued UK production of certain items; another where the purpose was to set up a 'brass-plate' dummy company to gain a 20 per cent investment grant for the building of ships; two applications to set up front companies for tax-avoidance purposes (in one case coupled with an attempt to take over a UK financial institution with the suspected ultimate purpose of forging certificates of deposit); and a somewhat dubious abortion operation. [72]

The Bank of England, acting as the agent of the Treasury, has delegated authority to approve applications involving sums up to £500,000, without the need to consult the Treasury or other government departments, except in the case of certain specified firms in defence-related industries, which it must refer to the Foreign Exchange Committee. All cases involving greater amounts are considered by the Foreign Exchange Committee, which meets weekly on Wednesday mornings, and is composed of Treasury, Bank of England, Board of Trade and Ministry of Technology representatives, with the addition of any other departments affected by the proposals. The process is quite rapid; the Bank of England prepares a brief with recommendations within three days of receiving the application, this is circulated to interested departments, and the final decision is usually made within a week of the application being made. In the case of very large projects, the company frequently approaches the Treasury direct; in 1969 Dunlop had extensive consultations with Treasury officials concerning its proposed merger with Pirelli, and it was as a result of Treasury advice that the resultant share-exchange formula, in which the underlying equity remained in the same hands, with no foreign exchange flows or losses, was devised. These discussions by Dunlop with the Treasury, and the fact that the proposed merger with Pirelli was in line with the industrial policy developed by the Labour Government, also produced a provision in the 1969 Finance Bill exempting *bona fide* mergers from capital gains tax, thus preventing Dunlop and Pirelli from incurring an extra tax burden. [73]

Although the Dunlop—Pirelli merger was a special case, both in its size and its time (when 'European' gestures were particularly encouraged by the government), the Foreign Exchange Committee has a reputation for amenability to exchange control applications. In the case of take-over bids, where speed and secrecy are essential, the time-table is accelerated considerably; in 1969, when Philip Morris bid for Gallaher, another tobacco company, representatives of Philip Morris went to see the Bank of England at 11 a.m. and the Bank of England official immediately contacted the Treasury. A Treasury official saw the Permanent Secretary of the Chancellor of the Exchequer at 3 p.m. recommending approval. At 5.30 p.m. news of the £27 million bid leaked out from company sources, but exchange control permission was granted by the Treasury at 11.30 a.m. the next day – just over twenty-four hours from the time of the initial application. In the event, the Philip Morris bid was unsuccessful, but the incident illustrates the relative speed and informality of the exchange control procedure; in many instances, inter-departmental consultation and approval of exchange control applications has been carried out by telephone; and even when the Foreign Exchange Committee meets physically, it usually only consists of three or four officials who use their past experience, rather than intensive research on the application itself, to judge the pronouncements of the investor company. [74]

Until 1968, exchange control applications were generally only scrutinised for their financial implications, and the general policy of welcoming inward investment because of the technological and managerial resources which were seen as accompanying it meant that a very liberal policy was applied. Although the blanket prohibitions of the Exchange Control Act gave the Foreign Exchange Committee the ability to refuse applications without stating a reason, it has been seen above that very few such applications have ever been refused, and in only a small number of cases have conditions been attached to the exchange control permissions. Indeed, the Chancellor of the Exchequer is only notified of the large transactions, as Lord Bridges makes clear:

> Investment in the United Kingdom from overseas is likely to raise fewer problems. It is generally welcomed because it helps our balance of payments and tends to make funds available for our traditional role of overseas investment, particularly in the Commonwealth. Consequently there are few restrictions on new investment and *none on the reparation of capital and profits.* [My emphasis.] The most important and the most spectacular cases in this part of the overseas finance field are bids by foreign buyers to take over control of a United Kingdom company. In such a case, while the general policy of welcoming foreign investment ensures that such an application will be given every consideration, any other government departments concerned will have to be consulted to ensure that the transaction is not against the national interest. Moreover, as the take-over of a

80

major United Kingdom enterprise is likely to attract a good deal of interest in Parliament and outside, Ministers will have to be brought in at an early stage. [75]

In fact, very few take-over bids have resulted in undertakings being required from the bidding company; during the Labour Government's term of office there were only three such cases, all occurring at the the end of 1966 — the Chrysler take-over of Rootes, the Philips take-over of Pye Telecommunications, and the Litton Industries take-over of Imperial Typewriter. Only in the first two cases were the undertakings made public, in the form of an exchange of letters between the Minister of Technology and the chairman of the acquiring companies, and these are set out below.

(a) *The Chrysler take-over of Rootes*
(i) Chrysler will not initiate any action to impair either the home or overseas operation or the management and direction of Rootes as a British company in its relations with the Government, labour, its British shareholders, and the public.
(ii) Chrysler undertakes to maintain a majority of British directors on the Board of Rootes.
(iii) Chrysler confirms the plans of expansion covering development work at various factories, and especially at Linwood in Scotland where the major development will take place, and where it is planned to increase employment by several thousands; these plans are essential if Rootes is to remain competitive, achieve its proper share of exports and return to reasonable profitability.
(iv) Chrysler plans to achieve a progressive increase in the export of Rootes products without restriction to all practicable markets and to continue to make available its full international organisation for this purpose. They note that, in the view of Her Majesty's Government, the test of fulfillment of this undertaking would be that the export percentage of the products of the Rootes Group should be at least as high as the average for the British Motor Vehicle Industry as a whole.
(v) Chrysler will nominate a Rootes Director (British) to each of the Boards of Simca S.A. and Chrysler International S.A., and it is understood that a Simca Director (French) will be nominated to the Board of Rootes.
(vi) Chrysler understakes to leave at least 15 per cent of the Rootes equity in the hands of the shareholders other than Chrysler, and

that if such equity is taken up by the Industrial Reorganisation Corporation, a member of the IRC should sit on the Rootes Board.[76]

(b) *The Philips take-over of Pye*
(i)   Philips undertakes to maintain a majority of British directors on the Pye Board.
(ii)   Philips undertakes to ensure that any reorganization will not involve a diminution in the volume of production in the United Kingdom, or export from the United Kindom.
(iii)   Philips will ensure that all contractual arrangements for exchange or granting of technical information and patent licences will only be entered into on such conditions as would be considered fair and reasonable commercially. [77]

The most important point to note about these undertakings, which had the objective of improving the companies' contribution to the balance of payments, ensuring continued expansion in the UK, and guaranteeing continued representation of British interest on their Boards of Directors, is that they are much specific than any undertakings which had been asked for by the Government on previous occasions, such as the take-over of Trinidad Oil in 1956 or the purchase by Ford of the minority shareholding in 1960.[78] Although none of the undertakings is particularly onerous, they are of the type which go beyond 'best endeavours' to undertakings whose fulfillment can be objectively determined; Chrysler's undertaking that Rootes' export record would be at least as good in percentage terms as the UK motor industry as a whole, is a good example of this. What is surprising, particularly since the undertakings laid down quite specific standards of performance, was that no attempt was made either by the Treasury or the Ministry of Technology to ensure that the companies lived up to them. [79] In part this was due to a feeling among Treasury officials that the undertakings merely required 'tolerably good behaviour in the industrial scene,' [80] and that reliance could be placed on the good faith and social responsibility of the companies concerned; to this was added the feeling of the Minister of Technology at that time, Mr Antony Wedgwood Benn, that such undertakings were rather static in conception and that policing 'that sort of thing wasn't good enough, and interrogating them about whether they'd kept their conditions was much less creative than ... keeping in touch.'[81]

In the view of both Treasury and Ministry of Technology officials interviewed for this study, the purpose of such undertakings was twofold: firstly, they were a means of communication to the companies concerned that they were expected to act in a responsible manner; and secondly, they acted as a political escape-valve to reduce the possibility of criticism of permitting UK companies to come under foreign control. Certainly, the fact that similar undertakings have never been asked from foreign companies establishing their investments in the UK, as opposed to taking over existing British companies, is an indication that the undertakings had some public relations function. The rarity of such undertakings itself demonstrates the non-controversial character of most foreign investment; the chairman of the Foreign Exchange Committee had only received three letters of protest from members of the public in the three years he held that position. [82] Although in extreme cases the government could impose sanctions on deviant companies, such as withdrawing exchange control permission to repatriate profits or to make further capital injections into the subsidiary, it was felt that these would be rather extreme and that 'moral suasion' would be preferable. In fact the repatriation of profits (as made clear in the quotation from Lord Bridges above) is covered by a general — i.e. continuing — permission granted at the same time as exchange control permission for the initial investment, and although permission for subsequent imports of capital has to be sought each time it is required, it is invariably granted.

The speed of the exchange control procedure, the reluctance to impose conditions or interfere with the subsequent management of the investment, and the confidential nature of exchange control criteria all indicate the desire of the Government to encourage inward investment. The phrase 'qualified welcome' was frequently used by the officials interviewed to describe government policy toward inward investment, and the purely financial character of the exchange control criteria for foreign investment underlies this general attitude. Both the Treasury and its agent, the Bank of England, concern themselves solely with the foreign exchange and financial aspects of the investment applications, and where conditions have been imposed, these have been due to the insistence of the Ministry of Technology. [83] Although the attempted take-over of Pollard Ball Bearing by the Swedish SKF in 1969 was dropped (because of the opposition of the IRC and the Ministry of Technology) before a formal exchange control application was made, one Treasury official indicated that it would propably have been approved on purely financial grounds. The Treasury's main concern — that gains to foreign exchange reserves through inward investment should not be eschewed unless there are overwhelming drawbacks to such investment — is not, therefore, identical to the major objective of the Ministry of Technology, discussed below, that viable British-owned companies should not come under foreign control.

Although the 'general desirability' criterion mentioned above would cover such a situation, and was introduced at the behest of the Ministry of Technology, there is no evidence that it has been used to prevent any inward investment; it may be, of course, that the commercial banks have advised prospective investors in sensitive industries to abandon their proposals at an early stage.

Some have argued that, given the welcoming official attitude to inward investment, the Exchange Control Act and its procedure are an ideal series of absolute prohibitions, making investment impossible without permission. Since the criteria for granting such permission are not contained in the Act, and are only publicised in an informal manner, it is possible to set quite stringent requirements where necessary without deterring other potential investors, who are only aware of the general liberality of the procedure. [84] Nevertheless, the fact that responsibility for administering exchange control lies with the Treasury, which has no industrial responsibilities and a consistently favourable view of any transactions which add to the foreign exchange reserves, does indicate that the Act is not an ideal way of exercising control over multinational companies. The exchange control procedure demonstrates a preoccupation with the financial rather than the industrial effects of inward investment; perhaps the clearest example of this can be seen in the take-over battle for British Aluminium, the largest firm in the British aluminium industry, which occurred between November 1958 and January 1959. The Board of British Aluminium favoured a bid by Alcoa (an American company) against a rival bid, which succeeded, by Tube Investments and Reynolds Metals (another American company). Both would in effect have meant that the company would come under American control, but the Treasury took a neutral position and left the matter to the shareholders. 'No attempt was made by any public body to inquire into or evaluate the issues in terms of the national interest.' [85]

Although this liberal attitude to inward investment became somewhat more restrictive after the 'general desirability' criterion was added in 1968, there is little evidence to suggest that the attitude of Treasury officials to foreign investment, regarding it primarily as a financial transaction, changed dramatically as a result. Their preoccupation with foreign exchange reserves and the balance of payments led them to welcome almost all foreign investment, while the exchange control regulations which were imposed on outward investment by British companies were far more restrictive. The UK's large capital outflow in 1963–64, which raised the value of British direct investments abroad from £4,100 million in 1962 to £4,600 million in 1964, was seen as 'a principal cause of its

economic crisis and necessitated restrictive short-term measures.'[86]   In
addition to a change in taxation of profits remitted to the UK, which
made overseas investment less attractive (see below), the 1965 Budget
imposed new restrictions on outward investment, with direct investment
outside the Sterling Area having to be financed either by foreign borrowing or the purchase of investment currency (proceeds of sale of overseas
assets by other persons) usually at a premium over the official rate of
exchange, if the benefits accruing to the UK economy equalled the
amount invested within two or three years. [87] From 1966 onwards direct
investment in non-developing countries in the Sterling Area was restricted
under a voluntary scheme, and British-owned companies were requested
to remit at least two-thirds of their overseas profits back to the UK.[88]
These restrictions, unlike those which could be applied to inward investment, were publicised in very specific terms, and underlined the Bank of
England official's view that 'the Exchange Control rules are designed to
provide the maximum benefits to the United Kingdom balance of payments at the minimum cost to the official foreign exchange reserves. [89]

It can thus be seen that, although the Labour Government's long-term
objective of restructuring British industry to make it competitive internationally brought about a shift in emphasis in the exchange control
criteria dealing with foreign investment, this only occurred after sterling
was devalued in November 1967, and until that time the addition to
foreign exchange reserves accruing from inward investment was the most
important consideration. Even after devaluation and the addition of the
'general desirability' criterion in 1968, it is important to note that general
industrial considerations continued to play a subordinate part in the exchange control procedure. Prime responsibility remained with the Treasury, and the Ministry of Technology played a secondary role, being con-
sulted but having very little leverage in the actual deliberations of the
Foreign Exchange Committee. The speed with which exchange control
applications were processed (usually less than a week from start to finish)
meant that detailed analysis of the industrial implications of an inward
investment project was rendered impossible, and only in the case of foreign take-overs of significant British companies were restrictions imposed
when exchange control permission was granted. The briefs which formed
the basis of the Foreign Exchange Committee's deliberations were prepared by the Bank of England, which 'on issues like devaluation or exchange
control does not pretend to be impartial. It is against them both.'[90] There
was thus a considerable bias in the procedure against restricting inward
investment, evidenced by the statement of a Bank of England official that
'provided the financial arrangements were adequate, no special scrutiny was

given to 99 percent of the applications.'[91]

The machinery for administering the Exchange Control Act, the only British statute which treats foreign companies operating in the UK economy as different from British companies, is effective in ensuring that foreign investment is carried out with foreign capital, and does not deplete existing stocks of capital within the UK. The sanctions available under the Act, namely withdrawal of permission to repatriate profits from the UK, or refusal to permit fresh capital injections, are so draconian that they are unlikely ever to be used; certainly no examples of such sanctions being imposed have come to light in the course of this study. The conclusion of the Steuer Report on inward investment, that 'given the implied [welcoming] attitude to inward investment, the Act and its surrounding procedure are satisfactory,'[92] may be accurate in financial terms, but the rarity of refused investment applications, and the lack of surveillance of companies which have been asked to fulfil certain undertakings as a condition of exchange control permission being granted, indicates that the Act is not suitable for policing the activities of multinational companies. The Labour Government seemed to have recognised this, as the activities of the Ministry of Technology and the Industrial Reorganisation Corporation made clear; the Treasury's preoccupation with the balance of payments and the maintenance of foreign exchange reserves meant that the consideration of foreign investment proposals was linked to short-term financial objectives rather than long-term industrials ones.

3.3.2   Registration of foreign-owned companies

The Insurance and Companies Department of the Board of Trade administers the legislation controlling the conditions under which companies are registered and operate in the UK, principally the Companies Acts of 1948 and 1967, which govern company registration and the filing of financial statements. Since a company organised under British law is regarded for almost all purposes as being a UK company even though all or a majority of its shares are owned by non-resident nationals of other countries, no particular surveillance of the subsidiaries of foreign multinational companies is carried out.[93] Companies are registered by submitting to the Registrar of Companies documents setting out the constitution and purposes of the company, the rules under which its members will agree to join together, the proposed name of the company (which must not be such that it can be confused with the name of any other company), and the address of its registered office. Once the Registrar has issued a certificate of incorporation, the company comes formally into being, and has a statutory duty to keep the Registrar informed of any changes in its constitution, details of its shareholding, directors and other offices, and its annual audited accounts and report. This information is open to public inspection at Companies House in London. The companies are of two kinds; private companies, in which the number of shareholders are limited, and shares are not offered to the public; and public companies, whose shares are transferable and offered to the public. Since 1964 the Insurance and Companies Department has kept a register of both quoted (public) and non-quoted (private) UK subsidiaries of foreign-owned companies having assets of over £500,000 or gross annual income of over £50,000; in 1969 there were 50 quoted subsidiaries, of which 41 were subsidiaries of US companies, and 429 unquoted subsidiaries, of which 299 were US owned.[94]

The total number of foreign-owned firms in the UK in 1969 was approximately 6,000,[95] of which 1,224 had assets over £500,000 or gross annual income of over £50,000.[96] This means that only 30 per cent of the large foreign-owned firms in the UK were incorporated in the UK under the Companies Acts. The remaining 795 are classified as 'overseas companies with a UK branch', under Part X of the Companies Act 1948, i.e. companies incorporated outside the UK which establish a place of business within the UK. Although such branches are not registered in the UK, the Registrar of Companies must be provided with similar information as with UK registered companies (articles of incorporation, lists of directors) as well as the name of at least one UK resident authorised on behalf of the company to receive legal notices required to be served on the company.[97] The major difference between the disclosure requirements for UK companies and UK branches of overseas companies is that, while both have to file copies of their annual financial statements, companies incorporated in the UK must provide a Directors' Report (giving details of major contracts, number of employees, divisional results, export sales, and distribution of profits) as well as the normal company balance sheet and profit and loss statement. UK branches of overseas companies, however, do not have to provide this information, and are also exempted by the Board of Trade from providing information on turnover, taxation charges, emoluments of directors, and details of parent, subsidiary and associated companies. There are thus certain advantages for foreign companies conducting business in the UK through branches rather than registered companies — Parke-Davis and Timex are examples of this — although the Companies Act requires such branches to display in all premises and on all letterheads and publications the name of the country under the laws of which it was organised, together with the name and nationality of non-

British directors. [98] Although the legal requirements of the Companies Acts are designed to make non-UK companies conducting business in the UK subject to the same regulations as UK companies, without placing any serious obstacle in the way of a company wishing to operate in the UK, the reduced amount of financial information required of such companies does mean that there is a serious gap in the data available to the British Government on the operations of multinational companies in the UK. [99] In addition, the Insurance and Companies Department is severely understaffed; in 1972 there were over half a million companies on the register, with over 30,000 being added each year, and only 15 senior civil servants to detect or prevent breaches of the Companies Acts. Even where companies fail to file their financial returns on time, the fine for non-compliance is only £5. [100] Nevertheless, the disclosure requirements of the Companies Acts compare favourably with those of other West European countries: an investigation by the European Federation of Financial Analysts in 1970 found that UK companies were compelled to provide 57 per cent of a theoretical maximum information volume, a higher percentage than for any of the other countries studied. [101] The Conservative Government announced in 1973 that it was planning a new Companies Act which would force multinational companies operating in Britain to make more information available in their published accounts; presumably this would involve the abolition of the special privileges of the 'overseas companies with a UK branch' under Section X of the 1948 Companies Act which exempted the majority of multinational companies operating in the UK from providing full information on their activities. [102]

3.3.3   The distribution of industry and investment incentives

Because the older industrial areas were overdependent on the basic industries, coal, iron, and shipbuilding, which have been affected by the exhaustion of minerals and the development of alternative fuels, together with intensified international competition, unemployment in these areas presented severe problems for British Governments since 1945. The problem of structural unemployment was intensified by the mechanisation of agriculture, which increased unemployment in areas which already had insufficient alternative work. Those industries which expanded after the war, such as automobiles and electrical engineering, mainly concentrated in the Midlands and the South East, and this, together with the attraction of London as a business centre, added to the uneven economic development of the UK as a whole. [103] The Distribution of Industry Act 1945 and the Town and Country Planning Act 1947 gave the Board of Trade powers to designate certain parts of the UK as 'development areas' and to require Industrial Development Certificates (IDCs) to be obtained for new industrial building or extensions to existing plant. IDCs were used as a form of negative planning, by refusing permission to build plant in congested areas and granting IDCs for areas where expansion was needed. The Board of Trade was given further means of inducing location of industry in development areas (chiefly the North East, North West, part of Scotland, Merseyside, South Wales and the far South West) under the Local Employment Act 1960, and the Finance Act 1963. These were financial incentives, including the provision of factories for rent or purchase on mortgage, loans and grants, training of workers, and free depreciation of capital expenditure, which enabled firms to set off up to 130 per cent of the cost of the investment (including normal investment allowance) against profits at any rate the firms chose. [104] The aim was to provide jobs by attracting efficient companies, since the financial incentives were mainly in the area of depreciation allowances rather than straight financial subsidies, and the Board of Trade exercised control over industrial development with the stick of IDCs and the carrot of fiscal concessions for firms locating in development areas. Because it was recognised that new investment projects were easier to place in development areas than extensions to existing businesses, the Board of Trade set up a British Industrial Development Office in New York in 1962 to attract American investment in the development areas; the fact that this remains the only such overseas office is a recognition of the importance of the US as a source of investment. The publicity material stressed the incentives available and the informality of the investment procedure:

> The British Government welcomes and assists foreign firms who wish to establish manufacturing facilities in Britain. No British participation is required either in capital or management: formalities are reduced to a minimum and there are no difficulties in the way of repatriating profits or capital. Apart from exchange control, foreign-owned companies are treated in the same way as domestic ones. [105]

There is little doubt that the character of the financial incentives offered by the Government for investment in the development areas were attractive to multinational companies; although the loans and grants made by the Board of Trade for the building of new factories were linked to the number of jobs created (a maximum of £1,000 per job), the free depreciation allowance, which was available whether or not employment was created, favoured the location of capital-intensive processes in the development areas, and frequently involved subsidising activities which made little contribution to the unemployment problem. [106] The Industrial Development Act of 1966 changed investment incentives radically; free depreciation was dropped, and instead capital investment on qualifying assets (i.e. manufacturing plant, including computers and ships) got cash investment grants at the rate of 40 per cent in development areas and 20 per cent in other areas, increased as a temporary measure in 1967 and 1968 to 45 and 25 per cent respectively. This made investment more attractive to firms which did not expect to be profitable in the short term, and for whom the free depreciation allowance was no incentive, and continued to favour capital-intensive projects since no employment criterion was involved. To some extent this latter defect was remedied by the introduction of a Regional Employment Premium, which was a weekly payment by the Government to firms in developing areas for every employee engaged in manufacturing, guaranteed for seven years. In effect, the Regional Employment Premium amounted to a reduction in labour costs of about 7 per cent as compared with non-development areas. [107]

The introduction of investment grants marked a vast increase in the amount of financial assistance for investment projects in development areas provided by the Labour Government, from £30 million in 1964/65 to £302 million in 1969/70. [108] The actual effect that investment grants had in attracting foreign investment cannot be accurately assessed, since in the issue of investment grants the Board of Trade made no distinction between British and non-British companies. [109] A Board of Trade inquiry in 1969 of 170 foreign-owned firms which had established a new plant in the U K in the period 1965-69 found that 57 per cent considered the financial inducements a major factor in deciding to invest in the U K, 10 per cent considered that they were a minor factor, and one-third stated that they had no bearing on the investment decision. For most of the foreign firms included in the survey, availability of labour and proximity of transport services were more important than financial incentives, and the possibility of obtaining an IDC was at least as important as the existence of investment grants. Just over half the foreign firms in the survey set up plants in the developing areas. [110]

Although both British and foreign-owned companies were treated alike in their applications for investment grants, a lawsuit decided in the House of Lords made it clear that the Board of Trade (or the Ministry of Technology, which took over this function of the Board of Trade in 1969) had substantial discretion in payment of investment grants. Lord Reid said in his judgement:

In this Act [Industrial Development Act 1966] Parliament has clearly laid down the conditions for eligibility for grants and it has clearly given to the Board a discretion so that the Board is not bound to pay to every person who is eligible to receive a grant. But I can find nothing to guide the Board as to the circumstances in which they should pay or the circumstances in which they should not pay to such persons. [111]

The most serious anomaly which was covered by this discretion arose in the case of investment grants for ships, which were paid on assets irrespective of whether they were manufactured in the UK, in order not to contravene GATT and EFTA obligations against discrimination in favour of home suppliers. The result of this situation was that foreign companies could set up a subsidiary in the UK, order their ships from abroad, and then operate these ships overseas with a 20 per cent cash grant from the UK Government. Between January 1966 and September 1969, the total amount of investment grants approved for ships on order amounted to £285 million of which £91 million was paid to UK companies controlled by non-residents, and £61 million of this latter figure was for ships built outside the UK. [112] In 1968 the Board of Trade tightened up the regulations on investment grants for ships, introducing a special balance of payments test on orders placed by foreign-owned companies registered in the UK after 1963. [113] This balance of payments test was extended to cover ships ordered by any company, British or foreign-owned, under the Industrial Development (Ships) Bill, 1969, if payment of the grant would be detrimental to the balance of payments. [114] This provoked several claims by foreign-owned companies that the balance of payments criteria applied to them were far more stringent than those applied to British-owned companies; the managing director of Esso (Great Britain) argued that the ships for which investment grants were refused in fact were contributing far more to the UK balance of payments than ships operated by BP and Shell, on which investment grants had been paid. [115]

Apart from this anomaly, however, there is no evidence that British and foreign-owned companies were treated any differently in their applications for investment grants, and the fact that the Board of Trade has kept no statistics distinguishing the applicant companies' country of origin is evidence that investment grants were administered on an impartial basis. The largest discovered abuse of the investment grants procedure, however, was made by Ford in 1969, when it sold equipment from its Halewood plant (in a development area) to Ford-Werke, its German subsidiary. The Parliamentary Select Committee on Public Accounts found that Ford had received £347,725 in investment grants for this equipment because it had been purchased for use in a UK development area. The sale was discovered by the Board of Trade when Ford claimed a further £139,118 in respect of the equipment, and it was found that it had already been moved to Germany.[116] A Ford spokesman later commented, 'It was a misunderstanding which is now a matter of history. Repayment of the grant was made within the same financial year — 1969–70.'[117]

The other main weapon of the Board of Trade in influencing industrial location was the granting of Industrial Development Certificates (IDCs); an IDC was required to support all applications for planning consent for industrial buildings over 3,000 square feet in the Midlands and the South-East, and over 5,000 square feet elsewhere. The Board of Trade has a statutory obligation to pay special regard to the employment needs of the development areas and in general to see that proposals are consistent with a proper distribution of industry, but, in the words of one economist, 'It is not easy to see from any published data with what vigour the policy is pursued, or what its effects may be.'[118] Although the Board of Trade officials interviewed for this study considered that foreign-owned firms were generally more co-operative than British firms in locating their plants in development areas, they conceded that the granting of IDCs was the result of a bargaining process between the Board of Trade and the firms concerned, resulting in a package deal: 'The multinational corporation can bargain by threatening to divert its investment elsewhere, but if these threats were taken at face value, IDC control would lose all credibility.'[119] The purpose of IDCs is to provide more jobs in development areas, and restrain large expansion in areas of labour scarcity, particularly the South-East. Although the officials interviewed stressed that a foreign firm would have to make a convincing case for not locating in a development area, the statistics of industrial location set out in Table 3.2 indicate that foreign firms were proportionately more successful in obtaining IDCs to set up in non-development areas than were British firms. Table 3.2 shows that during the period 1945–65 (the latest date for which figures are available), foreign-owned firms establishing new plants in the UK provided 19 per cent of the new employment for the UK as a whole, but only 18 per cent in the development areas and 53 per cent in the industrially congested areas of the South-East. The data for the 1960–65 period (when financial incentives were made available for firms establishing plants in the development areas) shows that the percentage of jobs created by foreign firms was lower, at 14 per cent for the UK as a whole, than for the longer period 1945–65, and that the imbalance between development areas and industrially congested areas continued. The more lenient policies

Table 3.2

Origin and destination of manufacturing establishments, 1945–65
(Employment in thousands, at end of 1966, excluding intra-regional moves)

Source	Destination							
	United Kingdom		Development areas		South-East		Scotland	
	No.	%	No.	%	No.	%	No.	%
1 United Kingdom								
1945–65	467	81	377	82	15	47	48	51
1960–65	138	86	117	87	4	50	26	81
2 Abroad								
1945–65	108	19	82	18	17	53	46	49
1960–65	23	14	18	13	4	50	6	19
3 Total								
1945–65	575	100	459	100	32	100	94	100
1960–65	161	100	135	100	8	100	32	100

Source: Board of Trade: *The Movement of Manufacturing Industry in the United Kingdom 1945–65* HMSO London 1968, pp. 40–3.

applied to foreign firms can be seen most clearly in the figures relating to location of manufacturing industry in the South-East. Although one official stated that 'foreign firms find it very tough to get an IDC for the South-East, and go relatively willingly to the development areas,'[120] Table 3.2 shows that foreign firms provided 53 per cent of new employment in the South-East during the period 1945—65 (as compared with 19 per cent for the UK as a whole), and that during the 1960—65 period this proportion was only marginally reduced to 50 per cent.

The only development area which has derived above average employment creation by foreign firms has been Scotland, but the reasons for this (which Board of Trade officials suggested ranged from the excellence of the Scottish educational system and the large pool of skilled labour available, to the multiplicity of golf courses and salmon streams) are difficult to quantify. Table 3.2 shows that foreign firms provided 49 per cent of new employment in Scotland in the period 1945—65, but that they accounted for only 19 per cent of new employment there in 1960—65, reflecting the general decline in labour-intensive foreign investment in the UK after 1960. In short, the figures do give some support to the argument that foreign firms were in a stronger bargaining postition than British firms when applying for IDCs for the industrially congested areas, the South-East in particular.

Although the officials interviewed were reluctant to discuss individual examples of this process, one particularly revealing case was described by a former Junior Minister at the Ministry of Technology. IBM's main manufacturing plant is at Greenock, in Scotland, employing 2,000 people, but in 1967 it established a smaller plant at Havant (in the South-East) which it decided in 1969 to expand to about the same size as its Greenock plant. IBM wanted to expand at Havant alone, and threatened to locate future expansion abroad if an IDC was refused; after discussions with the Board of Trade they agreed to expand employment at Greenock by 25 per cent, and to establish a new plant at Peterlee, County Durham (in the Northern development area) which would expand at the same rate as the existing Havant plant. On this basis IBM were granted an IDC for expansion at Havant, but no specific conditions were attached to the issue of the IDC. In the event, the plant at Havant was tripled in size, and the plant at Peterlee consisted of a prefabricated building housing a 360 computer and a small research staff. The Board of Trade officials granted the Havant IDC without reference to government ministers, leading the junior Minister from the Ministry of Technology to describe IDC control over industrial location by foreign companies as 'derisory'.[121]

This may be an extreme example, but the available data strongly suggests that IDCs were never used to turn away potential foreign investment; Hardie found that only 12 per cent of all (i.e. British and foreign) rejected IDC applications for the South-East between 1958 and 1963 resulted in total abandonment of the project and that 'in most cases, firms manage to achieve their original objectives in one way or another.'[122] Although industrial location figures for the period 1966—70 (when cash investment grants were given with a 20 per cent increment for plants in development areas) are not available, the bias in the investment grant systems toward capital intensive projects would suggest that post—1965 foreign investment in the development areas did not create any more jobs than the 1945—65 figures indicate. The Board of Trade, which was most interested in attracting export-generating or import-saving investment, was not responsible for general regional policy (which was the function of the Department of Economic Affairs), or for employment policy (carried out by the Department of Employment and Productivity), and in its administration of investment grants and IDCs did not discriminate between British and foreign companies. Indeed, where IDCs are concerned, it seems to have adopted far more lenient standards for foreign companies than it did for British ones, particularly for investment in the South-East region.

3.4 Government control over continuing operations of multinational companies

Having received permission to invest in the UK under exchange control regulations, foreign-owned companies are treated by the government for most purposes on the same basis as indigenous British companies. The objective of this section will be to determine to what extent the operations of multinational companies in the UK posed special problems for the Labour Government, and whether the formulation and implementation of its industrial policies took account of these problems. They may be classified for the sake of convenience under three headings: firstly, the problem of taxation; secondly, the question of competition policy; and thirdly, the methods of consultation and inquiry whereby the Labour Government gained information on the activities of multinational companies in the U K.

3.4.1 Taxation

Because the exchange control regulations are designed to ensure that foreign-owned companies import most of the capital required for their development (unless, as outlined in the previous section, there remains a British minority interest in the subsidiary, or it is established in a Development Area), the Treasury's control over monetary policy does not affect multinational companies any differently than purely domestic companies, except that the former have better access to overseas sources of capital. The Treasury's control over taxation policy, however, does have an effect on the investment climate in the UK, and changes in company taxation by the Labour Government underline their policy of encouraging inward investment and, at least while the balance of payments remained in a precarious position, discouraging outward investment.

The 1965 Finance Act introduced a Corporation Tax which taxed total company profits at 40 per cent, with distributed profits being taxed a second time at the marginal rate for the individual — in the case of profits remitted to US parent companies, this was fixed at 15 per cent under a protocol of 5 January 1966 amending the Anglo-American Tax Treaty. [123] This replaced a system in which all profits were taxed at 56 per sent (15 per cent profits tax, plus the standard rate of income tax prevailing at that time), and under which UK based companies could claim full allowance for tax paid on profits earned abroad. The result of the new tax regulations was that UK companies investing abroad could only claim relief for overseas taxes paid against the corporation tax on company receipts, and could not extend this relief to the income tax witheld on distributed profits. UK corporate profits were thus taxed twice — once when earned, and again when distributed to shareholders. This tax system resulted in retained profits being taxed at 40 per cent, and distributed profits at 65 per cent (for UK-based companies with overseas investments) or 49 per cent (for US-based companies remitting profits back to the parent company). [124]

The introduction of corporation tax was designed to discourage outward investment, by taxing overseas profits, and encourage profit retention by all companies operating in the UK. Since the US rate of corporation tax was at that time 48 per cent, with virtually no unrelieved foreign tax, the Treasury considered that not only would British companies choose to invest in the UK rather than overseas, but also that US investment in Britain would be made more attractive, particularly since the differential in corporation tax rates would offer a tax saving until the UK subsidiary distributed profits as dividends.[125] Treasury officials interviewed pointed out that the UK rate of corporation tax compared favourably with that of other industrialised countries, and that the higher rate of US corporation tax meant that it was in the interests of US-owned multinational companies to minimise royalties and service fees paid to the US parent company, since by substituting royalties and fees for dividends, their tax liabilities would merely be shifted to a higher tax area. As Brooke and Remmers concluded in their study of the internal finance of multinational companies:

> Where the total effective tax rate of the subsidiary was less than that of the parent company, there is no tax advantage in substituting other forms of payment for dividends. If the taxes are not paid by the subsidiary in the host country, then they will be paid by the parent company when remitted. [126]

In those cases where the parent companies are located in low corporation tax countries, the British Government has taken steps to tax royalties and fees at the same 15 per cent rate as dividends, in order to minimise tax evasion through manipulation of non-dividend intra-company payments. [127] In addition, the Inland Revenue Department scrutinises all intra-company non-dividend transactions to ensure that they are carried out on an arms-length basis; in certain cases involving intra-company sales, the Inland Revenue may ignore the actual price and regard the transactions as having taken place at open market prices, to the extent that it is advantageous to the Revenue to do so. [128] The Treasury officials interviewed felt that manipulation of tax liabilities through artificial transfer-pricing was not a serious problem, since the Customs and Excise Division were adept at import valuation:

> We are aware of the problem, but not much work has been done on it. ... It is a fact of life which makes the Treasury's life more difficult, but it is not serious enough to impede the free flow of capital. [129]

In so far as multinational companies played a part in the formulation of taxation policy, the Treasury's objective was to encourage inward investment and prevent the most blatant forms of tax evasion, without taking stern measures which might provoke retaliation against the overseas subsidiaries of British companies.

3.4.2 Competition policy

The power of the government to regulate the market behaviour of business enterprises in the UK derives from the Monopolies and Restrictive Practices (Inquiry and Control) Act 1948 and the extensions and modifications of the provisions contained therein under the Restrictive Trade Practices Act 1956, and the Monopolies and Mergers Act 1965. [130] The 1948 Act set up the Monopolies Commission, an independent body consisting (in 1970) of a full-time Chairman, a part-time Deputy Chairman, and fifteen part-time members drawn from business, universities, trade unions, and the professions, assisted by a small secretariat. The work of the Commission is to inquire into, and report on, the existence and effect on the public interest of monopoly conditions in the supply or export of specified goods and services and the effect on the public interest of mergers, or proposed mergers, of specified enterprises. It cannot, however, initiate such inquiries, but can only act on matters specifically referred to it by the Board of Trade,[131] and its recommendations do not carry the force of law, the Board of Trade being responsible for laying them before Parliament, for publishing them and for deciding on any steps to remedy the situation where the Commission's findings are that the public interest is being adversely affected. [132]

The 1948 Act places on the Board of Trade the responsibility of referring to the Monopolies Commission matters where the structure, behaviour or performance of companies with substantial market power might be harmful to the British economy, and to request it to determine whether this is the case and to recommend necessary remedial measures. [133] The definition of monopoly in the 1948 Act is that the firm should supply 'at least one-third of all the goods of any description which are supplied in the United Kingdom or any part thereof,' [134] and this definition of dominant market position is quite wide, since there could in theory be three monopolists in the same field. Once the Board of Trade considers that the one-third market test is met, the Board may at its discretion refer the matter to the Commission to investigate whether in fact this is the case, and instruct it to report whether in its opinion the activities of the parties 'operate or may be expected to operate against the public interest'. [135] It should be noted that reference to the Commission is not automatic, even if the market-test criterion is met, and that the 'public interest' criterion is very vague; consequently the Commission has considerable latitude, subject to the provisions of Section 14 of the Act, which define the public interest in terms of: (a) efficient and economical means of production of goods for home and overseas markets; (b) the organisation of industry and trade in such a way that their efficiency is progressively increased and new enterprise is encouraged; (c) the fullest use and best distribution of men, materials and industrial capacity and (d) the development of technical improvements and the expansion of existing markets and the opening up of new markets.

If the Commission decides that the behaviour of the parties is or may be in some way against the public interest, it may under Section 7(2) recommend what action should be taken to remedy the situation, but the

Board of Trade has absolute discretion in deciding whether any action should be taken, and in what form. The Board has extensive powers to act, including the power to break up the offending company, but this power has never been used, and it prefers to settle matters by direct negotiation with the parties concerned. [136] Since 1948 the Board of Trade has referred forty—two monopoly cases to the Commission (up to the end of 1970), which would indicate that it has used substantial powers of discretion given the rather low threshold of market dominance laid down by the Act. [137] Usually the Board gives some advance warning by including in its annual report of activity under the monopolies legislation a list of the 'non-trivial' complaints it has received: Sugarman and Kanter found that of nineteen monopolies references between 1960 and 1968, sixteen were on prior Board complaint lists. [138]

Of the twenty reports on monopoly situations published by the Commission between 1960 and 1970, six involved foreign-owned companies:

1   Supply of electrical equipment for mechanically propelled land vehicles (HC21); 18.12.1963. (Champion Spark Plugs).
2   Supply of petrol to retailers in the United Kingdom (HC264); 22.7.1965. (Shell, Esso, Texaco, Mobil, Continental, Total, with BP).
3   Supply and processing of colour film (HC1); 21.4.1966. (Kodak, Agfa-Gevaert, 3M, Ferrania, GAF).
4   Supply of household detergents (HC105); 3.8.1966. (Unilever, Procter & Gamble).
5   Supply of aluminium semi-manufactures (HC263); 20.12.1966. (Alcan).
6   Second report on the supply of electric lamps (HC4); 2.12.1968. (Philips).

An analysis of these reports is extremely interesting, because it is clear that the Monopolies Commission construes the market behaviour of a foreign-owned firm in the UK very narrowly. In one case (aluminium semi-manufactures) the Commission found that the situation did not come within the scope of the 1948 Act, and no evidence was presented in its report (see 5 above). In the electric lamps report (see 6 above), the Commission paid little attention to the status of Philips as a Dutch-owned company, and did not investigate the question of royalty and research and development payments made to the Dutch parent company, having satisfied itself that Philips UK was not making disproportionate profits from the manufacture of electric lamps. [139]

In the remaining four reports an analysis of the evidence given to the Commission and the conclusions it made bear out Rowley's criticism that the Commission has consistently omitted to consider the extraterritorial implications of the activities of the firms it has investigated: 'This omission must be considered as one of the major weaknesses in the approach of the Monopolies Commission — a weakness incidentally that appears to have passed without adverse comment.'[140] The overriding objective of the Commission seems to have been to consider the pricing policies of the companies concerned in the UK market, treating both the subsidiaries of foreign companies and the UK market itself in isolation. In the electrial equipment for motor vehicles report, the Commission concentrated on Champion's high profitability in terms of capital employed (an average of 57 per cent over the 1954–60 period),[141] and did not inquire into the implications of Champion's import of insulators from the US parent at a price some 30 per cent below customs valuation [142] — a piece of artificial transfer-pricing apparently designed to shift profit from the US parent to its UK subsidiary — or the so-called 'Toledo Charge' paid by Champion to the US parent for central research and development and administration: 'We have no means of verifying that it represents no more than expenditure currently incurrend by the parent on behalf of Champion.'[143]

In this case the Commission's definition of 'public interest' was confined to the question of Champion's selling prices, rather than to questions of tax revenue from Champion's UK profits or the degree to which Champion paid more or less than its full share of the parent company's general budget, and there was no attempt to assess the level of Champion's UK prices *vis-à-vis* other overseas markets:

> We think that a price policy which has allowed the company and its parent to retain over a long period so large a measure of the rewards of efficiency has been objectionable ... Having regard to the very high profits resulting from that policy, it operates and may be expected to operate against the public interest. [144]

Nevertheless, the Commission recommended no specific action against Champion, merely a general abolition of fixed retail prices for spark plugs. It did not avail itself of the opportunity to investigate Champion's relations with its US parent in order to determine whether other aspects of Champion's activities, aside from its pricing policy, were in the general interest of the UK economy, and defined its terms of reference very narrowly indeed.

The failure to consider some of the more general economic consequences of its findings can also be seen in the Commission's report on the supply of petrol to UK retailers by the oil companies. [145] Although six companies controlled 95 per cent of the British market in 1964, only the Anglo-Dutch consortium Shell-Mex and BP was a statutory monopolist with 45 per cent of the market. Esso had 27·4 per cent, Texaco (Regent) had 11·1 per cent, Mobil 5·9 per cent and Continental (Jet) 3·5 per cent; on the retail level, Shell-Mex and BP owned only 6 per cent of the retail outlets, and the other companies even fewer. [146] The Commission found that the companies did, however, restrict competition through recommended prices and exclusive dealership arrangements, and recommended that no petrol supplier whose delivery to company-owned stations exceeded 15 per cent of his total deliveries should be allowed to build or acquire any further stations, unless his total deliveries were less than 10 million gallons in any year. [147] In fact the Board of Trade set the lower limit at 50 million gallons after a year of negotiation with the oil companies in order to avoid 'a risk of discouraging new entrants to the UK market with the effect of diminishing rather than promoting competition.' [148] The Board also set limits not on the acquisition or building of new stations by the companies, but on the total number of company-owned stations, thus permitting the six major oil companies to replace undesirable sites by new ones. [149] Eventually the Board abandoned this requirement altogether, [150] partly because the limitation had encouraged other American oil companies to take over more than 2,000 outlets in the UK, increasing the pressure on the British-owned element of the oil industry. [151] The Board's interpretation and application of the Commission's findings in the petrol case certainly promoted competition, but it is questionable whether this competition genuinely served the public interest (no price wars ensued) or the balance of payments (since the number of foreign-owned companies in the industry increased).

The colour film case is interesting because it illustrates once again the very narrow view the Commission frequently takes of its terms of reference. The Commission found that Kodak controlled 70 per cent of the UK colour film market in the 1962–64 period, and that its profit on assets employed was 50 per cent greater than the average for UK manufacturing industry as a whole. [152] The Commission took no apparent cognizance of Kodak's argument that its US parent had made no charge to its UK subsidiary for research and development, technical know-how and central administration until 1962, and that since that time it had only paid a 3 per cent royalty on sales:

> ... the major part of the cost of research is borne by the parent company ... if Kodak were not a member of the Eastman Kodak Group, the cost to it per unit of the research and development re-

quired to produce goods of comparable quality would be immeasurably greater than it is. ... The parent company is allowing Kodak to retain, for the financing of future development, some part of the benefits of the world-wide organisation which it has created. [153]

The Commission did not itself investigate the prices of colour film in other overseas markets, but commented on figures supplied by Kodak that: 'It is clear that prices in this country are by no means identical with those elsewhere and that the British company has a fairly wide discretion to settle its own prices.' [154] Accordingly it recommended that Kodak should reduce its prices on colour film, and in negotiations with the Board Kodak consented to reduce its retail prices by 20 per cent. [155] Two members of the Commission had in fact dissented from this recommendation, on the grounds that it was impossible to scrutinise price changes in relation to Kodak's other products and its prices elsewhere in the world. [156] One indirect result of Kodak's lowering of prices was that Ilford, its only British-owned competitor, which had survived mainly because its prices were lower than Kodak's, was subsequently taken over by CIBA, the Swiss chemical company, in 1967. [157] Because the Commission had been preoccupied with the price of colour films, and not the structure of the photographic materials industry as a whole, it had not considered the wider implications of its findings, and in particular the assignment of profit among the subsidiaries of a multinational company, and the desirability of maintaining an indigenous competitor to Kodak.

In the detergents case, where Unilever and Procter & Gamble controlled 44 and 46 per cent of the UK market respectively, the Commission decided (as in the Kodak case) that the structural monopoly as such did not operate against the public interest. [158] Once again, the Commission declined to examine the behaviour of the two concerns in the context of the multinational groups to which they belonged, offering no evidence for its assertion that:

> Both Unilever and P & G belong to powerful groups operating on an international scale ... so far as household detergents are concerned these two are undoubtedly the leading producers in the world, though in some overseas markets there are other competitors who offer them more vigorous competition than any they have to meet at present in this country. [159]

The Commission recommended a 40 per cent decrease in the promotional expenses of the two companies (arguing that in a duopolistic situation such high promotional expenditure was unjustified), to be reflected in a

20 per cent reduction in selling prices. The Board declined to follow these recommendations, possibly (as Kanter and Sugarman suggest) because it would jeopardise relations with the business community and was anxious to reach a voluntary settlement; instead it negotiated a two-year price freeze and the launching of two budget detergents selling at 20 per cent below the heavily-advertised brands. [160]

There are several significant features in the administration of monopolies legislation in the UK which emerge from this brief survey. Firstly, the Board of Trade exercises substantial discretion in deciding whether or not to submit monopolistic practices to the scrutiny of the Monopolies Commission, and it gives the companies fair warning with the list of non-trivial complaints which it publishes in its annual report and which have almost invariably preceded a reference to the Commission by a year or more. Secondly, the Commission has never attempted to treat the subsidiaries of multinational companies as a special case, and consequently has never investigated the relationship between profitability and payment for central research, development, and administration. Neither has it attempted to investigate the activities of the parent company's subsidiaries in other national markets, or even the relationship between the product under investigation and other products of the same company; its behavioural analysis has been limited to that of the subsidiary in the UK market for a specified product, and considerations of the extraterritorial factors influencing that behaviour have been excluded. [161]

This view is generally in line with that of the government itself, which has vigorously protested when British-owned companies have been affected by extraterritorial applications of anti-trust law in other countries. In November 1969, for example the Labour Government protested against the EEC Commission's imposition of a fine on ICI for attempting to fix the price of aniline dyestuffs with nine other firms, on the grounds that the initiative was taken not by ICI's European subsidiary, but by the parent company in London. The government's confidential letter to the Commission outlined the general principles which must govern the application of anti-trust law to foreign companies thus:

1   Laws can be applied only to companies which carry on business in the country claiming jurisdiction.
2   The difference between a parent and its subsidiary must be respected.
3   Where a conspiracy is alleged to have taken place it must either have been formulated or carried out in the country trying to take action against it. [162]

In March 1970, when the Labour Government introduced the Commission for Industry and Manpower Bill, which was designed to strengthen the power of the Commission to investigate distortion of competition, but which was not enacted due to the Labour Government's defeat in the June 1970 General Election, the draft underlined its opposition to the principle of extraterritoriality:

> No reference shall be made ... of any question relating to the conduct of any undertaking which is not carried on in the United Kingdom; and where an undertaking is carried on both in the United Kingdom and in another country a reference ... shall not extend to the conduct of the undertaking in the other country, unless it is carried on by a body incorporated under the law of the United Kingdom or some part thereof, and then only so far as it appears to the Minister or Ministers that its conduct in that other country may affect the supply of goods or services in or the export of goods from the United Kingdom. [163]

In response to criticism from some of the Labour MPs on the Standing Committee which scrutinised the Bill, the Minister of State for the Department of Employment and Productivity, Mr Edmund Dell, said that the Bill was not designed to control multinational companies: 'What we can do here is not to force investment in this country but to encourage it, and we have met with considerable success.' [164]

The third point which should be made, the manner in which the Board of Trade implemented the recommendations of the Monopolies Commission, underlines the general policy of the Labour Government to avoid a confrontation with foreign-owned companies which might prejudice future foreign investment. In the four cases (electrical equipment, petrol, colour film, detergents) where the Commission did make some recommendations, the Board relied on voluntary compliance by the companies involved, and the actual undertakings given by the companies were the result of negotiations between them and the Board. In no case did any of the foreign-owned companies make an outright refusal to co-operate, and the Board never contemplated drastic solutions such as structural alterations in the companies concerned. [165] The fact that so few foreign-owned companies have been the subject of references by the Monopolies Commission, that the Board has eschewed the use of its wide-ranging powers of action under the monopolies legislation, and that the companies have reached an amicable settlement with the Board, underlines both the government's welcoming attitude toward foreign investment (and its consequent disinclination to delve into the activities of foreign investors) and the general aspiration of foreign investors not to step beyond the bounds of tolerable corporate behaviour.

With regard to mergers and take-overs, the Labour Government assumed powers to vet and control mergers under the Monopolies and Mergers Act 1965 as part of the promise contained in Labour's 1964 General Election Manifesto to 'control take-over bids and mergers'.[166] Under the 1965 Act, the Board of Trade may refer to the Monopolies Commission at its discretion any 'significant' merger (i.e. one in which the result includes control over one-third of any relevant UK market in the supply of goods or services, or the value of assets taken over exceeds £5 million) between two or more enterprises, one at least carried on in the UK or under the control of a body incorporated in the UK. [167] As with monopoly references, therefore, the Board of Trade had substantial discretion in deciding whether or not to refer a merger to the Commission, and the Commission's findings on whether or not the proposed merger might be expected to act in the public interest again have no legal force, but depend on the Board's discretion as to whether any action should be taken. The control of mergers must therefore be seen in the context of the Labour Government's industrial policy as a whole:

> Improving productive efficiency (e.g. by economies of scale) was seen as more important than improving market efficiency (e.g. by increasing competition). ... As a consequence, the desirability of a merger was judged on its individual circumstances – some were actively encouraged. ... [168]

On the one hand, principally through the IRC, the Labour Government encouraged rationalisation in industries which were faced with heavy international competition, and on the other hand it reserved the right to refer mergers to the Monopolies Commission. In response to criticisms of inconsistencies between the use of the IRC and the Monopolies Commission [169] the Labour Government gave details of the way in which mergers were given preliminary scrutiny. [170]

According to this publication, the Board, when it learns of a merger proposal (usually through the financial press, since there is no obligation on companies to notify mergers to the Board), decides whether or not it comes within the scope of the Act, on the basis of information requested in confidence from the parties concerned. Having done this, the results of the preliminary investigation are presented to a standing inter-departmental Mergers Panel, consisting of representatives of the Board, the DEA (which sponsored the IRC), the departments sponsoring the industries concerned, and any other government departments directly concerned.

This Panel then recommends the Board whether or not there is a prima facie case for reference to the Monopolies Commission. The process is conducted extremely rapidly: 90 per cent of all cases have been dealt with by the Board within three weeks, and 75 per cent within two weeks of their announcement and notification. [171] Even if the Panel decide that the merger warrants a reference to the Commission, the Board has in a number of cases decided not to refer mergers after obtaining assurances from the companies concerned, on such diverse matters as consultation with the unions, the form of company accounts after the merger, future policy on investment and exports (where the take-over was by a foreign firm), and due regard for regional policy. [172] Two such cases were the proposed take-over by Chrysler of Rootes and General Foods of Rowntree. [173]

In the case of take-overs by foreign-owned firms, the Board made clear that its main preoccupation was with the possible balance of payments consequences:

> Will there be any restriction on the British firm preventing its competing in markets of the overseas company? Will there be any transfer of manufacture out of the United Kingdom to the overseas company or its subsidiaries? Will the British firm in future be required to import from abroad e.g. components previously bought in the United Kingdom — or to alter its sources of imports? Where will effective management of the British firm rest, in the United Kingdom (with British nationals) or overseas? What are the consequences likely to be for the flow of technology and earnings from licensing? [174]

In fact of some 350 mergers which came within the scope of the Act during the period July 1965 to April 1969, only ten were referred by the Board to the Monopolies Commission, and only one of these concerned a foreign-owned company. [175] In the period 1965—68, there were 318 mergers considered by the Panel, of which 21 (7 per cent of the total) concerned acquisitions by foreign-owned companies. [176] One explanation for this very low level of acquisitions by foreign-owned companies was given by the Monopolies Commission in its survey of mergers:

> Having regard to the level of merger activity in the USA in recent years it is perhaps surprising that foreign companies have not been more active in the British merger market. The UK-based, foreign-owned companies seem generally to have concerned themselves with expansion from within. ... The largest American companies seem to have ignored the prospects of growth by acquisition both in the US

and other countries, concentrating instead on self-generated growth; they have become multi-national by setting up plants in countries where they foresee possibilities of expansion and an increasing flow of profits. On the other hand, most of the largest United Kingdom companies have relied to a considerable extent on acquisitions for growth. [177]

In the only case of a proposed take-over by a foreign company which was referred to the Commission, the bid in 1966 by the Dentists' Supply Co. of New York for the Amalgamated Dental Co. Ltd.[178] was approved by the Commission on the grounds that it would improve efficiency and would provide 'an immediate substantial gain of dollar currency for this country'. [179] The Commission rejected the arguments of the Ministry of Health, which opposed the merger on the ground that a British-owned company would export more and be more amenable to Ministry influence on such matters as price and quality. [180] In the event, neither proposed merger (a bid from a British firm was also considered in the report, and also approved) took place. Of the twenty proposed take-overs by foreign companies not referred to the Commission, thirteen involved American companies; one (the break-up of Caltex by Chevron and Texaco in 1967) involved only a technical restructuring, and two others were only minor acquisitions (TRW acquired Clevedon Engineering in 1966 and the Rheem Corporation acquired Blagden & Noakes in 1968). [181] Of the remaining nine, the Esso take-over of the Agip petrol stations in 1966 was permitted because it was in progress at the time of the Monopolies Commission report on petrol, and similar permissions were given to other oil companies with take-overs of retail outlets in progress.[182] The Chrysler take-over of Rootes (see Chapter 5) in 1967 was permitted because no viable British alternative bidder was available, and it ensured the continued operation of Rootes and employment for its workers; certain assurances were given by Chrysler to the Minister of Technology, and the IRC was represented on the Rootes board. The take-over of the pump firm Worthington—Simpson by the Studebaker—Worthington Company was supported by the IRC in the face of a counter-bid from the Scottish Weir Group, on the grounds that the British bid would not guarantee the future viability of the pump industry in the UK. [183] The fourth significant case, General Mills' bid for Smiths Crisps in 1968, was allowed by the Board because the rival bidder, Imperial Tobacco, already owned the only other major potato crisp manufacturer, Golden Wonder. [184] In the case of the battle in 1968 between American Tobacco and Philip Morris for the control of Gallaher (won by American) and the subsequent successful bid by Philip Morris for Godfrey Phillips, the Board considered that the dominant market position of the British-owned Imperial Tobacco Company made a reference unnecessary.[185] The eighth case, namely the bitterly contested bid by Leasco for Pergamon Press, was not referred by the Board because it was considered that there would be substantial technological benefits (including the development of data-retrieval systems) which would accrue from the merger, and the financial criteria (the Pergamon assets amounted to over £20 million) were not relevant.[186] The last case, the General Foods bid for Rowntree in 1968/9 was not referred by the Board, despite the opposition of the IRC to the bid, largely because the Board was aware through its IRC contacts that a counter-bid from the British Mackintosh company was in preparation, and that the majority shareholders preferred the Mackintosh bid.[187]

The pattern which emerges from the above cases appears to have three elements: take-over bids by American companies were approved by the Board either (a) because they were economically insignificant, or (b) because no viable British alternative existed, or (c) because they either maintained or increased competition and/or conferred potential technological or overseas marketing benefits. In none of the cases included here was there any evidence of an anti-American bias, although the following analysis of mergers between British companies will indicate that the Board imposed standards which might not have been so flexible if a foreign company was involved. The Monopolies Commission found that acquisitions by quoted companies with assests of £½ million or more in the UK indicated 'a continuing and substantial increase in the scale of acquisition activities since 1966, whether measured by reference to the total consideration or the average total consideration per acquisition'.[188] While the Mergers Panel considered 318 mergers between 1965 and 1968,[189] 3059 large mergers took place, indicating that the £5 million threshold set by the 1965 Act excluded almost 90 per cent of all mergers from scrutiny. Of the twelve mergers referred by the Board to the Monopolies Commission in the period 1965–69, four were found to be against the public interest.[190] This generally permissive attitude stems from the wording of Section 6(2) of the 1965 Act that the criterion for judging a merger is whether or not it 'operates or may be expected to operate against the public interest', rather than any positive burden on the parties involved to prove that it will act in the public interest.[191]

One of the most consistent themes in the Commission's reports on mergers has been the desirability of creating large British firms to withstand foreign competition, even at the expense of reducing domestic competition: 'The most valuable result of the merger for the public interest will be that it will make possible a more rapid increase in exports. [192] The assumption that British companies would show more consideration for British customers, would not have restricted export markets, and would not be responsible for remittances abroad led the Commission to approve the BMC/Pressed Steel merger in 1966: 'We think that in this case there is some appreciable advantage in Pressed Steel being taken over by a British rather than a foreign company.' [193] The Commision approved Thorn's bid for Radio Rentals on the grounds that the imminent reduction in import duties and adoption of common line standards for television sets would intensify foreign competition and what Thorn needed was 'a stable and secure home market as a basis for establishing itself in overseas markets'. [194] In another case, the Commission approved a merger which created a virtual monopoly in the UK of propellor shafts and constant velocity joints because 'there is at least no obvious reason why the merged company should be any less successful overseas than its constituents have been,' and the merger was the only possible partnership open to the acquired company. [195] The Commission approved the merger of Unilever and Allied Breweries on the grounds that it would 'provide the basis for developing an international drinks business', and would also maintain the balance between the British and Dutch elements of Unilever, since the Dutch element had grown faster in recent years. [196] Throughout these reports there runs a preoccupation with resisting external competition, to the extent of creating potential barriers of entry for future domestic competition (whether that would come from British or foreign companies), and a near-obsession with achieving a favourable balance of payments position, to the extent of accepting some of the more rosy export forecasts submitted by the companies without critical examination. Kanter and Sugarman commented:

> We do not criticize the basically promerger policy in Britain — in fact we recognize a need for it. What we question is the need for such an elaborate antimerger framework if merger control is virtually non-existent. [197]

Indeed, the major policy of the Labour Government lay not in frustrating mergers but in encouraging the creation of larger industrial units which could compete with the giant international companies. [198] This effort was spear-headed by the IRC, whose structure and functions were discussed in section (2) of this chapter. The Board of the IRC saw its aims as threefold: first, to increase productivity by improving the logical structure of industry, in particular through reducing product differentiation and reducing the duplication of production where this would lead to economies of scale, particularly in sectors where the balance of payments would benefit. Second, they aimed to promote (or at least not harm) regional development. Third, they had the objective of retaining company control in the UK as a means of achieving its first two aims. [199] From January 1967 (when the IRC began its full operations under the 1966 IRC Act), to April 1971 (when it was wound up by the Conservative Government), the IRC participated in 86 projects, mainly in the electrical and electronics, mechanical engineering, automotive, textile, paper, scientific instruments, rubber and nuclear power industries. [200] Of these 86 projcts, 10 were acquisitions or joint ventures involving foreign companies:

1   Rootes Motors (IRC took 15 per cent shareholding and nominated a board member at Government request after Chrysler take-over). January 1967.
2   Studebaker—Worthington Inc. take-over of Worthington—Simpson Pumps (IRC sponsored merger, but no financial support given). January 1969.
3   Pirelli joint venture with Enfield—Standard Power Cables (IRC sponsored, no financial support). July 1969.
4   Aeroquip Corp. of the US take-over of Super Oil Seals (IRC sponsored on grounds of increased investment and exports, no financial support). November 1969.
5   Ingersoll—Rand Pumps (US) purchase of SPP Pumps (IRC sponsored on grounds of increased production range and exports, no financial support). May 1970.
6   Reyrolle—Parsons joint venture in USA with North American Rockwell (IRC sponsored on grounds of strengthening UK company's international position, no finance). June 1970.
7   Miles Roman Ltd acquisition of General Precision Systems from Singer Corporation of USA. (IRC sponsored in order to strengthen UK computer softward industry, took £211,000 equity stake). May 1970.
8   Laporte merger with Solvay of Belgium (IRC informed and supported, no finance). July 1970.
9   Power Gas Corporation acquisition of Bemag Verfahrenstechnik of Germany (IRC supported this establishment of a presence in the EEC, no finance). August 1970.
10   Financial support to UK subsidiary of Kearney & Trecker Corp. USA. (IRC supported UK production of numerically-controlled machine tools to improve productivity of UK industry and increase exports, £300,000 loan). December 1970. [201]

These ten cases, only three of which involved any use of IRC funds, were stressed by IRC executives interviewed as examples of the IRC's non-discriminatory approach toward foreign companies. While this may be so, an analysis of them reveals that 3, 6, 7, 8 and 9 involved a strengthening of the overseas presence of British-owned companies, with no increase in foreign control over UK industry, and in the case of the remaining five acquisitions by foreign companies, no viable British alternative existed in the industries involved. [202] In other industries, principally electrical engineering, computers, motor vehicles, scientific instrumens and ball-bearings, the IRC aimed at rationalisation of the British-owned elements in order to make them internationally competitive, even at the cost of reducing competition in the domestic UK market. In electrical engineering, it was concerned with: ' ... a sector which is of great importance to the country's export effort, where the pace of technical change is rapid, and where there is intense competition from powerful companies in the United States, Europe and Japan.' [203] It therefore sponsored the merger between GEC and AEI in September 1967, and the take-over of English Electric by GEC/AEI in September 1968, creating a company with sales of £2190 million, the fourth largest such company in the world and the largest non-US company in the field. [204] Mr Anthony Crosland, the President of the Board of Trade, said that the mergers would: ' ... increase the efficiency and productivity of the electrical engineering and electronics industries and in particular the effectiveness of the export effort of the companies whose overseas sales are of the greatest importance to the balance of payments.' [205] In addition, while not directly involved in the creation of ICL as the major British computer manufacturer in 1968 (see Chapter 5), the IRC prepared the way for the merger by sponsoring the take-over of Elliott–Automation by English Electric in June 1967. [206] The IRC also sponsored and gave substantial financial support to the rationalisation of the British-owned elements in the motor industry which led to the formation of BLMC in January 1968, with a £25 million seven year unsecured loan, the largest financial outlay it made during its existence. [207]

The IRC's attempts to rationalise the scientific instruments industry led it to intervene directly in the market in 1968 in support of George Kent's bid for Cambridge Instruments, in opposition to a rival bid from the Rank Organisation. The IRC purchased 19·3 per cent of the Cambridge shares in order to thwart the Rank bid, leading to much criticism that it was departing from an objective position (and would therefore be less valuable in promoting future mergers) and was disturbing normal market forces which would otherwise decide the outcome of rival bids. [208] Indeed, it was this IRC initiative which strengthened the resolve of the Conservative Party to abolish the IRC when it returned to office. [209]

The most interesting case of IRC intervention in a take-over battle occured as a result of its attempts to rationalise the ball-bearing industry. In 1968 total UK-based production amounted the £70 million, of which £ 15 million was exported. Imports accounted for £11 million, making total UK consumption £66 million. There were six major manufacturers, three of whom were wholly owned subsidiaries of foreign companies: Skefko (owned by SKF of Sweden, which had bought out a minority UK shareholding in April 1968), British Timken (owned by Timken USA), and Fafnir (a subsidiary of Textron Inc., USA). the three other major manufacturers were British controlled: Ransome & Marles, Hoffmann, and Pollard, and between them had approximately 35 per cent of the UK market. Skefko supplied about 27 per cent, and the rest was shared between the two American companies and imports. [210] Because it was aware that SKF was preparing to bid for one of the three British companies, the IRC began an investigation of the industry in early May 1968, for three reasons:

> In the first place, the ball-bearing industry is a large sector of engineering technology, making an essential input to major exporting sectors such as the motor and aircraft industries; secondly, compared with the industries in Western Europe and North America the structure of the UK based industry appeared fragmented and this fell directly within IRC's remit; and in the third palce the possibility of a merger between Ransome & Marles and ... Skefko ... could only mean that there might shortly be no viable British owned company in the industry. [211]

In its investigations the IRC found that in other advanced economies the bearing industry was very highly concentrated, with SKF having a 70 per cent share of the French and Italian markets, a predominant share of the Scandinavian market, and sharing 80 per cent of the German market with Kugelfischer FAG. The main reasons for this concentration were the need for long production runs to achieve economies of scale, and the need to limit the range of bearings produced. Whereas output per employee in Europe was over £3,000 per annum, the British companies had an annual output of only just over £2,000 per employee, and this was reflected in the decreasingly favourable UK balance of trade in bearings. [212] In particular, the IRC noted that the only market apart from Sweden in which there was a strong surplus in the bearings trade was Germany, which had the only strong competitor to SKF, and that SKF's contribution to German exports of bearings was well below its market share. [213] In particular, the IRC was struck by the performance of RIV, the Italian bearing company, after SKF had taken over management of it in 1963 (it purchased control of RIV from Giovanni Agnelli of Fiat in 1965). Exports from RIV to SKF's German subsidiary rose from 12·2 million kroner in 1963 to 51·3 million kroner in 1965, but after SKF assumed ownership of RIV in 1965, the company's exports to Germany fell back to 9·6 million kroner in 1967. [214] The IRC saw this as the result of intensified competition in Germany from Kugelfischer, which forced SKF to switch production to Germany in order to improve its marginal costs, [215] and feared that:

> SKF, as with any strongly based international group, acting in the interest of its own efficiency and profitability might well find it advantageous to rationalise its production facilities, locate its R & D, buy its raw materials and machine tools and direct its marketing policy in ways which would not necessarily benefit the UK economy. [216]

The Managing Director of SKF, Mr Folke Lindskog (who had been managing director of Skefko in Britain between 1960 and 1964), gave rather a different explanation, emphasising the importance of intra-company trading to maintain production and employment in each country despite fluctuations in national business cycles. [217] He pointed out that the Italian company was on the verge of bankruptcy in 1962, and that this was avoided by other SKF subsidiaries, particularly the German one, placing orders with it which accounted for RIV's splendid export record 1963–65. In 1966, the German economy began to slow down, while the Italian economy began to pick up, with the result that RIV switched from exports to supplying the increasing demands of Italian industry. In 1962–63, when the UK market contracted, Lindskog had maintained full employment at Skefko in Britain by increasing intra-company exports from 15 per cent to 24 per cent, and similar geocentric trading had kept the German and Canadian plants operating when their home demand dropped in the late 1960s.[218] Lindskog stressed that in sixty years of operating in the UK, SKF had never laid off a worker, had reinvested almost 80 per cent of its profits, and remitted very small amounts. [219]

Nevertheless, the IRC was dubious about SKF's arguments, pointing to its marginally negative balance of payments position (due to a preference for Swedish rather than British steel for its products), when even US Timken's contribution was positive. [220] SKF was therefore informed by the IRC in September 1968 that it would not be allowed to bid for

Ransome & Marles, the leading British bearing company, and on 31 October 1968 the IRC's Managing Director wrote to the Chairman of Skefko: 'The IRC Board feels that the right way to proceed is through a grouping of the three British-owned companies in the ball bearings industry, leaving room at every stage for SKF participation. Such participation, would, of course, involve assurances. ... [221] The nature of these assurances included the issues of control, market share, balance of payments contribution, commercial freedom, rationalisation and management structure, but the subsequent discussions with SKF broke down on the issue of control. SKF insisted that if it participated in the rationalisation scheme, it wanted control over its holdings and autonomy in export and purchasing policy. Discussions were at times quite heated, with an SKF representative exclaiming: 'What we own, we control', and a Ministry of Technology official recalling that Sweden had supplied ball-bearings to the Japanese during the Second World War. [222]

In January 1969, when it had become clear that SKF co-operation was not forthcoming, the IRC made a bid for Brown Bayley, Hoffmann's parent company, and SKF countered by purchasing a 15 per cent stake in Pollard in April 1969. [223] The IRC considered that Pollard was vital to the new group (Ransome & Marles was to take over Hoffmann from the IRC) because it supplied both Ford and Chrysler with bearings, and the SKF share purchase would give Pollard a £½ million cash injection which would enable it to continue a price war with Ransome/Hoffmann – prices had only increased 1 per cent in the industry in 1963–68 – which would have seriously damaged the new grouping. [224] In May 1968 the three-way grouping was achieved with IRC backing, and Ransome–Hoffmann–Pollard came into existence. The Swedish Ambassador made a personal protest to the Minister of Technology, Mr Wedgwood Benn, on the grounds of discrimination against an EFTA partner, [225] but Mr Benn made it clear that he supported the IRC decision:

> I explained candidly ... that this was based on a study of what SKF had done when they bought Agnelli's ball-bearing outfit which had led to the ending of exports and we felt that the right thing to do was to get the British groups together. But there was never anything in our minds, certainly not in my mind, that a British group was a substitute for an international link. Really the choice presenting itself to us was whether you built up a British group first and then went international or whether you encouraged or allowed international companies to swoop in and pick up the most efficient bits and knock out the rest by competition. [226]

114

Although both the government and the IRC denied any nationalistic motives in their handling of the SKF affair, their subsequent actions indicated a certain conscience about the way in which SKF had been treated. When SKF announced an £18 million UK expansion plan in 1970, the Ministry of Technology sent its Minister of State, Lord Delacourt-Smith to address Skefko's diamond jubilee dinner, where he stressed that Mintech was constantly seeking 'international technological collaboration on a wider plane', and stressed that the government was not seeking a monopoly of British-owned interest in the UK bearing industry. [227] IRC officials pointed out that RHP and SKF had a joint marketing subsidiary in Australia, and hoped that similar collaborative projects would develop. [228] Mr Lindskog himself acknowledged that the government 'has every right to intervene to protect British interests', but pointed out that 'the individual European companies will find it hard to compete against Japanese competition unless they stand together.' [229]

The conclusion which can be drawn from this brief analysis of the IRC's attempts to restructure certain sections of British industry is that, despite its avowed intention to seek international solutions for rationalising these sectors, it almost invariably settled for British ones. Although it had always used comparisons with foreign industries in preparing its working papers, there was no concerted IRC feeling that it must seek international solutions until the end of 1969, when Mr Charles Villiers (its Managing Director) began to make a series of speeches advocating a European IRC and more UK-European company mergers. [230] Where international solutions had been sought, these were in areas (such as the pump industry) where no viable British solution was possible, and one former IRC executive considered that 'the IRC's public statements on the need for international solutions were rather in excess of its actual achievements in this sphere'. [231]

Had the IRC continued in existence after 1970, with most of its initial objectives for rationalising British industry fulfilled, it might have developed this side of its activities further, and become, in the words of Kanter and Sugarman, 'a more potent weapon than the merger-control law for meeting the American challenge.' [232] However, in its semi-autonomous role as a government-funded merchant bank and industrial marriage-broker (even though some were of the shotgun variety), the IRC was responsible for a significant number of mergers in industries which faced considerable foreign competition. The success of these mergers is difficult to assess at this short distance in time, but, as *The Economist* commented, 'Government departments acting on their own have not done much better than the IRC,' [233] and the IRC's autonomous status enabled it to discuss proposals on a confidential basis with businessmen without the constraints which direct consultation with a government department would have involved:

> Civil servants are totally unqualified and unable to make qualitative judgements and push them through to their conclusion because they are answerable to their Minister who might get faced with nasty questions in the House. The IRC's intervention is selective and personal, which civil servants can never be, and the IRC board members are businessmen and its executives tough and imaginative. [234]

Although this view is debatable, it is clear that the IRC was a valuable addition to the Labour Government's methods of controlling the activities of multinational companies operating in the UK, principally by creating countervailing British-owned companies capable of competing against them. Nevertheless, although the IRC was complementary to the Labour Government's industrial policy, it could never have been a substitute for it; there were frequent instances of conflicts between IRC policies and initiatives and those of government departments, [235] and the speed at which the IRC pushed through its proposals meant that the Board of Trade frequently did not have time to consider their full implications under the 1965 Mergers Act (from which IRC-sponsored mergers were, with the Board's permission, exempt). [236] Indeed, members of the Monopolies Commission were quoted in the press as having 'serious anxieties that their work is being undermined by other agencies'. [237]

In general it can be seen that the market behaviour of multinational companies in the UK has not been a major preoccupation of the British Government during the period under review:

> British competition policy is not aimed primarily at American business. It is designed, rather, to create the economic climate thought healthiest by Parliament from time to time. Aspects of that competition policy are aimed at preserving competition, creating particular efficiencies in the economy, and constructing a satisfactory balance of payments ledger. [238]

It might be argued, however, that even these objectives have not necessarily been achieved by the government departments charged with carrying them out. The government has wide legal powers to regulate the market behaviour of firms in the UK, whether British or foreign-owned, but there is little evidence that they have been used, or even that the government contemplated using them. The small number of monopolies references to the Commission, and, in the case of references involving

multinational companies, the extremely narrow interpretation of the behaviour scrutinised (almost all extraterritorial considerations being excluded), are evidence of this lenient attitude, as is the amount of discretion exercised by the Board of Trade in deciding whether to make such
references and which, if any, of the Commission's findings are to be
implemented — with implementation centring on a voluntary mode of
complaince by the firms involved. So, too, is the general tolerance of most
merger activity evidence of this lenient attitude; a Board of Trade official
emphasised that questions concerning a multinational company's operating strategy are rarely, if ever, considered by the Board, and that if
assurances are asked for, 'one would take the word of the firm — we have
no means of policing such undertakings.' [239]

In part, this lack of detailed supervision of foreign companies in the UK
may have been due to a fear that it would discourage foreign investment,
but in fact there was little supervision of any companies — British or
foreign-owned. Graham has offered a persuasive explanation of this relatively *laissez-faire* policy:

> In the UK, governments depend almost entirely for their statistical
> information on voluntary co-operation between industry and govern-
> ment departments (particularly the Ministry of Technology and the
> Board of Trade). In addition, during this period the co-operation of
> industry was required in planning, in prices and incomes policy, and
> in the programme of voluntary exchange control. Close scrutiny may
> have been thought counter-productive, politically, if not econom-
> ically — though whether this view is correct is another matter. [240]

Even in the absence of such scrutiny, there were serious gaps in the data
available to government departments on the operations of multinational
companies in the UK, and it is this aspect of governmental control which
must now be considered.

3.4.3 The activities of multinational companies — government consulta-
tion and inquiry

The main source of data on industrial activity in the UK is the Statistics
Division of the Board of Trade, and the previous chapter drew heavily on
the material published in the weekly *Board of Trade Journal*. The Board
of Trade presents a monthly report on exports and imports to Parliament,
based on documents submitted to HM Customs and Excise by importers
and exporters, it also carries out an annual census of production in the
UK, with a census of distribution and other services at longer intervals. In

collecting such statistics, no distinction is made between British and foreign-owned companies, although the 1963 Census of Industrial Production included for the first time questions on the country of origin of the companies concerned. [241] As far as the operations of multinational companies are concerned, the Board has made no concerted effort to gather statistical data on their activities; it started collecting statistics on inward and outward investment only in 1958, on royalty payments between 1958 and 1964 (and again in 1970), on exports between related concerns in 1966 only, and on repatriation of profits from 1958. All such data are published in aggregated form, and in the case of trade figures, HM Customs and Excise have refused to supply the Board with disaggregated figures because this would identify the import and export transactions of individual firms. Statistics on the oil industry were collected by the Ministry of Power, and were not communicated to the Board or included in the Board's trade and investment data on national security grounds. [242]

Although, as mentioned above, statistics on exports between related concerns were collected in 1966, there has never been any attempt to collect data on *imports* between related concerns. In those cases where investigations were carried out by the Ministry of Technology or the IRC on the balance of trade of individual firms, these depended on voluntary disclosure by the firms, or leaks from disaffected employees of the firms concerned. [243] As Dr Jeremy Bray, a former junior Minister at Mintech, has pointed out, there has been no co-ordination of statistics gathering by government departments, [244] with employment figures gathered monthly by the Department of Employment and Productivity, production figures annually and investment intentions quarterly by the Board of Trade, and taxation figures annually by the Department of Inland Revenue. The result has been that the time series of the various sources of data are incompatible, and since each department aggregates the data it receives, the individual firm disappears, so that it is impossible to measure its productivity. Several government officials interviewed for this study expressed disappointment with the quantity and quality of available statistical data concerning multinational companies, and in one Ministry of Technology study statistics furnished by the US Department of Commerce had to be used. [245] The only working paper on multinational companies produced by the Ministry of Technology drew heavily on data furnished by Professor John Dunning of Reading University, who had to generate his own data from questionnaires and company reports. [246]

It was partly as a result of this dissatisfaction with the current state of information on the multinational company that the Economic Services Division of the Board of Trade in 1967 requested Dr Max Steuer of the

London School of Economics to prepare a report on 'Inward Investment in the United Kingdom'. [247] The final report, which utilised unpublished data from the 1963 census of industrial production, was completed in 1970, and was considered by a Cabinet Committee on 20 May 1970, which concluded that it was 'satisfied that the Steuer report would raise no major problems for Government'. It was therefore somewhat surprising that the Steuer report was not published until three years later, with much of the data generated by the 1963 census of industrial production and a postal survey of all 6,000 discoverable foreign firms omitted. Despite the fact that Dr Steuer and his team had full access to the data held by the various government departments (with the exception of oil statistics), the report stressed that the lack of hard information on the activities of foreign-owned firms contributed a substantial amount of uncertainty to its findings: 'Clearly our knowledge is far from complete, and a close watch on inward investment is a minimal sensible policy ... We recommend a much intensified monitoring of the foreign activity in this country. [248] The reports findings were therefore heavily qualified, although it concluded that:

> ... concerns over the multi-national firm and inward investment on the grounds of monopoly power, technology, and the balance of payments are not well-founded ... While the foreign subsidiary means that some decision taking relevant to our economy goes on outside this country, there is not a great deal of interference and we have been unable to find substantial adverse effects due to it. [249]

For this reason the report came down against discriminating among individual foreign investors, or of excluding foreign investment from certain industries, although it was sympathetic to the idea of an overall limit on foreign investment:

> Obviously the choice of any precise number, like the safe alcohol level in the blood, is arbitrary in a range. But a general order of magnitude for a desirable upper limit is not obviously foolish. On pure economic grounds narrowly defined, we see no case for such a limit. ... But as the foreign proportion gets higher, say, over twenty per cent, the non-economic drawbacks may become more important. [250]

The agnostic stance of the Steuer report, and its argument that 'some of the objection to the growing success of the multinational firm is a dog in the manger attitude' [251] caused *The Times* to comment that:

119

It is likely to be prayed in aid of opposing points of view. Its typical conclusion — that there is not enough information to resolve a given dispute and that more information should be gathered, preferably by the Government—certainly leaves room for the popular debate on the sub-economics of the multinational enterprise to continue for many a long season. [252]

The impression remains that the paucity of statistics on the operation of multinational companies in the UK is a result of the fragmentation of responsibility for industrial policy among several government departments, and the peripheral interest of each of them in the subject of multinational companies. Where useful statistics have been collected, and the Board of Trade has done more than most to collect them, they have been aggregated in such a way that monitoring the performance of individual companies, or even foreign-owned companies as a whole, is impossible. The National Economic Development Office, on whose Council representatives of government, business and the trade unions sit, decided on 7 April 1970 to institute a study on multinational companies, [253] but three years later no such study had been published. The NEDO-sponsored Economics Development Committees, which cover twenty-one major industries and include government, business and trade union representatives, have all produced reports on the economic prospects for their respective industries, including some discussion of the role of foreign investment and the international competitive environment. [254] With few exceptions, however, have these reports provided very much hard information, and, perhaps, because they depend on the goodwill of companies to provide information on their intentions and representatives for the work of the committees, the EDCs have not indulged in any critical analysis of the role of foreign companies in their respective industries. [256]

Altough both the Ministry of Technology and the IRC began a series of dialogues with certain multinational companies in 1968—69, these did not involve more than a dozen companies and were not carried out on an industry-wide basis. [256] It is significant that the only two macro-studies of the costs and benefits of foreign investment, the Reddaway and Steuer reports, were compiled by outside academics (admittedly at the behest of the government, and with its co-operation) rather than by government officials themsleves. The fact that much of the Steuer report's data on profit distribution, royalty and service payments, exports and net asset values of foreign-owned companies had to be obtained by voluntary questionnaires indicates the paucity of information on multinational companies available to decision-makers in the British Government. Although the West German Government, for example, has even fewer statistics on inward investment, and its Ministry of Economics (BMW) finds it difficult to extract even the most basic information on individual companies, [257] the range of Board of Trade data on multinational companies compares unfavourably with that available to the US Department of Commerce — despite the fact that the UK has been, after Canada, the most important location for US direct investment.

3.5 Conclusion

The Conservative Minister for Trade and Industry, Mr John Davies, announced in October 1971 that the British Government would require under new companies legislation a greater degree of disclosure of information by multinational companies, but this legislation has so far not materialised. [258] Until it does, it must be said that the government has insufficient information on which to assess the activities of multinational companies in the UK, and no prospect, therefore, of formulating policies for controlling them effectively. It has been seen in this chapter that the Labour Government maintained the policy of its predecessors in extending a qualified welcome for foreign investment in the UK. This openhanded attitude was undoubtedly conditioned by the critical need for foreign capital, especially during the balance of payments and sterling crises which bedevilled the first three years of the Labour Government's term. Such a policy was justified by most of the politicians and civil servants interviewed as 'pragmatic', 'treating each case on its own merits', and similar arguments. It is hard to avoid the suspicion, however, that the emperor was clothing his nakedness with *ad hoc* garments, and that the government had little information which would enable it to examine 'each case on its own merits'. It has been seen that the Board of Trade reached judgements on the desirability of almost all the mergers it considered within three weeks — hardly enough time to analyse the present implications of a merger, let alone the future repercussions on the UK economy. It has also been seen that the Treasury judged applications to invest in the UK on solely financial grounds, and was disposed to granting all but the most dubious investment projects if they satisfied its financial criteria. Admittedly the views of other departments were frequently considered by the Treasury's Foreign Exchange Committee, but the speed with which applications were processed (less than a week in most cases) casts doubts on the suitability of the Exchange Control Act and its attendant procedures for controlling multinational companies and ensuring that they served the interests of the UK economy and government policy.

Indeed, the powers at the disposal of the British Government for controlling the activities of multinational companies operating in the UK resemble nothing so much as using a sledgehammer to catch an eel (if one may be excused a mixed metaphor). There were certainly powers to control and eliminate blatant malpractice by multinational companies, but the rare occasions on which those powers have been used indicates that multinational companies are rarely guilty of, or misguided enough to engage in, blatant malpractice. Just as tax avoidance is permissible for citizens, while tax evasion is not, so multinational companies *might* be avoiding their full responsibility to the UK economy while not actually evading their legal responsibilities. The word 'might' is underlined, because neither the British Government nor an individual researcher has any means at present of determining whether avoidance of social and economic responsibility is taking place, and because the Labour Government never attempted to define the limits of that responsibility.

In part this was due to the peripheral interest of all the government departments concerned with industrial policy in the multinational company, and the failure of some departments even to consider the problem at all. Like A.A. Milne's nursery character, Winnie-the-Pooh, who said, 'We will build it here, just by this wood, out of the wind, because this is where I first thought of it,' the Labour Government improvised an *ad hoc* policy toward multinational companies operating in the UK, rather than attempting to devise a long-term strategy for ensuring that the British economy derived the maximum benefit from their activities consistent with maintaining an attractive investment climate. It is true that, toward the end of its term of office, the Labour Government began to pay more attention to the implications of the emergence of multinational companies, and began a constructive dialogue with some of them, but summit meetings with Henry Ford were no substitute for the formulation of clear, consitent and coherent policy guidelines. In a sense, what the Labour Government lacked was a theory of foreign investment, which would clarify its objectives and indicate what information was needed, and it lacked such a theory because none of the government departments had the prime responsibility for formulating one. Since the Labour Government had consciously eschewed Keynesian management of the economy in favour of a more interventionist form of economic management, such an omission was both surprising and regrettable.

Notes

[1] Quoted in E. Moonman *The Reluctant Partnership* Gollancz, London 1971, pp. 52–3

[2] *Labour Party General Election Manifesto 1964,* p. 8. Harold Wilson had attracted much attention for his speech at the Labour Party's 1963 Conference when he announced his intention of harnessing the 'white heat of the technological revolution' to the modernisation of British industry. See *Report of the 62nd Annual Labour Party Conference* The Labour Party, London 1963, pp. 139–40

[3] Lord Bridges *The Treasury* Allen & Unwin, London 1964, p. 203

[4] *Control of Public Expenditure* Cmnd. 1432, HMSO, London 1961

[5] Bridges, op. cit., p. 83

[6] Samuel Brittan *Steering the Economy* Secker & Warburg, London 1969, pp. 4, 16

[7] ibid., p. 25

[8] H. Roseveare *The Treasury* Allen Lane, London 1969, p. 336

[9] Edmund Burke *The Oeconomical Reform of the Civil and Other Establishments* London 1780, p. 5

[10] Board of Trade *An Introduction to the Board of Trade* Board of Trade, London 1969, p. 3

[11] Quoted in Graham Turner *Business in Britain* Penguin Books, Harmondsworth 1971, p. 69

[12] Harold Wilson *The Labour Government 1964–1970* Weidenfeld & Nicolson, London 1971, pp. 5–9

[13] George Brown *In My Way: Memoirs* Gollancz, London 1971, p. 97

[14] J. & A.–M. Hackett *The British Economy: Problems and Prospects* Allen & Unwin, London 1967, p. 134

[15] Interview with a former Economist, Department of Economic Affairs, 14 April 1971

[16] *The National Plan* (Cmnd. 2764), HMSO 1965, p. 10

[17] see note 15

[18] Turner, op. cit., p. 80

[19] A. Fels *The British Prices and Incomes Board* Cambridge University Press, 1972, p. 27

[20] ibid., pp. 38–9

[21] Those where the price increases were accepted were Batteries (10.4.1968 Cmnd. 3597), Butyl Rubber (13.5.1968 Cmnd. 3626); modifications were asked for in the case of Detergents (11.10.1965 Cmnd. 2791 – standstill or reductions in some prices), Hoover Domestic Appliances (8.6.1968 Cmnd. 3671 – 3% instead of 7·6% for floor care appliances)

and IBM Rental Charges (10.7.1968 Cmnd. 3699 − 5 to 7% instead of 10%)

22 Interview with a former member of the Prices and Incomes Board, 6 December 1972

23 Interview with the Rt Hon A. Wedgwood Benn MP (former Minister of Technology), 2 December 1970

24 *The Industrial Reorganisation Corporation* (Cmnd. 2889), HMSO, January 1966

25 Industrial Reorganisation Corporation *Report and Accounts 1967/68* p. 5. Mr Grierson was replaced by Mr Charles Villiers in 1968

26 ibid., p. 8

27 Interview with an IRC senior executive, 28 October 1970

28 *The Times* 26 January 1966, p. 12

29 S. Young 'Reshaping industry: the IRC in retrospect' *New Society* vol. 16, no. 425 (19 November 1970), p. 908

30 IRC *Report and Accounts 1967−68*, pp. 12−13

31 Interview with a former IRC executive, 25 November 1970

32 IRC *Report and Accounts 1968−69*, pp. 16−17

33 Interview with a former Under-Secretary at the Department of Economic Affairs (responsible for liaison with the IRC), 15 December 1970

34 see *The Times* 26 January 1966, p. 17; 21 February 1966, p. 17

35 *The Times* 19 December 1970, p. 5

36 Personal knowledge

37 See his speech to the Labour Party's 1963 Annual Conference in The Labour Party *Report of the 62nd Annual Conference* The Labour Party, London 1963, pp. 139−40

38 H.C. Deb. vol. 702 (26 November 1964) cols. 216−17

39 *The Ministry of Technology 1964−69* Ministry of Technology, London 1969, p. 1

40 Ministry of Technology Press Notice 'The History, Policy and Organisation of Mintech', 1970, p. 1

41 *The Times* 29 September 1970, p. 19

42 *The Ministry of Technology 1964−69*, op. cit., p. 3

43 Wedgwood Benn interview, loc. cit.

44 'A message from the Minister to the staff' *Mintech Review* September 1969, pp. 3−4

45 Interview with a senior civil servant, Industrial Policy Division, Ministry of Technology, 23 November 1970

46 Interview with Dr Jeremy Bray, Joint Parliamentary Secretary, Ministry of Technology (1967−69), 15 February 1971

[47] 'Multinational companies: note by the Ministry of Technology,' 3 July 1969, mimeo; 'Information on multinational companies', OECD working paper IND (70) 3/17, March 1970, mimeo

[48] Sir Richard Clarke (Permanent Secretary, Ministry of Technology) 'Guidelines for multinational corporations — a government view' British-North American Committee Paper BN/M—12 (July 1970), London p. 7; personal interview 22 December 1970

[49] Bray interview, loc. cit.

[50] *Report of the Sainsbury Committee into the Relationship of the Pharmaceutical Industry with the National Health Service 1965—67* (Cmnd. 3410) HMSO, London 1967, p. 9

[51] ibid., p. 34

[52] ibid., p. 53

[53] ibid., pp. 84, 13

[54] ibid., pp. 55, 63

[55] ibid., p. 88

[56] Interview with a senior Ministry of Health official, 17 November 1970

[57] ibid.

[58] Monopolies Commission *A Report on the Supply of Chlordiazepoxide and Diazepam* HMSO, London 1973, p. 70; *The Economist* 19 May 1973, p. 98

[59] Interview with a member of the Chemicals EDC, 12 November 1970

[60] Interview with an ABPI official, 20 February 1971

[61] 'Economic effects of pressure on the prices of NHS medicines', Pfizer Ltd, London December 1970 (mimeo), p. 17

[62] M. Cooper *International Price Comparison of the Pharmaceutical Industry* National Economic Development Office, London 1972, *passim*

[63] F.C. Howard *Exchange and Borrowing Control* Butterworth, London 1948, pp. 16—20

[64] M. D. Steuer *et al The Impact of Foreign Direct Investment on the United Kingdom*, HMSO London, 1973, p. 177

[65] *The Economist* 28 January 1967, p. 339; *The Times* 21 February 1971, p. 10

[66] Interview with a Planning Executive of a London merchant bank, 25 November 1970

[67] John H. Dunning *The Role of American Investment in the British Economy* PEP, London 1969, pp. 161—2

[68] Interview with a senior civil servant (Home and General), HM Treasury 22 January 1971: this was increased to 100 per cent in 1972

[69] Interview with a senior official, Overseas Department, Bank of England 25 January 1971

[70] Interview with a senior Treasury official 15 December 1970

[71] Interview with a former senior official, Ministry of Technology 22 December 1970

[72] Interview with a senior civil servant (Finance), H.M. Treasury, 22 January 1971

[73] Interview with a senior Treasury official 22 January 1971

[74] Interview with a senior Treasury official, 22 January 1971

[75] Bridges, op. cit., p. 84

[76] H.C. Deb. vol. 739 (17 January 1967), cols. 45—6

[77] *The Economist* 28 January 1967, p. 339, and Ministry of Technology officials

[78] see H.C. Deb. vol. 554 (14 June 1956), cols 775—6; vol. 630 (21 November 1960), cols 769—70

[79] Interview with a Department of Trade and Industry official, 12 January 1971

[80] Interview with a senior Treasury official, 22 January 1971

[81] Interview with the Rt Hon Antony Wedgwood Benn, MP, 2 December 1970

[82] Interview, 22 January 1971

[83] ibid.

[84] Interview with a senior official, Bank of England, 25 January 1971

[85] S. Hatch and M. Fores 'The struggle for British Aluminium' *The Political Quarterly* vol. 31 (1960), p. 487

[86] Dudley Seers and Paul Streeten 'Overseas development policies' in Wilfred Beckerman (ed.) *The Labour Government's Economic Record: 1964—70* Duckworth, London 1972, p. 146

[87] 'Direct and trade investment in the non-sterling area' *Board of Trade Journal* 26 April 1968, pp. 1263—7

[88] Seers and Streeten, op. cit., p. 147. This was ended in 1972

[89] see note 84

[90] Brittan, op. cit., p. 28

[91] see note 84

[92] Steuer *et al,* op. cit., p. 181

[93] Interview with an Assistant Registrar of Companies, Board of Trade, 20 January 1971

[94] Board of Trade, Insurance and Companies Department, unpublished statistics, December 1970

[95] Steuer, op. cit., p. 4

[96] Board of Trade, op. cit.

[97] L.C.B. Gower *Modern Company Law* (3rd edn) Stevens, London 1969, p. 673

[98] ibid., p. 675

[99] Interview with a senior official, Insurance and Companies Department, Board of Trade, 20 January 1971

[100] *The Guardian* 4 August 1972, p. 12

[101] *The Financial Times* 12 October 1970, p. 8

[102] Department of Trade and Industry *Company Law Reform* (Cmnd 5391) HMSO, London 1973, p. 8

[103] J. and A.M. Hackett *The British Economy: Problems and Prospects* Allen & Unwin, London 1967, pp. 76–9

[104] 'Regional development' *Notes on Current Politics* no. 20 (15 December 1969), Conservative Research Department, London pp. 367–9

[105] *Get Ahead in Britain* Board of Trade, London 1967, p. 2

[106] Jeremy Hardie 'Regional policy' in Beckerman, op. cit., p. 223

[107] ibid., p. 230. In 1970 the Conservative Government discontinued both the REP and investment grants, replacing them by a depreciation allowance for plant and machinery. The 1972 Budget re-introduced investment grants for development areas, and permitted foreign firms to raise all their capital needs for investment in assisted areas from sterling sources

[108] *H.C. Deb.*, vol. 801, col. 643

[109] Interview with a member of the Policy Briefing Section, Department of Trade and Industry, 1 January 1971

[110] Interview with a member of the Distribution of Industry Division, Department of Trade and Industry, 29 March 1971

[111] *British Oxygen Co. Ltd v.Minister of Technology* (1970), 3 *All England Law Reports* at p. 165

[112] *Report of the Rochdale Committee on Shipping* (Cmnd 4337) HMSO, London 1970, p. 366 and *The Financial Times* 20 November 1969, p. 6

[113] Board of Trade *Investment Grants: A Guide for Industry* Board of Trade, London 1968, pp. 90–8

[114] *The Financial Times* 12 November 1969, p. 14

[115] Interview with Dr Austin Pearce, Managing Director, Esso Petroleum Company, 1 June 1970

[116] Select Committee on Public Accounts *Third Report* (1969–70 Session), para. 24

[117] *The Times* 17 March 1971, p. 19

[118] Hardie, op. cit., p. 233

[119] Interview with a civil servant, Distribution of Industry Division,

Department of Trade and Industry (formerly Board of Trade), 29 March 1971

120   Interview with a senior civil servant, Distribution of Industry Division, Board of Trade, 29 March 1971

121   Interview, 15 February 1971

122   Hardie, op. cit., p. 234

123   Central Office of Information *Britain's Overseas Investments* COI, London April 1966, p. 26

124   Arthur Andersen & Co. *Tax and Trade Guide for the United Kingdom* Arthur Andersen, New York 1969, p. 117

125   ibid., p. 128. Changes to an imputation tax system for corporations, announced in the 1972 Budget, would tend to further discriminate against profit distribution to non-residents, unless they could set off UK tax against their home country tax liability.

126   M.Z. Brooke and H.L. Remmers *The Strategy of Multinational Enterprise* Longman, London 1970, p. 164

127   see, for example, the amended Anglo-Swiss Double Taxation Agreement, governing the flow of licence fees from the UK to Swiss-based companies *Financial Times* 20 September 1966, p. 6. The Sainsbury Report op. cit., p. 84, found that Swiss drug companies in the UK were less than half as profitable as their American counterparts, and 30 per cent less profitable than British and other European companies

128   Andersen, op. cit., p. 123

129   Neale interview, loc cit.

130   C.K. Rowley *The British Monopolies Commission* Allen & Unwin, London 1966, p. 51

131   This function was taken over by the Department of Employment and Productivity in 1969, but was transferred to the Department of Trade and Industry created by the Conservative Government in 1970

132   Interview with a member of the Monopolies Commission, 12 November 1970

133   Monopolies Act 1948, Sections 2, 6(1), 7(2)

134   ibid., Section 3(1) (a). This was also extended to the supply of services by Section 2(2) of the 1965 Act

135   ibid., Section 6(1) (b)

136   Interview with a senior Board of Trade official, 7 August 1970

137   A.B. Kanter and S.D. Sugarman 'British antitrust response to the American business invasion' *Stanford Law Review* vol. 22 (February 1970), pp. 464–5.

138   ibid., p. 465

139   Monopolies Commission *Second Report on the Supply of Electric*

Lamps (HC4), HMSO, London 1968, pp. 65–8

[140]   Rowley, op. cit., p. 253

[141]   Monopolies Commission *Supply of Electrical Equipment for Mechanically Propelled Land Vehicles* (HC21) HMSO, London 1963, p. 237

[142]   ibid., p. 232

[143]   ibid., p. 237

[144]   ibid., p. 358

[145]   Monopolies Commission *Supply of Petrol to Retailers in the United Kingdom* (HC264) HMSO, London 1965

[146]   ibid., para. 101

[147]   ibid., para. 428

[148]   President of the Board of Trade, quoted in Kanter and Sugarman op. cit., p. 475

[149]   ibid., p. 476

[150]   *The Times* 4 May 1968, p. 11

[151]   *The Sunday Times* 31 March 1968, p. 30

[152]   Monopolies Commission *Supply and Processing of Colour Film* (HC1) HMSO, London 1966, p. 94

[153]   ibid., pp. 101–2

[154]   ibid., p. 58

[155]   Kanter and Sugarman, op. cit., p. 470

[156]   Monopolies Commission op. cit., p. 119

[157]   S. de la Mahotière *Towards One Europe* Penguin, Harmondsworth 1970, p. 106

[158]   Monopolies Commission *Supply of Household Detergents* (HC105) HMSO, London 1966, p. 40

[159]   ibid., p. 42

[160]   Kanter and Sugarman op. cit., pp. 472–3

[161]   An important exception in the Hoffmann–La Roche case *A Report on the Supply of Chlordiazepoxide and Diazepam*, HC 197, HMSO London, 1973 where the commission asked the Company to supply figures on worldwide sales and R & D, but the Swiss company refused; see p. 75

[162]   *The Sunday Times* 23 November 1969, p. 31. At the same time that the Ministry of Health was attempting to obtain foreign sales figures from Hoffmann–La Roche (see n.161), the British Government prohibited Beecham (UK) from supplying UK sales figures to the US Justice Department; see *The Economist* 19 May 1973, p. 98

[163]   *Commission for Industry and Manpower Bill* (HC123) HMSO, London 1970, Section 2(3)

[164]   *Parliamentary Debates: Commons Standing Committees Official*

Report (Session 1969–70), Standing Committee H (5 May 1970), cols 451–2

[165] Interview with a senior civil servant, Economic Services Division, Department of Trade and Industry, (formerly Board of Trade), 12 January 1971

[166] Labour Party, op. cit., p. 12

[167] Monopolies and Mergers Act 1965, Section 6

[168] Graham, op. cit., p. 193

[169] The merger of the trawling interests of Ross and Associated Fisheries, sponsored by the IRC in April 1969, had been preceded by a Monopolies Commission report in 1966 on a similar proposal which it found to be against the public interest. See IRC *Report and Accounts 1968/69* p. 35, and Monopolies Commission *Proposed Merger of Ross Group Ltd. and Associated Fisheries Ltd* (HC42), HMSO London, 1966

[170] Board of Trade *Mergers: A Guide to Board of Trade Practice* HMSO, London 1969

[171] ibid., pp. 20–1

[172] ibid., p. 23

[173] ibid., p. 28

[174] ibid., p. 13

[175] ibid., pp. 26–7. In addition, two newspaper mergers were referred. But these references were mandatory under the 1965 Act

[176] ibid., p. 26

[177] Monopolies Commission *A Survey of Mergers 1958–1968* HMSO, London 1970, pp. 13–14

[178] Monopolies Commission *Proposed Mergers of Dental Manufacturing Co. Ltd. or the Dentists' Supply Co. of New York and The Amalgamated Dental Co. Ltd.* (HC147), HMSO, London 1966

[179] ibid., p. 43

[180] ibid. p. 42

[181] Kanter and Sugarman op. cit., p. 442

[182] *Board of Trade Journal* no. 194 (1968), p. 1178

[183] Interview with an IRC executive, 28 October 1970

[184] Interview with a Board of Trade official, 7 August 1970

[185] Kanter and Sugarman, op. cit.,p. 444

[186] Interview with a Department of Trade and Industry official (formerly Ministry of Technology), 23 November 1970

[187] IRC *Annual Report and Accounts 1969/70* p. 14 and interview with an IRC executive, 28 October 1970

[188] Monopolies Commission *A Survey of Mergers* p. 41

[189] see note 176

[190]   Board of Trade, op. cit., p. 27
[191]   see the criticism of this approach in A. Sutherland 'The management of mergers policy' in A. Cairncross (ed.) *The Managed Economy* Basil Blackwell, Oxford 1970, pp. 106–34
[192]   Monopolies Commission *Proposed Merger of British Insulated Callender's Cables Ltd. and Pyrotenax Ltd.* (HC490) HMSO, London 1967, p. 52
[193]   Monopolies Commission *Merger of the British Motor Corporation and Pressed Steel Company Ltd.*, (HC46) HMSO, London 1966, p. 16
[194]   Monopolies Commission *Proposed Merger of Thorn Electrical Industries Ltd. and Radio Rentals Ltd.* (HC318) HMSO, London 1968, p. 73
[195]   Monopolies Commission *Merger of Guest, Keen & Nettlefolds Ltd. and Birfield Ltd.* (Cmnd 3186), HMSO, London 1967, p. 53
[196]   Monopolies Commission *Proposed Merger of Unilever Limited and Allied Breweries Limited* (HC297) HMSO, London 1969, pp. 23, 27
[197]   Kanter and Sugarman, op. cit. p. 450
[198]   The most cogent statement of Labour policy may be found in the White Paper establishing the IRC *The Industrial Reorganisation Corporation* (Cmnd 2889) HMSO, London 1966
[199]   Interview with a senior IRC executive, 28 October 1970
[200]   IRC *Report and Accounts* 1967/68, 1968/69, 1969/70, 1970/71
[201]   ibid.
[202]   Interview with a former IRC executive, 25 November 1970
[203]   IRC *Report and Accounts 1967/68,* p. 9
[204]   *The Times* 7 September 1968, p. 11. (US General Electric had sales of $7,880 million in 1967, Westinghouse $2,880 million, and ITT $2,760 million)
[205]   ibid., 14 September 1968, p. 11
[206]   IRC op. cit., p. 9
[207]   ibid., p. 21
[208]   *The Sunday Times* 23 June 1968, p. 25: *The Times* 9 July 1968, p. 23
[209]   *The Economist* 21 June 1969, p. 63
[210]   IRC *Statement on the U.K. Ball and Roller Bearing Industry*, IRC Press Release, 21 May 1969, p. 2
[211]   ibid., p. 1
[212]   ibid., p. 2
[213]   Interview with a former IRC executive with responsibility for the bearing industry, 18 November 1970
[214]   *The Sunday Times* 8 June 1969, p. 35

131

215   see note 213
216   IRC op. cit., p. 2
217   Interview, 25 May 1972
218   see note 214
219   Lindskog interview, loc. cit.
220   see note 213
221   Quoted in IRC op. cit., p. 3
222   Interview with a former IRC executive, 18 November 1970
223   *The Observer* 13 April 1969, p. 13
224   see note 222. When Pollard was eventually taken over by Ransome/ Hoffmann, its accounts showed that it had lost £200,000 on manufacturing orders at uneconomic prices, largely to give it an impressive order book and make itself an attractive take-over prospect
225   *Business Europe* 27 June 1969, p. 202
226   Wedgwood Benn interview, 2 December 1970
227   *The Times* 10 April 1970, p. 13
228   Interview with a senior IRC executive, 28 October 1970
229   Lindskog interview, loc. cit.
230   see IRC *Report and Accounts 1969/70* Appendix 3; *The Times* 6 January 1970, p. 14
231   Interview, 25 November 1970
232   Kanter and Sugarman, op. cit., p. 458
233   *The Economist* 14 February 1970, p. 62
234   Interview with a senior IRC executive, 28 October 1970
235   The Treasury's Foreign Exchange Committee had given SKF permission to take a 15 per cent stake in Pollard in April 1969, and would probably have approved an outright take-over by SKF on purely foreign exchange grounds; interview with a senior Treasury official, 22 January 1971
236   Graham, op. cit., p. 194
237   *The Times* 16 September 1968, p. 17. One example of this is the fisheries merger sponsored by the IRC which was very similar to one which the Monopolies Commission had deemed to be contrary to the public interest — see note 169
238   Kanter and Sugarman, op. cit., p. 485
239   Interview with a senior official, Department of Trade and Industry (formerly Board of Trade), 12 January 1971
240   Graham, op. cit., p. 194
241   Board of Trade *Report on the Census of Production 1963* HMSO, London 1969, vol. 131, Table 1
242   Interview with a member of the Statistics Division, Department of

Trade and Industry (formerly Board of Trade), 1 January 1971

[243] Interview with an official in the Industrial Policy Division, Department of Trade and Industry (formerly Ministry of Technology), 23 November 1970

[244] Jeremy Bray *Decision in Government* Gollancz, London 1970, p. 166

[245] Interview with a former Ministry of Technology official, 23 November 1970

[246] *Multi-National Companies: Note by the Ministry of Technology* 3 July 1969 mimeo, Annex B; interview with Professor John Dunning 10 December 1970

[247] Interview with a senior official, Economics and Statistics Division, Department of Trade and Industry (formerly Board of Trade) 11 December 1970

[248] M.D. Steuer *et al The Impact of Foreign Direct Investment on the United Kingdom* HMSO, London 1973, pp. 14—15

[249] ibid., p. 12—13

[250] ibid,, p. 14

[251] ibid., p. 15

[252] *The Times* 15 August 1973, p. 21

[253] Interview with a senior NEDO official 11 November 1970

[254] National Economic Development Office *EDC Activity Report* NEDO, London June 1969

[255] One exception to this is the Pharmaceuticals Working Party of the Chemicals EDC — see note 59

[256] see notes 45 and 230

[257] Interview with a senior official, Federal Ministry of Economics, Bonn 28 April 1971

[258] *The Guardian* 12 October 1971, p. 22. This objective was reiterated in the White Paper on *Company Law Reform* (Cmnd 5391) published in July 1973

4 Governmental Attitudes toward Multinational Companies in the UK

4.1 Introduction

As the previous chapter indicated, the activities of foreign companies operating in the UK played only a marginal role in the formulation of the Labour Government's industrial policy. The general policy of 'qualified welcome' for foreign investment in the UK meant that very few policy measures were intended to deal with foreign companies as distinct from British-owned firms, and this absence of discrimination may be explained in terms of the attitudes of governmental decision-makers toward foreign investment, and their perceptions of the consequences of such investment. From the evidence presented in the second and third chapters of this study, it would appear that most foreign firms adopted practices which are characteristic of polycentric attitudes (i.e. a willingness to adapt to UK conditions and norms), while government policies tended to reflect xenophilic attitudes (i.e. that foreign firms conferred substantial benefits on the UK economy and presented no outright challenge to the government's decision-making autonomy).

This combination of attitudinal orientations, within the foreign subsidiaries operating in the UK and the government departments charged with the responsibility for supervising such foreign firms, falls within what Perlmutter has called the 'quasi-balanced' state of host government-multinational firm relationships,[1] and helps to explain why foreign investment was not a great source of concern to the Labour Government. The objective of this chapter will be to delineate and analyse the governmental attitudes which underlay this xenophilic orientation, utilising three main sources of information:

1 A series of in-depth interviews with senior civil servants having responsibility for overseeing the activities of foreign firms, conducted in accordance with a fixed interview schedule, in 1970–71.[2] This included key

135

decision-makers in central government departments and government-affiliated bodies such as the Industrial Reorganisation Corporation and the National Economic Development Office.

2 An unpublished survey of élite attitudes toward foreign investment, carried out by Conrad Jameson Associates in 1969, which included a random sample of 120 senior civil servants (those with the rank of Principal and above) and 355 businessmen in middle and senior management (55 of them working for foreign-owned companies).[3]

3 Speeches of government Ministers and back-bench MPs reported in Hansard, various newspapers and party press releases, and supplemented by a number of interviews with politicians.

Some caveats must be made about the data utilised; the in-depth interviews were limited to key decision-makers, and because of the marginal importance of foreign companies in the formulation of the government's industrial policy there were very few senior civil servants both willing and able to discuss multinational companies — 28 in all[4] — and the small number of interviews prevents statistically valid conclusions from being drawn. The Conrad Jameson survey sample was drawn from central government departments at random, and there is no departmental breakdown of the respondents, but the larger size of the sample makes it useful as a general indication of the attitudinal orientations of senior civil servants in general toward multinational companies. As far as the attitudes of politicians are concerned, the small number of Parliamentary debates involving the consideration of foreign investment (nine during the Labour Government's term of office, only three of which dealt with the subject at any length), and the rarity of extra-parliamentary speeches by politicians on the subject,[5] indicates that foreign investment was not an important political issue, but makes detailed analysis difficult. The attitudinal profiles which follow, therefore, are tentative rather than definitive, and the lack of an extended time series for most of the data (with the exception of published political speeches) means that they take no account of changes in attitudes over time,[6] but rather represent attitudes as they were at the end of the Labour Government's term of office.

4.2   Attitudes of senior civil servants

The following discussion of the attitudes of senior civil servants toward the operations of multinational companies in the UK is divided into three sections: firstly, the *salience* of multinational companies, defined in terms of the civil servant's knowledgeability about multinational companies, his contacts with such companies in the course of his duties, and his estimate of their significance in the UK economy. Secondly, the civil servant's estimates of the *relative contribution* made by foreign companies to the UK economy, in terms of the perceived costs and benefits of foreign investment. Thirdly, the civil servant's perception of the *responsiveness to Government policy* on the part of foreign firms, and the appropriate methods of controlling multinational companies.

4.2.1   Salience

All the twenty-eight civil servants interviewed in depth had some direct responsibility for the formulation and implementation of industrial policy; one of the objectives of the interviews was to establish what their conceptions of the term 'multinational company' were, how much contact they had with multinational companies in the performance of their duties, and how well-informed they were about the level and distribution of foreign investment in the UK. The civil servants interviewed were not given any prompting when a definition of 'multinational company' was requested, and similarly the UK industries in which they thought foreign investment played a significant role were left for them to suggest spontaneously. The responses to these questions are set out in table 4.1, which indicates that just over half the civil servants interviewed had frequent (i.e. more than a dozen times a year) contact with foreign companies; the frequency of contact appeared to be dependent on the seniority of the civil servant concerned (with fewer contacts for more senior officials) and the degree to which his post involved specific industrial responsibilities. Officials from the Treasury and the Department of Economic Affairs (DEA), who were mainly concerned with general economic policies, had less contact with foreign firms than officials from departments which sponsored various industries, such as the Ministry of Technology and the Ministry of Health, while officials in NEDO and the IRC (whose main functions were in-depth investigations of industry) had most of all.

When asked to define 'multinational company', only one civil servant limited the definition to non-British firms, and over half cited a minimalist definition of a firm which operated outside its home country. There was a slight tendency for officials who had specific industrial responsibilities and frequent contact with foreign firms to define 'multinational company' as one which operates on an international, rather than a two or three country, level, with integrated management. It is notable that none of the civil servants interviewed equated 'multinational company' with American

Table 4.1

Salience of multinational companies – selected senior civil servants, 1970–71

		Department							
		Treasury	Trade	Mintech	DEA	Health	NEDO	IRC	Total
1	No. of officials interviewed	4	6	4	2	2	6	4	28
2	Of which, having contact with foreign companies more than 12 times annually	1	2	2	0	2	5	4	16
3	Definition of MNC:								
	(a) Non-UK firms	0	1	0	0	0	0	0	1
	(b) Firms operating outside home country	4	3	1	2	0	4	1	15
	(c) Firms operating world-wide	0	2	3	0	2	2	3	12
4	UK industries with prominent foreign element:								
	Electronics and computers	4	6	4	2	2	5	4	27
	Motor vehicles	4	5	4	2	1	5	4	25
	Engineering	2	3	4	2	1	4	4	20
	Chemicals and drugs	1	6	1	1	2	3	1	15
	Oil	4	3	0	0	0	1	1	9
	Other	6	0	4	0	0	3	0	14

Source: personal interviews (see Appendix for question schedule)

Table 4.2

International and American companies – élite civil service attitudes, 1969

(N=125)   %

	Strongly agree	Agree	Neither	Disagree	Strongly disagree	Don't know
(a) How strongly do you agree or disagree with the statement that 'When people talk about international companies they usually mean American companies'?	0	40	6	42	10	2
(b) How strongly do you agree or disagree with the statement that 'The growth of international companies is a real alternative to domination by American business'?	2	54	11	19	4	10

Source: Conrad Jameson Associates (London), unpublished survey 1969

companies, despite the predominant role played by American companies in foreign investment in the UK. Indeed, material from the Conrad Jameson survey, set out in Table 4.2, indicates that a majority of civil servants in the survey thought that there was a distinction to be made between international companies and American companies (52 per cent) and 56 per cent thought that international companies presented a real alternative to domination by American business; the low percentage of 'Don't know' reponses underlines the clarity of this distinction. A possible explanation for this might be that 'international' companies are seen as an alternative to companies with nationalistic identities and (in the case of American companies) powerful home governments to promote their interests if they conflicted with UK interests.

Nearly all the twenty-eight senior civil servants interviewed named the electronics (particularly computer) and motor industries as ones in which foreign firms played a prominent role, followed by engineering (two-thirds of those interviewed) and chemicals and drugs (just over half). Surprisingly, only one-third cited oil, perhaps because the internationalisation of this industry is of long standing and therefore taken for granted. Among the specific companies given as examples of multinationalism, most were American (in particular the Big Three motor companies and IBM), with a few European companies (notably Philips and SKF, both of which had recently been involved in take-over bids in the UK) and even fewer British-owned companies (principally BP, ICI, and the Anglo-Dutch Unilever). Material from the Conrad Jameson survey, set out in Table 4.3, confirms this pattern; although fewer civil servants gave the correct answer on the percentage of British industry owned by American firms – 10–20 per cent – than their counterparts in industry (34 per cent and 39 per cent respectively), they made fewer wild guesses (9 per cent of civil servants thought more than half of UK industry was American-owned, compared to 26 per cent of industrialists), indicating that civil servants were better-informed, or perhaps more conservative, than British businessmen. The motor, computers, electronics and oil industries were singled out by both groups as being subject to extensive American investment; the overwhelming majority of civil servants thought that American investment would increase somewhat, but a much smaller percentage of civil servants than businessmen thought that American ownership would increase greatly (11 and 23 per cent respectively), and none at all though it would decrease.

The implication of the above findings would seem to be that civil servants are somewhat better-informed about foreign investment than British businessmen, that they generally distinguish between American

Table 4.3

Salience of American investment to central government
and business élites, 1969

(a) Can you tell me roughly what percentage of British industry you
would think is owned by American firms?

	Central government (N=125) %	Industry (N=355) %
0–10%	12	7
10–20%	34	39
21–30%	30	20
31–40%	13	16
41–50%	2	8
Over 50%	6	23
Don't know	3	3

(b) Which two industries are most keenly controlled by American firms?

Food processing	11	25
Chemicals	7	11
Computers	38	37
Aircraft	0	2
Motor industry	74	66
Electronics	16	15
Oil	40	34
Textiles	0	0
Paper	2	1
Farm machinery	9	7
Rubber products	1	1

(c) In what way do you think that ownership of British industry by
American firms is likely to change in the future?

Increase greatly	11	23
Increase somewhat	82	65
Stay same	6	11
Decrease somewhat	0	1
Decrease greatly	0	0

Source: Conrad Jameson Associates unpublished survey 1969

and international companies (although most of the examples of international companies cited in interviews were in fact American), and that those who make a distinction between integrated companies operating on a global scale and companies operating in countries outside their home base tend to have more frequent contact with foreign companies and more specific industrial policy responsibilities than those who do not. The examples cited by civil servants of UK industries in which foreign investment plays a major role accord quite well with the objective data set out in Chapter 2, and (as will be seen below) have definite links with the examples of industries in which further foreign investment should be discouraged. Nevertheless, it must be emphasised that most of the civil servants interviewed in depth or included in the Conrad Jameson survey take a relaxed attitude toward foreign investment; all twenty-eight civil servants interviewed in depth thought that on balance foreign investment was beneficial to the UK economy, and Table 4.3 indicates that the vast majority of civil servants considered that increased American investment was inevitable. As Table 4.4 below demonstrates, very few of the civil servants in the Conrad Jameson sample thought that international companies would dominate business life, which underlines the lack of hostility toward foreign investment on the part of civil servants.

It can thus be been that, although the majority of civil servants appear to be well-informed as to the significance of foreign investment in the UK economy, they do not see foreign investment as a threat, or endorse the fear that international companies will dominate the UK economy. The small number of civil servants actually engaged in supervising the activities

Table 4.4
Dominance of international companies –
élite civil servant attitudes, 1969

How strongly do you agree or disagree with the statement that 'there's still plenty of room for small businesses – big international companies don't dominate business life'?

(N=125)

Strongly agree	Agree	Neither	Disagree	Strongly disagree	Don't know
% 7	60	12	8	5	7

Source: see Table 4.2

of foreign-owned companies in the UK, estimated by the chairman of the Treasury's Exchange Control Committee to be less than two dozen[7] (an estimate confirmed by research for this study), is an indication of the non-threatening nature of foreign investment so far as the British Government is concerned, and the xenophilic orientation of the civil servants interviewed underlines this. It is now necessary to probe this xenophilic orientation, and delineate the attitudes which underpin it.

4.2.2 Relative contribution to the UK economy

As was mentioned in the previous section, all the twenty-eight senior civil servants interviewed thought that on balance the UK benefited from foreign investment; Tables 4.5 and 4.6 set out the major advantages and disadvantages of foreign investment cited spontaneously by these civil servants. The advantages of foreign investment were seen to lie chiefly in access to technology and benefit to the balance of payments (cited by twenty-seven of the twenty-eight civil servants interviewed), with the major advantage to the balance of payments being in terms of capital inflow, helping to compensate for UK overseas direct investment (cited by twenty of the respondents). Next most important were provision of employment, especially in the depressed regions, increased efficiency and productivity, and access to management skills, all of which were cited by more than half of the civil servants interviewed. With the exception of the Treasury officials, citation of management skills and increased efficiency was linked to the frequency of contact which civil servants had with foreign companies, and in general the advantages cited had some link with the functional responsibilities of the officials concerned — those with responsibilities for regional development tended to mention the contribution of foreign investment to this objective, for example, and Treasury officials stressed the importance of foreign capital inflows as an aid to the balance of payments, while Board of Trade officials stressed the increased exports arising from foreign investment.

Turning to the disadvantages of foreign investment set out in Table 4.6, it can be seen that the overriding concern of the civil servants interviewed was that foreign companies could take decisions inimical to UK interests, although the types of decisions cited varied considerably. Almost a third of those interviewed thought that foreign companies might decide to shift production or future investment away from the UK, while a quarter thought that foreign companies might harm the balance of payments by importing plant and materials instead of purchasing them locally, and limit the export markets of their UK subsidiaries. The ability of multi-

143

Table 4.5

Major advantages of foreign investment — selected civil servants, 1970–71

	Department							
	Treasury (N=4)	Board of trade (N=6)	Mintech (N=4)	DEA (N=2)	Health (N=2)	NEDO (N=6)	IRC (N=4)	Total (N=28)
1 Access to technology and new products	4	5	4	2	2	6	4	27
2 Management skills	3	1	3	0	1	3	3	14
3 (a) employment	2	3	3	2	1	4	0	15
(b) especially in development areas	2	3	1	2	0	3	0	11
4 Increased efficiency and productivity	3	1	1	2	1	5	3	16
5 Benefits balance of payments of which	4	6	4	2	2	6	3	27
(a) capital inflow	3	4	4	1	1	5	2	20
(b) increased exports	0	4	1	1	0	3	1	10
(c) import substitution	1	1	2	1	2	3	1	11

Source: Personal interviews (for interview schedule see Appendix)

Table 4.6: Major disadvantages of foreign investment – selected civil servants, 1970–71

Department:	Treasury (N=4)	Board of trade (N=28)	Mintech (N=4)	DEA (N=2)	Health (N=2)	NEDO (N=6)	IRC (N=4)	Total (N=28)
1 Dominate economically important industries	4	2	2	0	1	1	2	12
2 Technological dependence	2	0	2	1	0	2	1	8
3 Take decisions against UK interests	4	6	3	1	2	5	4	25
of which								
(a) tax avoidance	2	2	1	0	0	2	0	7
(b) excessive profits remission	1	2	0	0	0	0	0	3
(c) sterling speculation	3	0	0	0	0	0	0	3
(d) limit exports	0	1	2	0	0	0	3	6
(e) increase imports	2	2	1	0	0	1	1	7
(f) shift production/ investment	2	2	0	0	0	2	3	9
(g) circumvent government policy	1	0	2	2	1	1	0	7
4 Monopolistic behaviour	0	1	0	0	1	2	1	5
5 Poor labour relations	0	0	1	0	0	2	0	3
6 No real disadvantages	1	1	0	0	0	0	0	2

Source: personal interviews (see Appendix for interview schedule)

national companies to circumvent government policies (in particular prices and incomes policy) and avoid UK taxation by artificial transfer-pricing was also cited by a quarter of the respondents. The possibility of technological dependence was raised by eight of the twenty-eight respondents, but this was not of such concern as the possibility that foreign companies might dominate economically important UK industries (of which the motor industry was most frequently given as an example), cited by twelve of the respondents. This apprehension was most evident among the Treasury officials interviewed, and the fact that this was not shared to the same degree by civil servants with specific industrial responsibilities and frequent contact with foreign companies suggests that the possibility of such foreign domination was not perceived as a serious problem: Only five respondents considered that foreign companies behaved in a monopolistic fashion (only one of these was from the Board Trade, which had responsibility for administering monopolies legislation), and only three respondents considered that foreign companies generally had poor labour relations. Two respondents (one each from the Treasury and the Board of Trade, neither having frequent contact with foreign companies or specific industrial responsibilities) thought that foreign investment caused no real disadvantages. Links between cited disadvantages and departmental functions are marked in one area, that of speculation against sterling, which was only cited by Treasury officials as a problem.

Data from the Conrad Jameson survey generally supports these findings; of 125 senior civil servants, 70 per cent thought that the UK economy benefited from American investment, 18 per cent thought that it lost, 6 per cent thought that the effect was neutral, and 5 per cent did not express an opinion. Table 4.7 sets out some of the Conrad Jameson findings on the technology issue, which shows that the majority of civil servants in the survey thought that foreign investment was a source of technology which could not be emulated by purely British firms. Table 4.8 sets out the findings on two aspects of the balance of payments issue — capital inflow and profit remissions — in relation to American investment, and shows that over three-quarters of the senior civil servants in the Conrad Jameson survey agreed that American capital benefited the UK economy, while 53 per cent considered that profit remissions by American firms were not a real burden on the UK balance of payments.

Table 4.9 deals with some of the efficiency and productivity aspects of foreign investment, and shows that between two-thirds and three-quarters of the civil servants considered that international companies (or American companies) were a source of efficiency because of their scale of production, and their superior marketing expertise and competitiveness in

146

Table 4.7

Technology and foreign investment – élite civil service attitudes, 1969 (percentages)
(N = 125)

	Strongly agree	Agree	Neither	Disagree	Strongly disagree	Don't know
1 The big international companies are the pace setters in technology throughout the world.	5	42	10	30	5	6
2 American firms have certainly brought us a great deal of valuable technological know-how.	9	70	3	13	2	2
3 British firms have an outstanding record in developing new technology. So there's little to be gained from links with American business on that score.	5	16	9	52	15	2

Source: see Table 4.2

Table 4.8

American investment and the balance of payments – élite civil service attitudes, 1969
(N = 125) %

	Strongly agree	Agree	Neither	Disagree	Strongly disagree	Don't know
1 The capital which is brought into Britain by American firms is a very good thing for the British economy	15	62	8	10	0	5
2 One major snag with American firms in Britain is that their profits are taken home. This is a real burden on our balance of payments.	6	21	10	51	2	8

Source: see Table 4.2

Table 4.9

Foreign investment and efficiency/productivity – élite civil service attitudes, 1969

(N=125) %

	Strongly agree	Agree	Neither	Disagree	Strongly disagree	Don't know
1 International companies are a good means of getting long production runs plus low prices.	2	59	14	11	1	11
2 Marketing is the strong point of American-owned firms operating in Britain. They are far better at it than most British-owned firms.	17	59	5	14	0	5
3 Competition from American firms is really forcing inefficient British firms to pull up their socks.	3	64	10	18	1	3
4 Competition from American firms is unfair – their sheer size allows them to buy up efficient British firms that would generally perform better left on their own.	2	9	18	58	6	6
5 Price fixing and monopolies result from the growth of international companies	3	34	10	42	2	6

Source: see Table 4.2

relation to British firms. Sixty-four per cent thought that such competition was not unfair, and a small majority considered that international companies were not monopolistic in their behaviour. The Conrad Jameson survey found less favourable attitudes among civil servants on the questions of rationalisation of production and labour relations, however, as Table 4.10 indicates. Sixty-three per cent of the respondents considered that international companies were more tough-minded about shutting down uneconomic plants or making workers redundant than British companies, and while opinion on whether US firms had bad labour relations was evenly divided, a clear majority thought that labour relations were not the strong point of American companies. Such opinions might well be the result of the disproportionate amount of publicity given to labour disputes and production shut-downs involving foreign firms, since (as Chapter 2 demonstrated) their record is better than most UK firms in these respects. The fact that very few of the civil servants interviewed in depth for this study cited labour problems is indicative that they were not considered to be as serious as Table 4.10 might lead one to believe, but the belief that multinational companies might act against UK interests by transferring production out of the UK (cited by nine of the twenty-eight civil servants interviewed in depth) is confirmed by the Conrad Jameson survey.

Almost all the twenty-eight civil servants interviewed in depth preferred foreign investment to be in the form of a new establishment rather than the take-over of an existing British firm (twenty-five preferring new establishments, and three expressing no preference), although some respondents, mainly in the Ministry of Technology and the IRC, stated that foreign take-overs of non-viable UK firms would be acceptable (six in all, two each from Mintech and the IRC). The Conrad Jameson survey indicates that there is some disquiet among British senior civil servants about American take-overs in Europe, but that the majority (6 per cent) feel that the government should maintain a neutral position with regard to American take-overs of British firms. (see Table 4.11 below). Thus there are strong indications that while senior civil servants preferred new establishments to take-overs, they did not feel that foreign take-overs were a sufficiently serious problem for the British Government to take a public stand against them; as was shown in the two previous chapters, less than 20 per cent of foreign investment has been by way of take-over, and only one such take-over was referred to the Monopolies Commission by the Board of Trade in the 1965–70 period, although assurances have been sought by the Treasury or Ministry of Technology in several cases.

The civil servants interviewed were asked whether there were any

Table 4.10

Labour and production policies of foreign companies – élite civil service attitudes, 1969
(N=125) %

	Strongly agree	Agree	Neither	Disagree	Strongly disagree	Don't know
1 International companies are much readier to take tough decisions like shutting down a plant or laying off employees when business conditions make it necessary.	10	53	10	17	2	8
2 One thing American firms are particularly good at is labour relations.	0	24	22	38	8	8
3 American firms in Britain tend to be very bad at labour relations. They just don't know how to handle the unions.	6	29	25	30	5	6

Source: see Table 4.2

Table 4.11
American take-overs of existing firms – élite civil service attitudes, 1969
(N=125)

	Agree strongly	Agree	Neither	Disagree	Disagree strongly	Don't know
(a) The independence of business throughout Europe – not just in Britain – is being threatened by American take-overs. %	9	34	18	25	0	11

	Discourage	Encourage	Impartial	Don't know
(b) Do you feel the Government should encourage or discourage American take-overs of British firms? %	24	6	61	9

Source: see Table 4.2

UK industries in which further foreign investment should be prevented or discouraged, but (apart from the computer and motor industries) they were reluctant to specify individual industries, preferring instead to set out general criteria for prevention or discouragement of further foreign investment. Their responses are set out in Table 4.12, which indicates that foreign investment would be most unwelcome if it led to foreign domination of an economically important industry, such as the motor industry (cited by nineteen of the twenty-eight repondents), led to a state of technological dependence (cited by fourteen) or prevented UK firms from becoming viable internationally (thirteen respondents). The only other general criterion, that foreign investment should be discouraged in defence-related industries, was cited by less than a quarter of those interviewed, perhaps because such investment was thought unlikely. One of the most interesting factors emerging from these responses is that officials from the Board of Trade (which administers the monopolies and mergers legislation) were much more reluctant to specify conditions under which foreign investment should be discouraged than their colleagues in other departments — confirmation of the *laissez-faire* attitude often imputed to the Board. As might be expected, Mintech officials stressed the technological dependence factor more than other departments; in general, the more frequent the official's contact with foreign companies and the more specific his industrial responsibilities, the more elaborate the criteria for prevention/discouragement of foreign investment put forward by him. Even so, there was a general feeling that such criteria should not be publicised, and that each case should be treated on its merits.[8]

None of the civil servants interviewed favoured discrimination between British and foreign firms in the matter of investment incentives offered by the Government, on the grounds that discrimination against foreign firms would worsen the investment climate and cause foreign firms to invest elsewhere (cited by eleven of the twenty-eight respondents), that investment of *any* kind, British or foreign, fulfilled the general objectives of the investment incentive schemes (seven respondents), or that such discrimination might provoke retaliation against British investors overseas (five respondents). The opinion that investment incentives (particularly those available for establishments in the Development Area) in fact discriminated *in favour* of foreign firms, because they had fewer preconceptions concerning location, was expressed by several respondents, but none favoured preferential investment incentives for foreign firms. No patterns of responses on departmental lines were discernible in this item.

On the question of research and development by foreign firms in the UK, Table 4.13 shows that a majority (nineteen of the twenty-eight

Table 4.12

Conditions under which further foreign investment should be prevented or discouraged – selected civil servants, 1970–71

	Department							
	Treasury (N=4)	Board of trade (N=6)	Mintech (N=4)	DEA (N=2)	Health (N=2)	NEDO (N=6)	IRC (N=4)	Total (N=28)
1 Would lead to foreign domination of an important sector	4	1	3	1	2	6	2	19
2 Cause technological dependence	3	1	4	0	1	3	2	14
3 Would prevent development of international capability by a UK firm	2	1	3	1	1	2	3	13
4 Involve strategic/defence industries	2	2	1	0	0	0	1	6
5 No opinion	0	2	0	0	0	0	0	2

Source: personal interviews (for interview schedule, see Appendix)

Table 4.13

R & D by foreign firms in the UK – selected civil servants, 1970–71

	Department							
T	Treasury (N=4)	Board of trade (N=6)	Mintech (N=4)	DEA (N=2)	Health (N=2)	NEDO (N=6)	IRC (N=4)	Total (N=28)
1 General desirability:								
Important	3	2	4	2	2	3	3	19
Desirable but not vital	1	4	0	0	0	2	1	8
Not important	0	0	0	0	0	1	0	1
2 Reasons:								
(a) Increase innovative levels in UK and halt brain drain	1	1	2	1	1	2	0	8
(b) Ensure access to parent's R & D	2	0	1	0	0	1	1	5
(c) Show firm's commitment to UK	2	1	0	0	0	0	1	4

Source: personal interviews

155

respondents) thought that foreign firms should have such programmes, while an additional eight respondents thought this kind of activity was desirable but not important. Respondents who were most emphatic about the need for UK-based R & D programmes by foreign firms tended to come from departments concerned with the technology-based industries (Mintech, Health, NEDO and the IRC), and the most common justification of such programmes was that they increased the level of innovative activity in the UK and helped to stem the emigration of British scientists.[9] Other justifications included ensuring that the foreign subsidiary gained access to the R & D of the parent, since it had innovations to offer in exchange, and the importance of a foreign firm's R & D programme as a symbolic commitment to the UK economy. None of the respondents, however, thought that such R & D programmes should be autonomous or self-contained, since this would be a wasteful use of resources from the point of view of both the foreign company and the UK.

There was general agreement that foreign firms made a smaller contribution to the balance of payments than UK firms (greater six, the same two, less twenty), although it was generally positive since it saved imports through local production; respondents who thought that foreign firms made less of a contribution than UK firms tended to be those having frequent contact with foreign companies (fifteen of the twenty holding this opinion), while a majority of those who thought foreign firms made a greater contribution (four of the six with this opinion) did not have much contact with foreign companies. The majority of those interviewed (twenty-two of the twenty-eight) considered that foreign firms did seek to minimise their UK taxes by manipulating intra-company transactions, but that there were few blatant offenders and that it was not a serious problem. Similarly, twenty-three of those interviewed were opposed to restrictions on profit remittances by foreign companies, and eight of these pointed out that in any case, most profits earned by foreign firms were reinvested in the UK. While a majority (seventeen respondents) agreed that foreign firms did speculate against sterling, and twelve respondents thought that they were more willing to do so than British firms, eleven respondents stated that such activity was an inevitable result of the internationalisation of trade and production, being a symptom of currency instability rather than a cause of it.

In short, it can be seen that the majority of civil servants viewed foreign investment in the UK as beneficial, principally because it aided the balance of payments (a constant preoccupation during the Labour Government's term office) and provided access to technological and managerial skills (which accorded well with the Labour Government's policy of injecting 'the white heat of the scientific revolution' into British industry). This xenophilic orientation can be seen in the imputation of greater dynamism and efficiency to foreign firms, particularly American ones, and the reluctance to translate private preferences, such as that for new establishments rather than take-overs, into public and explicit guidelines. Where foreign investment was perceived as harmful, this was stated in terms of potential rather than actual disadvantages; even those officials having frequent contact with foreign companies and a specific responsibility for some aspect of industrial policy, who tended to have a more highly developed view of the benefits and disadvantages of foreign investment, outlined the adverse implications of foreign investment in abstract rather than concrete terms.

Where the operations of multinational companies in the UK were seen as having adverse effects on the UK economy, such as in matters of tax avoidance and currency hedging, these were generally perceived as a consequence of the internationalisation of trade and investment – as the obverse of the technology/capital/managerial efficiency coin – and therefore as the unavoidable price to be paid for the undoubted benefits of foreign investment. Since the problems caused by foreign investment were not generally regarded as serious, the costs of eliminating them would be far greater (in terms of creating an adverse investment climate and courting retaliatory discrimination against UK overseas investment) than the potential benefits. The desirable objective was not to eliminate the capabilities of multinational companies, but to emulate them; one can characterise the attitudinal orientation of British civil servants as xenophilic, tempered by an acceptance of the disadvantages of actual or potential geocentrism on the part of foreign firms operating in the UK, in particular their ability to decide in favour of their global interests at the expense of purely UK interests. In the words of one senior Ministry of Technology official:

> The government of the recipient country must accept that the multinational company must lay out its resources as it thinks right; and that if the performance of the local subsidiary is bad, nothing can stop the multinational company from drawing its own conclusions. [10]

4.2.3   Responsiveness to Government policy

It has been seen that the British Government did not have a policy toward foreign companies so much as a series of predispositions, largely favourable.[11] The Conrad Jameson survey provides some support for this statement, as can be seen in Table 4.14 below; a third of the civil servants and businessmen in the sample did not known whether they agreed or disagreed with the government's policy toward American-owned firms in Britain, which would suggest that government policy was not sufficiently explicit for them to form an opinion. In relation to government policy in general, Table 4.15 indicates that the majority of senior civil servants interviewed in depth considered foreign firms to be more co-operative with government than British firms (sixteen of the twenty-eight respondents), this co-operativeness being most frequently attributed to the desire of foreign firms not to attract attention to themselves by entering into a confrontation with the government, and their consequent efforts to be on their best behaviour. It is noteworthy that all four IRC executives interviewed dissented from this view, holding that foreign firms were generally less co-operative than British firms; such an opinion is probably the result of their experience in trying to restructure certain sectors of UK industry, and the IRC's general objective of creating viable British-owned enterprises wherever possible. As the SKF affair showed, foreign companies were frequently perceived as being obstacles to this objective, and the foreign companies themselves would not necessarily see the IRC's interests as being compatible with their own.[12] In contrast, it should be noted that all four officials from the Ministry of Technology (whose objectives were broadly similar to those of the IRC) agreed that foreign companies were generally more co-operative than British firms.

Table 4.14
Government policy toward American firms in the UK — élite
civil service and business attitudes, 1969

Would you say that you basically agree or disagree with the Government's present policy towards American-owned firms in Britain?

	Civil servants (N=125) %	Businessmen (N=355) %
Agree	62	52
Disagree	5	13
Don't know	33	34

Source: see Table 4.2

Table 4.15 also shows that the majority of civil servants interviewed for this study considered that American-owned companies were generally more co-operative than other foreign companies (sixteen of the twenty-eight interviewed), although ten of the remainder thought that there was no difference in co-operativeness attributable to the nationality of the parent company. The only civil servants not sharing this opinion were two NEDO officials who were concerned with the motor industry, where the non-American foreign element is very small; in general the civil servants interviewed considered European companies to be more secretive and unwilling to co-operate than American firms, although several pointed out that American firms checked back with their headquarters before providing information for government inquiries. Even so, the Conrad Jameson survey indicated strong opposition among senior civil servants to any distinction in government policy between American and other foreign firms; 78 per cent opposed such a distinction, 16 per cent were in favour, and 5 per cent were undecided. [13]

As Table 4.16 demonstrates, eighteen of the twenty-eight civil servants interviewed thought that the degree of autonomy exercised by a foreign subsidiary in the UK was not a significant factor in determining its willingness to co-operate with the government; most of the civil servants expressing this view considered that the corporate philosophy of the parent company was much more important a determinant, and two civil servants (from the Treasury and Board of Trade) even thought that subsidiaries with a substantial degree of autonomy might be more prepared to defy the government than those which were more tightly controlled by the parent company. Ministry of Technology officials were more disposed to consider subsidiary autonomy as a factor in the foreign firm's willingness to co-operate, on the grounds that such autonomy permitted the management to adopt a more flexible approach. Table 4.16 also shows that a majority of the civil servants interviewed thought that more subsidiary autonomy was desirable (labour and export policies being the most frequently cited examples), although Board of Trade officials and in particular Treasury officials were sceptical of the utility of increased subsidiary autonomy.

The view that the philosophy of the parent company was the most important factor in determining the willingness of a foreign firm to co-operate is given additional support by the responses set out in Table 4.17. Although seventeen of the twenty-eight respondents thought that the presence of British nationals on the board or in senior management might make foreign firms more co-operative, there was strong emphasis that this very much depended on the personalities concerned, and two civil servants

Table 4.15

Co-operativeness of foreign firms – selected civil servants 1970–71

| | Department | | | | | | | |
	Treasury (N=4)	Board of trade (N=6)	Mintech (N=4)	DEA (N=2)	Health (N=2)	NEDO (N=6)	IRC (N=4)	Total (N=28)
1 UK/ foreign firms:								
Foreign more than UK	4	4	4	2	0	2	0	16
No difference	0	2	0	0	2	2	0	6
UK more than foreign	0	0	0	0	0	2	4	6
2 US/ other foreign: US more than other foreign	1	4	2	1	2	2	4	16
No difference	3	2	2	1	0	2	0	10
Other foreign more than US	0	0	0	0	0	2	0	2

Source: personal interviews (for interview schedule see Appendix)

Table 4.16

Co-operativeness and autonomy of foreign subsidiaries – selected civil servants 1970–71

	Department							
	Treasury (N=4)	Board of trade (N=6)	Mintech (N=4)	DEA (N=2)	Health (N=2)	NEDO (N=6)	IRC (N=4)	Total (N=28)
1 Actual autonomy:								
Important	0	0	2	1	0	0	0	3
Not very important	1	1	2	1	0	0	0	5
Unimportant	2	4	0	0	2	6	4	18
Counterproductive	1	1	0	0	0	0	0	2
2 Desirable autonomy:								
More desirable	0	2	4	2	2	5	4	19
Same desirable	0	0	0	0	0	0	0	0
Less desirable	1	1	0	0	0	0	0	2
Irrelevant	3	2	0	0	0	1	0	6

Source: personal interviews (for schedule see Appendix)

Table 4.17

Co-operativeness and nationality of management and shareholders – selected civil servants, 1970–71

	Department							
	Treasury (N=4)	Board of trade (N=6)	Mintech (N=4)	DEA (N=2)	Health (N=2)	NEDO (N=6)	IRC (N=4)	Total (N=28)
1 British managers/directors:								
Important	0	2	2	1	1	0	1	7
Not very important	1	2	1	0	1	3	2	10
Unimportant	3	1	0	1	0	2	1	8
Counterproductive	0	0	1	0	0	1	0	2
Don't know	0	1	0	0	0	0	0	1
2 UK minority shareholding:								
Important	0	0	0	1	0	0	0	1
Not very important	1	1	1	0	1	0	0	4
Unimportant	3	4	3	1	1	5	2	19
Counterproductive	0	0	0	0	0	1	2	3
Don't know	0	1	0	0	0	0	0	1

Source: personal interviews (for schedule see Appendix)

even thought that British managers would be less effective in gaining concessions from the parent company than would home country nationals. There was a slight tendency for civil servants having frequent contact with foreign companies to prefer British managers and directors, possibly because there would be fewer cultural barriers to communication. There was definite agreement that a British-held minority shareholding in foreign companies was of no use in ensuring co-operation; several respondents cited the IRC's 15 per cent stake in Rootes as an example of ineffective and politically-motivated window-dressing, and three thought such a shareholding prevented foreign companies from operating efficiently and inhibited further investment. The alternative possibility, of internationalising the share ownership of the parent company, was only mentioned by two Ministry of Technology officials.

When asked whether they considered that the British Government had sufficient means of controlling the activities of foreign firms in the UK, the majority (eighteen of the twenty-eight respondents) thought that the wide powers of government discretion under the exchange control and monopolies legislation provided for all likely contingencies; ten respondents (including nearly all the Ministry of Technology and IRC officials) thought that the government's powers were too insensitive or unselective to provide adequate control, and that the government had insufficient information on multinational companies to scrutinise their activities effectively. The vast majority of those interviewed (twenty-three of the twenty-eight) considered that deviant behaviour on the part of foreign firms was best dealt with by frank and informal discussions with the firms concerned, coupled with the negotiation of private assurances on future conduct. Only one of those interviewed (a Ministry of Health official) favoured legal or public sanctions against deviant foreign firms, and there was general agreement that public assurances, of the Chrysler/Ford/Philips variety, were too static and unenforceable to be of any use.

On the question of further measures which might be necessary to control multinational companies, the most frequently expressed need was for more information on multinational companies and dialogues with them to gain more understanding of their internal operations (twenty-one of the twenty-eight interviewed). IRC officials tended to favour the creation of countervailing British international companies (three of the four interviewed), which underlines their rather more xenophobic disposition in comparison with their colleagues in other departments, while Ministry of Technology officials were more disposed toward the development of international codes of corporate behaviour and intergovernmental co-operation than those in other departments (three of the four Mintech officials held this view, which was shared by only three other officials, in the Board of Trade, DEA and NEDO). It is notable that the majority of Treasury (three out of four) and Board of Trade (four out of six) officials interviewed considered that no further measures were necessary, beyond a marginal extension of information disclosure by multinational companies.

To sum up, it can be seen that the attitudinal orientation of civil servants toward foreign investment in the UK was generally xenophilic – foreign companies were considered to make a positive contribution to the UK economy in terms of helping the balance of payments, providing access to technology and managerial skills, and promoting industrial efficiency and regional development. There was a widespread assumption that foreign firms were more anxious to avoid a confrontation with the government than British firms, and were consequently more co-operative; the problems caused by foreign investment were not sufficiently serious to make special surveillance of foreign companies necessary, since existing government procedures and powers were adequate to deal with recalcitrant foreign companies. The xenophilic orientation was reinforced by an incipient geocentric orientation – that the UK was the home of many international companies, and that if these were desirable, there was no cause to discriminate against multinational companies, since this might provoke retaliatory measures against British multinationals.

In particular, international companies as such were not seen as a threat to UK interests, since industrial domination by foreign companies was considered to be a remote and somewhat unlikely possibility; if such a situation arose (as it had the motor and computer industries), the government had sufficient powers to deal with it on an *ad hoc* basis. When civil servants in the Conrad Jameson survey were asked for their opinion on the statement that 'the power of the international company has grown, is growing and ought to be diminished,' the majority of civil servants disagreed with the proposition – a further indication that international companies were not seen as a threat to UK interests. [14] Although most of the civil servants considered that foreign companies were likely to take decisions inconsistent with UK interests, this was seen as a consequence of the development of international companies, rather than as a deliberate disregard of UK interests by foreign companies (which were, after all, seen as more co-operative than British companies by the majority of civil servants). It is probably significant that the bulk of foreign investment in the UK is by American firms, and the so-called 'special relationship' and shared Anglo-Saxon culture perhaps accounts for the failure of any of the civil servants interviewed to cite manipulation of foreign companies by their home government as a potential disadvantage of foreign investment.

164

Indeed, transatlantic affinities might account for a good deal of this xenophilic orientation; in the Conrad Jameson survey a majority of civil servants agreed with the statement that 'American business expansion isn't the biggest threat to British business . . . we have much more to fear from German and Japanese competition'.[15] As a long-standing ally, the American Government would be more likely to accede to British requests to curb undesirable activities by American firms in the UK, and there were few potential political conflicts between the two countries. The image of affluence and efficiency in the United States conveyed by the media would serve to reinforce the perception of the beneficial effects of American investment, and the belief that Britain and the United States shared a common political and cultural heritage would tend to minimise perceptions of the disadvantageous aspects of American investment. Although such factors did not exist in the case of other foreign investment, this was economically less significant and therefore did not undermine the basically xenophilic orientation of civil servants; of Britain's war-time adversaries, there was no significant Japanese investment in the UK, and the German and Italian shares were very small.

4.3   Attitudes of politicians

The question of foreign investment in the UK was never a significant political issue in Britain during the 1964—70 period, and consequently very few Parliamentary debates or extra-Parliamentary speeches by politicians dealt with the activities of foreign companies in the UK.[16] During the six Parliamentary sessions held while the Labour Government was in power, foreign investment was raised in only thirteen debates and was the subject of thirty-one written or oral questions (out of some 100,000 questions during the period). Six of the debates involved foreign investment in the UK motor industry, two the computer industry, three international companies in general, and there were also debates on corporation tax and foreign investment and the labour relations of Roberts—Arundel. Of the questions asked, half were to seek information on the level of foreign investment and associated transactions, five were about international companies generally, four were on the computer industry, four on the motor industry, three on the ball-bearing industry, and one on the typewriter industry. As Table 4.18 indicates, there was an increase in Parliamentary interest in foreign investment over the period, peaking in the 1968—69 Parliamentary session with fourteen mentions of foreign investment (largely caused by the Ford strike and rationalisation of the ball-bearing

Table 4.18

Parliamentary consideration of foreign investment, 1964—70

Session	Debates	Written and oral questions	Total
1964—65	1	2	3
1965—66	1	4	5
1966—67	3	3	6
1967—68	3	5	8
1968—69	2	12	14
1969—70	3	5	8
Total 1964—70	13	31	44

Source: *House of Commons Debates* (1964—70)

industry during that session, accounting for five and three mentions respectively). Of the total forty-four mentions of foreign investment, the largest group (seventeen) were concerned with take-overs by foreign firms of UK companies or mergers between British companies to maintain a viable UK-owned element. As one former Labour MP commented: 'The House was only intermittently concerned with foreign investment, usually only when foreign take-overs were in the news.'[17]

The explanation for this lack of interest probably lies in the general consensus among the political parties that foreign investment was benficial to the UK economy, particularly during periods when the balance of payments situation was serious (see below), but also in the occupations and interests of MPs in general. As Table 4.19 indicates, only 13 per cent of MPs had business connections in 1966 (the majority of them Conservative), and a very small number — just over 2 per cent — had any experience of management; as Eric Moonman, a Labour MP, has commented:

> My estimate is that in the 1966—70 Parliament no more than a dozen MPs out of 630 had had any top-line management experience or had had to work through management problems against a background of typical organisational conflict. [18]

Indeed, it is interesting to note that there were twice as many Labour MPs with such management experience as Conservatives (eight and four respectively), although three times as many Conservative MPs had business connections compared to Labour MPs (sixty-two and twenty respectively).

Table 4.19

Business background of MPs, 1966 Parliament

		Conservative No.	%	Liberal No.	%	Labour No.	%	Total No.	%
1	Total MPs	253	100·0	12	100·0	363	100·0	628	100·0
2	MPs with business connections (consultants or directors)	62	24·5	2	16·7	20	5·5	84	13·4
3	MPs having business connections with foreign firms	16	6·3	1	8·3	3	0·8	20	3·2
4	MPs having business connections with UK firms investing overseas	26	10·3	0	0	5	1·4	31	4·9
5	MPs with management experience	4	1·6	1	8·3	8	2·2	13	2·1
6	MPs with trade union affiliations	1	0·4	0	0	150	41·3	151	24·0

Source: Calculated from listings in A. Roth *The Business Background of M.P.'s Parliamentary Profiles*, London 1967

Conservative MPs were more likely to have business connections with foreign firms (over a quarter of those having business connections, compared to one-sixth of Labour MPs with business interests); although the foreign firms concerned — with the exception of Philips, Timken, Rootes and five chemical/pharmaceutical companies — tended not to be important investors in the UK. [19] This may be because the larger foreign firms were prepared to devote more resources to general public relations exercises involving MPs, and did not therefore require direct representation of their interests; the prominence of pharmaceutical companies on the list is probably due to the state monopoly of ethical drug purchasing in the UK. Of the thirty-seven MPs who raised matters connected with foreign investment in the House of Commons during the Labour Government's term of office, five were connected with foreign companies (See Table 4.20), a ratio four times greater than for the House of Commons as a whole. Indeed, MPs with business connections (with UK or foreign firms) formed almost half of the MPs involved, followed by those with some constituency interest, trade union affiliation or managerial experience. In no case, however, did MPs with foreign business connections speak on matters related to the particular firms concerned; if they did engage in lobbying activities, these were evidently informal and unpublicised.

A content analysis of House of Commons speeches by Labour Government ministers and Conservative and Labour MPs (supplemented by published speeches of ministers) during the 1964—70 period is set out in Tables 4.21 and 4.22 and reveals some interesting differences between the attitudes of Labour Government ministers and their back-bench MPs, and between Labour and Conservative MPs. Whereas Labour Government ministers tended to stress the advantages of foreign investment in the UK, citing twice as many advantages as disadvantages overall, Labour MPs in general cited four times as many disadvantages as advantages; and Labour MPs with trade union affiliations were particularly concerned about the possibility of technology dependence, of foreign companies transferring production out of the UK, and the unfavourable labour-relations of foreign firms. The disparity between the xenophilic orientation of Labour ministers toward foreign investment, and the xenophobic orientation of Labour back-bench MPs (particularly those with union affiliations) may be explained by the dynamics of intra-party relations in the Parliamentary Labour Party, and the desire of back-bench Labour MPs to moderate the predominantly favourable orientation of their leaders toward foreign investment. [20] The somewhat xenophobic character of the speeches of Labour MPs may therefore be more significant as an indicator of dissatisfaction with the general policies of the Labour Government, and a conse-

Table 4.20

Parliamentary consideration of foreign investment 1964—70: back-bench MPs

	Total	Trade Union affiliation	Business UK	Connection: foreign	Management experience	Constituency matter
Conservative	15	0	7	4	1	4
Labour	20	6	3	0	4	5
Liberal	2	0	1	1	1	0

Source: House of Commons Debates (1964—70) and sources used for Table 4.18

Table 4.21
Foreign investment – attitudes of Labour Ministers and Labour/Conservative MPs, 1964–70

	Government Ministers (N=16)	Labour MPs		Conservative MPs	
		Total (N=20)	Union affiliated (N=6)	Total (N=15)	MNC affiliated (N=6)*
Benefits of foreign investment:					
1 Access to technology	9	3	1	5	1
2 Aids balance of payments	8	1	0	5	3
3 Brings management skills	9	1	0	4	1
4 Improves efficiency	7	2	0	4	1
5 Provides employment	8	2	1	0	0
6 Aids regional development	5	2	2	1	0
7 Brings capital	4	1	1	1	0
8 Foreign firms anxious to co-operate	2	0	0	8	2
9 Aids free movement of capital and UK overseas investment	1	0	0	4	3
10 Reinvest profits	1	0	0	1	0
Benefit score	54	12	5	33	11

Disadvantages of foreign investment:

1 Potential domination of key industries	9	6	2	1	0
2 Can take decisions against UK interests	6	10	4	2	0
3 Limit export markets	0	6	2	1	1
4 Increase imports	0	6	2	0	0
5 Remit profits	0	3	1	0	0
6 Transfer-pricing	0	5	2	1	1
7 Transfer production from UK	3	6	4	3	2
8 Technology dependence	8	4	3	0	0
9 Poor labour relations	0	7	3	2	1
10 Undermine sterling	0	1	0	0	0
Disadvantage score	26	54	23	10	5

Note: * includes those connected with inward and outward investor firms

Source: *House of Commons Debates* (1964–70); also (for Ministers) published speeches and press releases

quent attempt to reassert the influence of the Labour back-benches *vis-à-vis* their leaders, than as a valid reflection of their attitudes toward foreign investment. As the infrequency of Parliamentary references to foreign investment demonstrates, it was not considered to be an important political issue, and the favourable consensus of both major political parties meant that it provided a good platform for Labour MPs to score points off their leaders without endangering the security of the Labour Government.

Even so, a comparison of the expressed attitudes of Conservative and Labour MPs on foreign investment reveals a marked difference between the two major parties; Table 4.21 shows that Conservative MPs were predominantly in favour of foreign investment, while Labour MPs were much more inclined to cite the disadvantages of foreign investment. Conservative MPs connected with foreign companies (or with British companies investing overseas), were particularly inclined to stress the favourable effect of foreign investment on the balance of payments, and the advantages of unrestricted foreign investment as a means of promoting the free movement of capital and the interests of UK overseas investors. Even where these Conservative MPs mentioned the disadvantages of foreign investment, the implications drawn from them were quite different from those mentioned by Labour MPs: foreign firms could transfer production out of the UK, but only because of the irresponsible activities of trade unionists in disrupting production; foreign firms could minimise their UK tax burden by transfer-pricing, but this was due to the high level of British tax rates caused by the size of the Labour Government's budget; and so on. In general, the attitudes of Conservative MPs were a mirror-image of the attitudes of Labour MPs, stressing the benefits of foreign investment and the unimpeachable behaviour of foreign firms, who would act against UK interests only if the Labour Government's policies forced them to safeguard their own commercial interests.

As Table 4.22 indicates, Labour Government ministers differed from their back-bench colleagues in that they did not favour stricter control over foreign-owned companies in the UK, considering that existing control procedures were adequate, that informal dialogues with foreign companies provided the best method of reaching mutual understanding, and that the creation of internationally viable British firms would prevent the threat of foreign domination (the creation of European firms with British participation was somewhat less popular). Labour MPs, on the other hand, wanted more government surveillance of foreign companies, and stressed the importance of British nationals in the management of foreign firms as a guarantee of their good behaviour. Not unexpectedly, Conservative MPs were opposed to greater government supervision of foreign investment,

Table 4.22

Desirable measures on foreign investment: Labour Ministers and Labour/Conservative MPs, 1964–70

	Government Ministers	Labour MPs		Conservative MPs	
		Total	Union Links	Total	MNC links
	(N=16)	(N=20)	(N=6)	(N=15)	(N=6)
Desirable measures:					
Government control adequate	7	0	0	2	1
Government surveillance of foreign companies	0	6	2	−1	−1
Dialogues with foreign companies	7	1	1	0	0
More information on foreign companies	2	3	2	0	0
UK preference in public contracts	4	2	1	−2	0
British nationals in management	1	3	2	−1	−1
British minority shareholding	1	1	0	−4	−2
Create UK-owned competitors	11	5	2	2	0
Nationalise offending foreign companies	0	2	1	0	0
Create European MNCs (including UK)	6	1	0	3	0
Improve investment climate in UK	5	0	0	9	6
Intergovernmental codes of corporate behaviour	2	1	1	2	0

Source: see Table 4.21

Note: −indicates undesirable

and in particular any insistence on a British minority shareholding in foreign firms (especially if this was in the form of governmental participation); they stressed the necessity of improving the UK investment climate to attract more foreign investment — this emphasis was most marked in the case of Conservative MPs having links with inward or outward investment. The difference between the attitudes of Conservative and Labour MPs is perhaps best illustrated by this exchange between two of them during a discussion on the desirability of greater government surveillance of foreign firms:

> *Mr W. Howie*, [Labour]: The only factor which protects a British Government is self-interest on the part of the international company . . . beyond that point what we require is that the firm should be much more closely regulated and much more closely controlled than such firms are now.
> *Mr J. Bruce-Gardyne* [Conservative]: Beyond the point at which acquiescence in the rules and regulations of the host country makes sense in terms of the international company's commercial self-interest, the rules become so onerous that the company will be encouraged to move its investments elsewhere. [21]

In general, the attitudes of Labour back-bench MPs may be seen as predominantly xenophobic, and those of Conservative MPs as generally xenophilic (with some geocentric undertones, as in their emphasis on promoting the free flow of investment, and blaming undesirable activities of international companies on adverse investment conditions which were not of their own making).

An examination of the speeches of Labour Government ministers indicates that they accepted the policy of 'qualified welcome' for foreign investment laid down by their Conservative predecessors, and continued to hold the view that foreign investment was beneficial and that the government had adequate powers to control it. [22] Indeed, Mr Wilson himself had told the House of Commons in 1956, when Labour was in opposition, that:

> It has been the policy of both parties in this country since the war to encourage American investment in this country . . . where a clear advantage could be shown. The House will be familiar with the kind of tests that have been applied to projects. Do they bring know-how to the country? Do they bring knowledge of new processes? Do they make possible the creation of some new export industry or export outlet? Do they provide some means of saving imports,

especially dollar imports?

We have welcomed very many of these investments. In the Development Areas there are scores, if not hundreds, of factories controlled by American companies which both the Labour Party and the Conservative Party have welcomed into the country since the war. [23]

There were two reservations expressed by Mr Wilson with regard to foreign (and particularly American) investment; firstly, that viable British firms might be taken over by giant foreign companies, and secondly that there was a danger of foreign companies coming to occupy a position of technological dominance in certain key industries. On the first point, the take-over of British firms by foreign companies, Mr Wilson (as Leader of the Opposition) said in the Commons debate on the Chrysler investment in Rootes in 1964:

> [We must] distinguish between those forms of foreign investment which are and have always been welcomed, which introduce 'know-how' which we do not possess, or which lead to the creation of new industries or new factories and employment for our people on the one hand, and, on the other, those which involve a partial or complete take-over of existing British firms which are already very well run. . . . [24]

Even so, it became clear when the Labour Government took office that foreign take-overs would not be resisted when it was considered that the British company being acquired had no prospect of becoming viable; as Mr Peter Shore (then a junior minister at the Ministry of Technology) said of the 1966 take-over of Imperial Typewriters by Litton Industries: 'We had to recognise the deplorable fact . . . that that section of the industry was already substantially undermined and was not seriously competitive with its rivals.' [25]

The second reservation, concerning the possibility of technological dependence on foreign firms, was first raised by Prime Minister Wilson when the Labour Government decided to make a second British application to join the EEC in 1966–67:

> There is no future for Europe, or for Britain, if we allow American business, and American industry so to dominate the strategic growth industries of our individual countries, that they, and not we, are able to determine the pace and direction of Europe's industrial advance, that we are left in industrial terms as the hewers of wood and drawers of water. . . . This is the road not to partnership but to an industrial helotry. . . . [26]

175

Indeed, there is some evidence to suggest that Mr Wilson was more anxious to establish his anti-American credentials with General de Gaulle than to deal with the problems of foreign investment; in his memoirs the 'industrial helotry' issue was only mentioned by Mr Wilson in the context of negotiations with the French President to gain support for British entry into the EEC, and nowhere in them does he discuss foreign investment as such.[27] As one former Labour MP commented, Mr Wilson's proposals for a European Technological Community were meant 'to show us he was serious about Europe, not that he was worried about American investment.'[28] In a speech after the failure of the second British application to join the EEC, Mr Wilson played down the technological dependence issue, stressing that 'we welcome foreign investment within limits . . . when they have anything new to bring either in terms of technical expertise or, in some cases, management expertise', and that the government had full powers to prevent foreign take-overs which 'might have the effect of controlling and perhaps ultimately operating against the national interest.'[29]

The devaluation of sterling in November 1967, and the amelioration of the balance of payments situation (which had previously made the Labour Government anxious to attract the capital inflows caused by foreign investment) did mark a watershed in the attitudes of Labour Government Ministers toward foreign investment. Mr Wedgwood Benn, the Minister of Technology, actively encouraged the creation of internationally viable British motor and computer companies during 1968, to act as a counterweight to the giant American firms in those industries,[30] and began to talk about the growing importance of international companies:

> Even if we had hundreds of millions of pounds of surplus every year . . . we would still, in the world we live in, find our future decided by what is happening in Detroit and Tokyo, Dusseldorf or Milan because . . . the intermeshing of international industrial activity is getting tighter and tighter. . . . We have got to think internationally, not only in terms of peace and war or brotherhood, but internationally in industrial terms.[31]

If there was a slight hardening of Labour Government attitudes toward foreign investment during 1968, there were no major policy changes,[32] and no real indication that the Labour Government as a whole had conducted any reevaluation of its basically favourable attitude toward foreign investment. As Mr Wilson was to admit early in 1973:

Where we failed was inadequate recognition of the power of remote financial interests to impose their own controls and, within industry itself, the growth of the power of irresponsible, multinational organisations, owing allegiance neither to national governments nor to international authority, to dictate the speed and direction of technological development. [33]

The xenophilic orientation of Labour Government Ministers was reinforced by a similar orientation on the part of civil servants who advised them, and the favourable attitudes of the Conservative Opposition Party toward foreign investment served to depoliticise the foreign investment issue, despite the somewhat xenophobic attitudes exhibited by several rank and file Labour MPs. The non-controversial nature of most foreign investment, and the consequent failure to examine the implications of the development of multinational companies for the UK economy meant that this predominantly xenophilic orientation toward foreign investment was remarkably stable over the six years of the Labour Government's term of office. Although there is some evidence of a learning process occurring in the Labour Government's conceptions about multinational companies and the appropriate ways of dealing with them, [34] this had not reached the stage of concrete policy formulation by the time of Labour's defeat in the General Election of June 1970, and it is impossible to speculate about the direction such policies might have taken. Mr Wilson perhaps provided a fitting epitaph when he wrote:

> If in all these things we had not gone as far as we had wished, we achieved far more than most would have expected. . . . In the event we were denied the mandate to continue what we had begun; once again, a Labour Government was prevented from building on the foundations which it had laid. [35]

Notes

[1] H.V. Perlmutter *Attitudinal Patterns in Joint Decision Making in Multinational Firm-Nation State Relationships* Division for Research and Development of Worldwide Institutions, Wharton School of Finance and Commerce, Philadelphia 1971 (mimeo) pp. 58—60

[2] The interview schedule is included in an appendix at the end of this study

[3] Interview with Mr J. Landell Mills, Director of Research, Conrad Jameson Associates 5 January 1972

⁴ Treasury 4; Ministry of Technology 4; Board of Trade 6; Department of Economic Affairs 2; Ministry of Health 2; National Economic Development Office 6; Industrial Reorganisation Corporation 4

⁵ Because none of the major British political parties keep comprehensive files of speeches, newspaper reports have had to be relied on

⁶ To compensate for this deficiency, case studies of the evolution of the Labour Government's policies toward the motor and computer industries are undertaken in Chaps. 5 and 6

⁷ Interview with Mr J.G. Littler, Assistant Secretary (Finance), HM Treasury 22 January 1971

⁸ This reticence is confirmed by the Conrad Jameson survey, where only a quarter of the sample of 125 senior civil servants were prepared to name industries in which the government should discourage further American take-overs (motors, aviation and computers were those most frequently cited), and only seven responded to a similar question on government encouragement of take-overs by American firms (all in the 'Don't know' category)

⁹ This argument is in contradiction of the suggestion in Chap. 2, that R & D by foreign firms in the UK denies scarce personnel to UK-owned industry, while conferring no general benefits on the economy as a whole, since innovations remain the property of the foreign firm — in other words, that R & D by foreign firms in the UK reduces the potential level of innovative activity by British firms

¹⁰ Sir R. Clarke *Guidelines for Multinational Corporations — A Government View* British-North American Committee, London 1970 (mimeo), p. 7

¹¹ see Chap. 3 *passim*

¹² see Chap. 3

¹³ Conrad Jameson Associates (London) unpublished survey 1969

¹⁴ *ibid.* The responses were: agree strongly 2%; agree 15%; neither 22%; disagree 52%; disagree strongly 3%; don't know 5%

¹⁵ *ibid.* The responses were: agree strongly 11%; agree 53%; neither 15%; disagree 12%; disagree strongly 1%; don't know 6%

¹⁶ Neither Gallup nor National Opinion Polls, the two major public opinion research organisations, carried out surveys on public attitudes toward foreign investment in the 1964–70 period, an indication of the lack of salience of this issue

¹⁷ Interview, 20 May 1971

¹⁸ E. Moonman *Reluctant Partnership* Gollancz, London 1971, p. 198

¹⁹ According to Roth, *op. cit.*, the firms were: *Conservative*: Luwa (Swiss — chemical engineering); Smith, Kline & French (US — pharma-

ceuticals); Olin Mathieson (US — engineering): E.R. Squibb (US — pharmaceuticals); Migdal Insurance (Israel); Dillon, Walker (US — stockbrokers); Deutz (German — engineering); Roots (US — vehicles); CIBA (Swiss — chemicals); Philips (Holland — electrical); J. Walter Thompson (US — advertising); Carr—Fastener (US — engineering); Philips Petroleum (US); Timken (US — bearings); ESAB (Sweden — engineering). *Labour*: Agfa (German — photographic); Philips (Dutch — electrical); Warner Bros (US — films); Bayer (German — chemicals). *Liberal*: Brown, Harris Stevens (US — securities)

[20]   Indeed, the attitudes of Labour Government ministers closely correspond to the attitudes of the senior civil servants outlined in the previous section; this is not surprising, since the ministers would have been briefed by them on these matters

[21]   *Commons Standing Committees Official Report* (Session 1969—70) vol. 5; Standing Committee H (5 May 1970) cols. 423—4

[22]   see, for example, the statement by Mrs G. Dunwoody Parliamentary Secretary to the Board of Trade, *H.C. Deb.* vol. 757 (29 January 1968) cols. 1057—60

[23]   *H.C. Deb.* vol. 554 (14 June 1956) cols. 1447—8

[24]   *H.C. Deb.* vol. 696 (8 June 1964) col. 39

[25]   *H.C. Deb.* vol. 738 (13 December 1966) col. 242

[26]   *The Times* 14 November 1967 p. 4; the idea was not altogether a novel one: 'We are becoming the hewers of wood and drawers of water, while the most skilled, the most profitable and the easiest trades are becoming American' — F.A. Mackenzie *The American Invaders* Grant Richards, London 1902, p. 120

[27]   H. Wilson *The Labour Government 1964—70*, Weidenfeld, London 1971, p. 334

[28]   Interview, 20 May 1971

[29]   *The Times* 28 January 1969, p. 17

[30]   see Chaps. 5 and 6

[31]   *Report of the 67th Annual Conference of the Labour Party* The Labour Party, London 1968, p. 202 (2 October 1968); see also *H.C. Deb.* vol. 774 (27 November 1968) col. 491 — quoted at the start of Chap. 5

[32]   see Chap. 3

[33]   *The Guardian* 22 January 1973, p. 7

[34]   see Chaps. 5, 6 and 7

[35]   Wilson, *op. cit.*, p. xviii

5 The Labour Government and the UK Motor Industry

'The hon Gentleman will be aware that, as the international companies develop, national Governments, including our own, will be reduced to the status of parish councils in dealing with the large corporations which will span the world.'
— Mr Anthony Wedgwood Benn, Minister of Technology (*Hansard*, 27 November 1968)

5.1 Introduction

Over half the politicians and civil servants interviewed for this study cited the motor industry as an example of a key industry in which the national interest required the maintenance of a British-owned capability; in addition, it is perhaps significant that in general discussions of the control exercised by parent corporations over their UK subsidiaries, 'Detroit' was frequently given as an example of rigid and insensitive long-distance control. The object of this case-study will be to offer some explanation for this sensitivity of British government decision-makers towards the operations of multinational corporations in the UK motor industry, and to analyse the policies adopted by the British government to deal with the problems arising from such operations.

The importance of vehicles production to the British economy may be seen from the results of the 1963 Census of Production, the last for which results are available, and also the first in which an attempt was made to distinguish between foreign and British-controlled enterprises. The vehicle industry (a classification which includes components and spare parts, but excludes such important items as tyres and electrical equipment) accounted for over 7½ per cent of manufacturing production, over 5 per cent of all industrial production, and nearly 6 per cent of manufacturing employment.[1] In that year 1963, the British motor industry exported 39 per cent of its output, accounting for almost 17 per cent of total UK exports, and one authoritative estimate concluded that over 10½ per cent of in-

181

dustrial production in the UK originated from or depended on the motor industry, directly or indirectly.[2]

The British government's concern over the operation of multinational companies in the motor industry is therefore quite comprehensible in terms of the economic significance of the industry, and when it is noted that an above average amount of foreign-investment has been channelled into the motor industry, it is possible to understand why it has become such a sensitive area. The following table, based on an unpublished Board of Trade exercise derived from the 1963 census data, indicates the degree of concentration of foreign investment in the motor industry. Sales, capital expenditure, and employment accounted for by foreign-controlled subsidiaries are expressed as percentages of the total figures for each industrial category.

Table 5.1
1963 sales, capital expenditure and employment
of foreign-owned motor companies

(as percentage of total UK + foreign)	Sales	Capital expenditure	Employment
Vehicle production	21·47	31·78	15·35
All manufacturing industry	16·07	20·40	11·09

Source: Board of Trade internal study (unpublished) *Report on the Census of Production* 1963, vol. 132, Table 20

It should be noted that 'foreign-controlled' is here defined as more than 50 per cent of the equity being owned by a company not registered in the UK; to this extent it disregards situations where a foreign company has substantial influence over the operations of a British company, but does not have a majority shareholding. Nevertheless, the above table does indicate that the UK motor industry accounts for an above-average level of foreign-controlled industrial production, and explains the British government's concern for this area. In a very real sense, therefore, the British motor industry epitomises the potential conflict between a host government attempting to control the course of its economy and a multinational corporation attempting, from a decision-centre outside the host country, to maximise its comparative advantage on a global scale. (This is not a new problem; in 1924 the British government proposed a horse-power tax on cars, and Ford threatened to move its European production centre out of the UK.)[3] The immense significance of the motor industry in the British economy makes the government/multinational corporation interface a very complex one. For the government, a multinational car company has great attraction; it can draw on extensive financial, managerial and marketing resources; it can create employment, increase productivity, provide capital, boost exports. At the same time, the highly sensitive and integrated control network which enables the multinational car company to achieve these objectives also permits it to change its investment, production and marketing strategies in order to maximise its comparative advantage.

The host government, therefore, is in the invidious position of competing with other countries for the location of investment by the car manufacturer, whilst attempting to derive maximum benefit from such investments and retain control over the country's economic development. The car manufacturer, operating in an industry which is increasingly capital-intensive and requires a high level of capacity utilisation in order to operate profitably (particularly since tooling costs form a large part of investment, and have to be recouped during the limited model-life of the car, which has to be redesigned frequently in order to remain internationally competitive), needs a thriving domestic market in order to achieve the economies of scale which make export production competitive.[4] The government may need to curb domestic demand in order to combat inflation and thus depress the domestic vehicle market. The government wishes the car manufacturer to expand production in order to create employment and increase exports; the car manufacturer is unwilling to commit long-term capital to expansion plans which may be unprofitable because of deflationary government short-term economic policies or loss of production due to labour unrest inspired by continuing inflation in the economy (which may itself push up his costs to a point where his products are uncompetitive in world markets).

The issue of mutual confidence lies at the heart of the problem in the British motor industry; the multinational car company, before committing investment to the UK, has to be confident that the British government's economic policy is such that it can derive an adequate return from its investment — while the British government has to be confident that the investing company will confer adequate benefits on the British economy. In the following case-study it will be seen that the British government in the 1960s attempted to achieve its objectives by requiring assurances of 'best endeavours' from multinational car companies investing in the UK whilst welcoming such investment, and by promoting rationalisation of the British-owned sector of the industry in order to create a countervailing force which would ensure good behaviour on the part of the foreign-controlled sector through competitive forces.

5.2 Foreign investment in the UK motor industry, 1911−60

The American motor manufacturers have been prominent in the development of the UK auto industry from a very early stage; Ford began assembly and partial manufacture of cars in Britain in 1911, and by 1914 was the largest UK producer of motor vehicles. In 1928 General Motors acquired Vauxhall, which in the next decade became the largest UK producer of commercial vehicles and the fourth largest car producer. In 1931 Ford's new plant at Dagenham began production, and the Ford share of the market increased from 5·7 per cent in 1929 to 18·9 per cent in 1933.[5] To some extent this expansion of production by the American motor manufacturers was an attempt to offset a decline in their home sales caused by the depression, which did not hit the UK market so hard; between 1929 and 1932 car production in the UK fell by 15 per cent compared with a 75 per cent drop in the US and Canada. The British market remained buoyant, with 1937 vehicle production double the 1929 level, whereas in the US, Canada and France the 1929 level of production was not surpassed until after the outbreak of World War II.[6] At the same time a massive rationalisation of the industry was taking place, with only twenty independent firms existing in 1938 (compared with eighty-eight in 1922) and, of these, six being responsible for 90 per cent of the UK output of cars − in order of size, these were Nuffield, Austin, Ford, Vauxhall, Rootes and Standard, with Ford and Vauxhall together accounting for a quarter of total UK car output.[7] Because of the proliferation of models, and the consequent inability to take advantage of economies of scale, British-made cars were not competitive on world markets, and of the 15 per cent of UK car production exported in 1938, over three-quarters were sold in Imperial Preference markets (while the UK market was protected by a $33\frac{1}{3}$ *ad valorem* tariff), with the UK motor industry accounting for only 4 per cent of total UK exports.[8]

The disruption in the UK motor industry caused by World War II and its aftermath left the manufacturers with the problem of an insatiable demand for cars at home and abroad, coupled with shortages of materials and skilled labour. The British government placed restrictions on capital expenditure and on the import of machine tools, with priority for projects which would earn foreign exchange, and massive increases in purchase tax on cars sold in the UK market (it was doubled to $66\frac{2}{3}$ per cent in 1951) to discourage home demand.[9] It was from this period that the perennial complaint of the British motor industry — that it was the target of selective economic regulation which made investment on the basis of a steadily expanding home market impossible — originated.

Nevertheless, these production problems did speed up the rationalisation process in the UK motor industry, with Austin and Nuffield merging in 1951 to form the British Motor Corporation, the largest British motor producer with over 40 per cent of the market. The access of Ford and Vauxhall to capital provided by their US parent companies led to a marked increase in their production and share of the market; by 1953 Ford had doubled its share compared to 1946 (27 per cent from 14 per cent) and Vauxhall registered the only other market share increase (from 9 per cent in 1946 60 10·4 per cent in 1953).[10] Vertical integration in the industry increased in the years after 1950, with attempts by the major manufacturers to standardise components and to control their sources of supply (in 1953 both Ford and BMC acquired body-producing plants). Frequently this drive to expand and rationalise production was carried out without sufficient regard for establishing sound labour relations, and the number of working days lost through strikes in the motor industry almost quadrupled, from 75,000 in 1948 to 285,000 in 1958, accounting for almost 15 per cent of the total for UK industry as a whole. Partly this was due to the highly integrated character of modern vehicle production, whereby a strike in the factory of a supplier of a vital component can virtually halt all production when supplies of that component dry up, and this increased the tendency of motor manufacturers to develop alternative sources of supply, frequently under their own control (General Motors expanded its AC–Delco electrical component company to supply virtually all of Vauxhall's requirements).[11]

By 1956 the sellers' market for British cars had largely disappeared; in that year West Germany overtook the UK both as a producer and exporter, and by 1961 Britain was also overtaken by France.[12] In many of Britain's major car export markets domestic production provided severe competition, particularly in Australia and the USA (with the introduction of compact cars), with the result that almost all the major British car manufacturers found themselves with increasing capacity, the product of intensive investment programmes in the mid-fifties, and far from buoyant markets both abroad and at home (where import quotas on foreign cars were lifted in 1959 and a credit-squeeze was instituted in 1961). The

185

result was a further round of mergers in the UK motor industry, with Leyland taking over Standard–Triumph and Jaguar acquiring Daimler. In the same year, 1960, Ford of America (which held 54·6 per cent of the equity in its UK subsidiary) decided to make a £130 million offer for the minority stake in Ford UK.

5.3 The Ford take-over, 1960

This move was quite comprehensible in the context of Ford's UK operations, particularly in view of its disappointing record in industrial disputes. In 1957 a British government Court of Inquiry had been told that Ford UK's body plant had 237 stoppages in the previous eighteen months, and the number of major stoppages at Dagenham (Ford's main plant) increased from 25 in 1958 to 79 in 1960. [13] A Ford official noted that local shareholders had been 'used as an umbrella to resist change. Local personnel will point to the minority shareholders when they want to argue against innovation.' [14] Ford's rationale for the bid was contained in a letter sent by Ford US to Ford UK which stated:

> Our objective is to obtain greater operational flexibility and enable us better to co-ordinate our European and American manufacturing facilities, and integrate further our product lines and operations on a world-wide basis. [15]

The 'flexibility' referred to related not only to a world-wide view of comparative advantage; Ford UK was the largest of Ford's overseas operations, and full ownership would enable the parent company to control dividend policy and reap maximum advantages. Moreover, allocation of markets on a world scale between wholly owned subsidiaries was less likely to fall foul of US anti-trust legislation, as the Timken case had shown in the early 1950s. Nevertheless, the take-over bid provoked a major argument in Parliament, with the Conservative Chancellor of the Exchequer, Mr Selwyn Lloyd, under attack by the Labour opposition for giving permission (required under the Exchange Control Act 1947) [16] for the bid to be made. The parliamentary debates which followed the announcement of the Ford bid in November 1960 are illuminating because they illustrate the major concerns of the British government of the time vis-à-vis international companies.

Ford at that time wholly owned all their overseas subsidiaries except the British one, where 39 per cent of the equity was in British hands and 6 per cent was in other foreign hands. On 14 November 1960 it announced an offer of £7. 5s. 6d. for each £1 share, having informed the British government the night before of its intentions. On 17 November it made formal application to the Bank of England for Exchange Control permission, and the next day contacted the Treasury for the first time. At that time the Chancellor of the Exchequer, Mr Selwyn Lloyd, said: 'The danger here may be that the investment or the development will go to the German factory if it does not come to Fords at Dagenham.'[17] Four days later, after discussions with Ford officials, he told the House of Commons that permission for transfer of the minority equity in Ford UK to Ford USA under the Exchange Control Act had been granted, on the basis that the offer price for the shares was 'not outside the reasonable range of negotiation between a willing buyer and a willing seller.'[18] This was merely a reiteration of a long-standing Treasury guideline that the inflow of foreign exchange should be of at least adequate value for the assets of a company transferred to a foreign buyer.

However, for perhaps the first time (certainly the first time in public), the British government sought further assurances from Ford on its contribution to the British economy, and in particular on the status of Ford's employees in the UK:

> I have discussed the position with representatives of both the US and UK companies. As a result I have been given the following explanations and assurances. The purpose has been described as to obtain greater operational flexibility and to enable Ford US to co-ordinate better its American and European operations so that it may be able to compete more effectively in world markets. ... I was told that ... if the offer were to be accepted, their decisions – that is to say, the decisions of the American company – with regard to expansion, production and exports in Europe would not be affected by the fact that profits from activity in the United Kingdom would belong only to the extent of just over half to the parent company. When developments were being planned, the possibly limiting factor of the UK company being only 55 per cent owned by the parent company would be eliminated.
>
> I therefore formed the view that full American ownership would lead to a still more vigorous development of the Ford enterprise here, and to even greater efforts in the export markets, inasmuch as the American company would have the incentive of having to secure a return on its heavy and extended investment here. Without full ownership of the United Kingdom company there might be a greater incentive for the United States company to concentrate efforts on

the development of the German company, which is nearly 100 per cent owned. [19]

These two government policies, to attract foreign investment capital and to boost exports, thus led to a reversal of what Mr Douglas Jay (the President of the Board of Trade in the Labour government 1964–67) called 'a passing fashion during the 1950s for governments to favour a minority UK shareholding in order to control foreign companies.'[20] The Conservative government considered that specific assurances from foreign companies as to their future conduct were more important, and Chancellor Lloyd obtained from Ford the following undertakings:

1   Exports: Greater efforts in the export markets.
2   Capital Investment: The planned expansion programme of £70 million would go forward.
3   Dividend Policy: The past practice of ploughing back a high proportion of UK profits for future development would continue.
4   Management Policy: Continuity would be preserved, and to this end the majority of members of the UK Board of Directors would continue to be British, with Sir Patrick Hennesey remaining as Chairman.
5   Employment Policy: There would be no change in policy, which would remain in the hands of the UK Board.
6   Imports Policy: The policy of obtaining almost all components from UK sources would be continued, and full American ownership would put the UK company in a better position to compete in world markets for the sale of British-made components. [21]

As to the question of control of a large proportion of a UK industry passing into foreign hands, Mr Lloyd said that this 'was not really relevant in this particular case because control was already with the US company, as it has been since the UK company started in 1911. Had it not been so, the company would never have come here and this huge industrial concern would never have been built up.'[22] He made it clear that such conditions made Ford a special case, inasmuch as the purpose of the bid was to strengthen the UK company and particularly to enable it to compete more effectively in world markets:

> There may well be cases where proposals may seem attractive from a commercial point of view, but where, nevertheless, it may be necessary to refuse consent to transfer of control for reasons of national security or the significance of a particular firm or industry to our economic life. [23]

188

In the subsequent debate, Chancellor Lloyd amplified on his decision, by adding further justifications; firstly, that US investment enabled Britain to derive benefits in terms of increased efficiency and exports as a result of drawing on massive American research and development programmes; secondly, that an inward flow of dollars helped the British balance of payments and added to British capacity to invest abroad; and thirdly, that Britain's extensive overseas investments gave her a paramount interest in the freest possible movement of capital, thus making it unwise to raise difficulties or impose restrictions unless they were absolutely necessary. Consequently, each transaction had to be considered on its own merits. [24]

The leader of the Labour opposition, Mr Harold Wilson, attacked the Conservative government's decision on the grounds that Ford US already had full operational control, and that they had failed to gain specific assurances from Ford of increased exports to the US and third countries, preferring instead to bring about a transient decrease in the balance of payments deficit. (In fact, October's trade figures, which had just been released, showed a trade deficit of £110 million, the worst for some years.) He feared a repetition of the 1958 incident when Ford of Canada was forbidden to fulfil an export order to Communist China, and went on to say:

> I want to make it clear that we on this side of the House are not against American investment in this country ... But we are against a major industry being owned by the Americans ... Do not let us press this argument of the desirability of some American investment to the point of 100 per cent ownership. [25]

Mr Douglas Jay made a further point, that foreign-owned companies had in his experience arranged their transfer-pricing policies so that exports from the UK earned little taxable profit in the UK, and that such companies had been very difficult to deal with. [26]

The Conservative President of the Board of Trade, Mr Reginald Maudling, wound up the debate by reiterating the British government's policy toward foreign investment. He stressed that the UK was competing with other countries for American investment and that UK investment in the US was of the same order of magnitude as US investment in the UK. The chief benefits of US investment were that it brought technological and managerial knowledge, increased productivity and exports, fresh capital, and employment in development districts. Because rigid restrictions on inward investment might invite retaliatory measures against UK investment overseas, it was better to examine each case individually, and in this case:

> The American company already has the power, with its 54 per cent holding, to restrict expansion and exports. With a 100 per cent holding it will have a much greater incentive to expand exports. That is the fundamental point at issue. [27]

Ford was successful in its bids for the minority shareholding, and the £130 million it paid for the equity was responsible for a jump in the overseas investment in the UK private sector item in the long-term capital account – up from £253 million in 1960 to £374 million in 1961 – and was a major factor in converting an overall basic balance of payments deficit of £457 million in 1960 to a surplus of £64 million in 1961. [28] The British financial press generally supported the take-over, on the grounds that the increase in the Ford US holding would encourage the deployment of more managerial resources in Ford UK and improve its performance. *The Economist* commented:

> One does not bid £129 million for administrative tidiness ... Given 100 per cent ownership of its biggest overseas manufacturing operations in Britain, as well as 99 per cent ownership of Ford of Germany, the American parent company would feel quite free to supply the export markets of the world strictly in terms of what appeared to it the best utilisation of its widely deployed manufacturing facilities ... But, even within the present pattern of ownership, such a policy could not be prevented in Britain if the American parent chose to dictate it, either regardless of or in the longer-term interest of the minority shareholders. [29]

Whilst it is true that the Ford bid did not involve a transfer of control in any strict legal sense, the government's supposition that full ownership would increase the significance of Ford UK in its parent company's overall strategy did suggest that government decision-makers were no longer convinced of the significance of a UK minority shareholding as a means of ensuring that foreign companies served UK interests. The provision in the assurances given by Ford to the Chancellor of the Exchequer that the majority of the Board of Directors and the Chairman would remain UK nationals indicates a Galbraithian shift of emphasis from shareholders to management as the point of salience. The chief economic aims of the government at that time were to correct a marked deterioration in the balance of trade (caused by an increase in imports while exports remained almost static in face of a minor recession in world markets), to reduce inflation (in part by reducing costs in terms of increased productivity), to maintain employment, and to increase capital investment (if at all possible by using foreign sources rather than increasing domestic sources of credit). The Ford acquisition offered the hope of positive effects on some of these objectives, with the likelihood of few negative effects on others. Except in the field of labour relations, Ford UK's management had a high reputation for progressive methods, and full ownership would encourage increased efficiency. Ultimate control had always resided in the American parent, and (although Ford was second only to BMC in terms of vehicle production and employment) the total American share of British vehicle production was approximately 40 per cent (25 per cent for Ford), about the same as for BMC, so there was no question of a major British industry coming under foreign domination. [30] The decisive factors were a large once-only benefit to the balance of payments from Ford's purchase of the minority equity, and the hope of increased exports in the context of Ford's world-wide production and marketing framework, together with a strong possibility that the £70 million three-year expansion programme announced by Ford UK in 1960 (to establish a plant at Halewood, a high unemployment area of northern England) would be diverted to Germany if the bid was not approved.

5.4   Chrysler enters the market, 1964

The next major development in the UK motor industry occurred in June 1964, when Chrysler announced that it was bidding for a 20 per cent stake in the Rootes Group, which was the smallest of the 'Big Five' motor manufacturers (BMC, Ford, Leyland, Vauxhall and Rootes accounted for 96 per cent of domestic sales in 1960) and the only such company to be family-controlled. Chrysler informed the Chancellor of the Exchequer, Mr Reginald Maudling, that it wished to acquire 30 per cent of Rootes' ordinary voting shares and 50 per cent of its non-voting shares, for a total of £12·3 million of the £66 million value of the group. [31] Chrysler, which at that time was the third largest car manufacturer in the world, had been much slower than Ford and GM in expanding its overseas production facilities; in 1958 it had taken a 25 per cent interest in the French Simca company (increased to 63 per cent in 1963), and had not followed their pattern of buying out all minority shareholdings. The Rootes Group were in the position of lacking sufficient capital to increase their market share (the establishment of a £22 million plant at Linwood in Scotland had been their major project in the early 1960s) and in particular lacked resources to penetrate export markets in the face of increasing competition. The relatively poor performance of the Rootes Group did not make it an attractive take-over prospect for the other British motor manufacturers (who were in any case still digesting the results of the wave of mergers and expansion programmes begun in 1960) and the approach from Chrysler was favourably received by Lord Rootes, the Chairman, who pointed out that Simca's exports had risen by 41 per cent in 1963, with a six-fold increase in car sales in the US, following Chrysler's increased stake in the company. He gave specific assurance that Rootes would not be managed by Chrysler. 'Chrysler do not govern our markets. They have no interest, except that where we cannot sell we shall try to get them to help.' [32]

The Chrysler bid, which came four months before the 1964 General Election, was the source of some political controversy. The Conservative President of the Board of Trade, Mr Edward Heath, welcomed it as being 'in the best interests of the car industry. It will strengthen the Rootes position and the whole industry as well. The offer will need no sanction from the Government.' [33] The Labour Leader of the Opposition, Mr Harold Wilson, contrasted the Conservative horror of public ownership of British industries with their welcoming attitude to foreign financial interests in key British exporting companies:

> We are entitled to know ... which firms they will guarantee — if by any mischance they remain in office — will not be allowed to fall into the hands of either financial manipulators in this country or American, German or other foreign interests. [34]

In the subsequent debate in the House of Commons, the shadow Chancellor Mr James Callaghan asked Chancellor Maudling:

> Is the right hon Gentleman aware that as a result of this latest purchase of shares, more than 50 per cent of the cars which will be manufactured in this country will be to some extent, either wholly or partly, within American control? ... As the motor car industry has been one of the most sensitive spots in the stop-go economy of the last 12 years, what is the policy of the Government to ensure that the future of the motor car industry in this country is dictated by our national interest and not by the interests of those overseas? [35]

Mr Maudling took essentially the same line that his predecessor Mr Lloyd had taken in the Ford case — namely that the question of control did not arise, (because in this case Chrysler was only taking a minority stake) that the bid would provide new capital, access to American knowledge and research, and improve exports:

> I see no sign of British industry falling under the domination of any other country. Our overseas investments are on a greater scale than foreign investments here ... I would rather see Chrysler investing money here rather than with our Continental competitors ... I think that the experience of Ford and Vauxhall in the export market show how well American companies export from this country.[36]

In an exchange of letters between Chancellor Maudling and Mr I.J. Minett, group vice-president of Chrysler, Chrysler undertook 'not to initiate any action to impair either the home overseas operations ... of Rootes as a British company in its relations with the government, labour, its British shareholders, and the public.' It also gave assurances that should it decide in the future to acquire control of Rootes, it would consult beforehand with the government and abide by its decision. Mr Maudling replied:

> On this understanding I am very ready to give you an assurance on behalf of the government that in considering whether to give their agreement they will take into account the interests of a prosperous and viable development of the motor car industry in general and of the Rootes business in particular.
>
> Finally, I should like to make it clear that there has been no change in our policy of welcoming foreign investment here which is of benefit to our economy; we certainly do not hold that there is in principle and in all circumstances an objection to the acquisition by a group such as yours of a majority interest in a British industrial enterprise. [37]

Mr Maudling's open-hand attitude may not have been unaffected by the steadily deteriorating UK balance of payments position (an increase in the basic balance's deficit from £35 million in 1963 to £750 million in 1964) and the rather gloomy forecasts about Rootes' profit (which for 1963–4 amounted to 1·1 per cent return on capital employed). [38] His decision was approved by the financial press, which commented that the association would 'bring solid benefits to both parties ... For Chrysler it provides another foothold in the important European motor market ... For Rootes, association with the Chrysler giant will provide obvious benefits in research, technical advances, production techniques ... and in export markets.'[39] The British approach was contrasted favourably to the hostile attitude of the French government when Chrysler took a 30 per cent stake in Simca in 1958:

All it achieved then was strongly to discourage further American investment in France; it did not deter Chrysler from going ahead, through a series of brilliant market manoeuvres conducted by Swiss nominees, to buy up enough Simca shares to gain a controlling interest — a tactic they have formally eschewed in the case of Rootes.

So it looks as though Mr Maudling's apparent softness has yielded the desired results. We retain control over further American investment: we show ourselves happy to receive it. [40]

In general the British financial press expressed the view that the City's interests were best served by minimum restrictions on inward investment, in order to preserve the very large British overseas investments from any reciprocal restrictions by foreign governments. [41]

5.5 The UK motor industry in 1964

By October 1964, when the Conservative government was replaced by a Labour government as a result of the General Election, the British motor industry still had scope for further rationalisation. Although BMC was the largest British vehicle producer, it was only third largest in Europe (after Volkswagen and Fiat), and in its total production came nowhere near rivalling the three major American motor companies, which were all now represented in UK manufacturing. Although elimination of inefficient motor companies through competition had reduced the number of car producers by over one-third in twenty-five years (from thirty-three in 1939 to eighteen in 1964), the five major producers, who produced over 90 per cent of the total UK output, had no great incentive to promote further mergers among themselves. As one study of the industry commented: 'The entire history of the British motor industry reveals very few mergers between *successful* firms: almost invariably one of the parties to a merger has been bankrupt or on the verge of liquidation.'[42] None of the British-owned companies were producing vehicles on a scale close to the technical optimum (about 500,000 identical vehicles per annum)[43] nor did they have the resources to attain a marketing optimum of a world-wide selling organisation with assembly plants in import markets, to attain maximum export sales. This was particularly important in view of the continuing restraints placed on the domestic UK vehicle market (in the form of credit restrictions, purchase tax, petrol tax, and so on) by a government attempting to curb inflation and promote a favourable trade balance by controlling the sales of consumer durables; for the British motor industry the uncertainties of its market made export sales doubly important. The problem for the British-owned motor companies was that none of them possessed long-term viability in world markets because of their moderate size, and none possessed sufficient financial and managerial resources to bring about a successful horizontal merger with another major car manufacturer. The only alternative — acquisition by one of the US Big Three, was unlikely both on political grounds and because the American companies possessed sufficient resources to expand internally without the additional costs of post-merger rationalisation. Only in the case of Chrysler, which had reserved the option to gain control of Rootes, was a further acquisition by an American car company at all likely.

The British government had, during the period 1960–64, maintained a very open-handed attitude toward foreign investment in the UK motor industry. In part this was due to its concern with the balance of payments; foreign investment provided a counterweight to UK private investment overseas (inward investment in the UK private sector averaged three-quarters of UK private overseas investment in the years 1960–64), [44] as well as the possibility of access to superior technical, managerial, and global marketing resources, factors which were specifically mentioned by Chancellors Lloyd and Maudling in the Ford and Rootes cases.

In general the British government during the period 1960–64 adopted a policy of considering applications for investment by foreign companies in the British motor industry on a case-by-case basis. It was possible to do so because neither the Ford nor the Chrysler investments involved an actual transfer of control to the foreign company involved; in the Ford case ultimate control had always resided in the American parent, and in the Chrysler case only a non-controlling interest was taken up in 1964 (although the exchange of letters between Mr Minett and Mr Maudling quoted above clearly foresaw the possibility of Chrysler gaining control of Rootes). In both cases there was an assumption by the government that the American investment would be accompanied by increased efficiency and particular improved export performance; yet the assurances sought from Ford and Chrysler included no guarantees of increased performance or even 'best endeavours'. The assurances given by both Ford and Chrysler were essentially negative in character: that the parent companies would not run down the operations of the UK firms in which they had an interest from their current level, and (in the Ford case) that previously announced expansion plans would be implemented. The government's concern seemed to be to preserve continuity rather than to require improved performance, although there was an implicit assumption that increased efficiency was a concomitant of American investment. In both cases the government had expressed concern lest the investment be lost to one of Britain's competitors in Europe, following an increasing trend for American companies to invest in EEC countries rather than in the UK. [45]

5.6   The UK motor industry and the Labour Government, 1964—70

In 1964, the year in which the Labour Government came to power, the British motor industry attained a record level of production (2·3 million vehicles) which was not to be equalled during the following six years (production in 1969 was 2·2 million vehicles, and in 1967 it had been 1·9 million). [46] The period was marked by a decline in the home market of over 20 per cent, increasing disruption of production by strikes, and extensive rationalisation in the structure of the industry. In 1964 there were seven major vehicle producing companies; by 1968 there were four, three of them American controlled (see Table 5.2). In some respects this was the result of the Labour Government's policy of creating a viable British-owned motor company which would act as a countervailing force to the presence of the three major American motor companies in the British market; in other respects it was the product of economic forces in the motor industry, where rising percentage of total factory costs accounted for by fixed costs made unit costs more responsive to levels of production and therefore encouraged rationalisation. [47]

Table 5.2

Main motor companies' share of UK market, 1965 and 1970

(Percentage of total new registrations of cars)

	1965		1970
Ford	26·3		26·5
Rootes (Chrysler)	11·9		10·5
Vauxhall (GM)	11·8		10·0
BMC	35·6		
Jaguar	1·2	BLMC	38.1
Leyland	5·9		
Rover	1·7		
Other UK	0·3		0·6
Imports	5·1		14·3

Source: SMMT

Table 5.3
UK vehicle production by manufacturer, 1966–69
(Cars and commercial vehicles, in thousands)

	1966	1967	1968	1969
Ford	580	535	642	669
Rootes	213	210	216	206
Vauxhall	275	286	342	274
BMC	693 }	717 }		
Jaguar	23		987	1016
Leyland	169 }	243 }		
Rover	75			
Other	14	14	19	18
Total	2042	1937	2225	2183

Source: SMMT

It is possible to distinguish five main aspects of the Labour Government's policy toward the motor industry; (a) a deflationary economic policy to remedy a chronic balance of payments deficit; (b) the failure to find an alternative to the Chrysler take-over of Rootes; (c) creation of a single British-owned motor company; (d) creation of a favourable investment climate in the UK; (e) establishing a dialogue between the government and the motor companies.

5.6.1   *Correcting the balance of payments deficit*

From 1963 until 1969 the UK balance of payments was continuously in deficit, reaching a peak of £749 million in 1964; during that period the Labour Government was forced to adopt a deflationary home economic policy which had severe effects on the UK motor industry. Income elasticity of demand for motor vehicles is quite high, since there is an economic threshold for car ownership, and British governments since 1950 had used the motor industry both as a source of revenue and as an economic regulator. The chronic balance of payments deficit during this period necessitated no less than fifteen changes in purchase tax or consumer credit regulations applying to cars, seven of them in the period June 1965 to November 1967. [48] These caused marked fluctuations in demand for motor vehicles which, when added to normal seasonal variations in demand, left UK motor manufacturers with a substantial amount of unusual capacity, even when increased exports were taken into account:

Table 5.4

Capacity utilisation for the seven major motor firms, 1963—67

1963	1964	1965	1966	1967
83%	88%	78%	68%	64%

Source: Motor Manufacturing EDC op. cit., p. 20

Because extensions to capacity have to be made in large stages, and carried out in advance of reliable estimates of demand, the UK motor manufacturers expanded their net fixed assets at almost twice the rate for UK industry as a whole during the period 1960—67. [49] The result was a general decline in their return on capital, and a growing inability to satisfy capital expenditure requirements from retained earnings. Since tooling investment becomes obsolete over a relatively fixed and short period of time, because of the need to redesign models to remain competitive internationally, all the UK motor companies were short of capital and were faced with the problem of obsolescent product lines and an inability to raise new capital on the market because of their dismal earnings position.

The result of the depressed home market was that vehicle production did not return to 1964 levels during the Labour Government's term of office; the 1965 National Plan forecast that 1970 vehicle production would be 2·6 million units, whereas actual 1970 production was just under 2 million units, and the 1965 forecast of 1·7 million units as the size of the home market was a 41 per cent overestimate — in fact just under 1 million units were sold in 1969, 21 per cent less than in 1964. [50] Not only was this a strong disincentive to further investment in the motor industry, but it served to worsen labour relations in the industry, by forcing the companies to vary the size of their labour force in accordance with fluctuations in demand and also to increase the number of occasions when short-time working was instituted. [51] The number of working days lost through strikes steadily increased during the period 1964—70; in some years the number of days lost per 1000 employees in the motor industry was almost ten times the average for UK industry as a whole. (see table below).

Table 5.5

Profitability of the seven major motor firms, 1963–69

(Pre-tax profits as a percentage of capital employed)

	Ford	Rootes	Vauxhall	BMC	Jaguar	Leyland	Rover
1963–64	25·1	1·1	17·2	16·4	27·4	11·7	9·6
1964–65	14·0	4·9	26·2	20·3	24·5	19·9	15·9
1965–66	5·4	loss	22·6	19·7	19·8	21·8	17·9
1966–67	5·0	loss	6·3	13·0	17·4	14·9	11·8
1967–68	3·2	loss	7·7	0·2 {		14·9 {	
1968–69	22·1	4·4	9·7	15·8 {			

Source: *Exchange Telegraph Statistics*

Table 5.6
Strikes in the UK motor industry, 1964–70

	Working days lost (thousands)	Days lost per 1000 employees	
		Motor industry	All industry
1964	429	500 – 1,000	50 – 100
1965	862	1,500 – 2,000	100 – 250
1966	344	500 – 1,000	100 – 250
1967	504	1,000	125
1968	898	1,800	200
1969	1,636	3,100	300
1970	1,105	2,150	475

Source: *Ministry of Labour Gazette*; *Employment and Productivity Gazette*

As the largest (in terms of capital employed, but not production) motor manufacturer in the UK, Ford came in for a good deal of criticism. The Labour MP for Dagenham, Mr John Parker, in a 1965 speech criticised the Americanisation of its labour relations, with its hire and fire policies:

> The feeling of anyone connected with Fords is that policy is controlled very rigidly by the United States company. That is not in the British interest ... We should ask ourselves how far the British Ford Company is a British asset. It has a large export trade, but only in limited markets. The profits are taxed in this country, but the dividends are distributed in the United States ... There is no real United States market to set off the sales of British Ford cars against dollar earnings which have to be made elsewhere by other firms to pay for these dividends paid to the United States. In the long run, especially if mergers take place in the industry and power rests in fewer – and largely foreign – hands, we shall have to take up the question of whether nationalisation is necessary. [52]

To some extent this feeling that the American-owned motor companies were not fully contributing to the British economy was echoed in the press; *The Times* pointed out that BMC sold 33,400 cars in the United States in 1964, almost half total UK exports to that market:

200

The ... key is to persuade the two American-owned companies, British Ford and Vauxhall, to institute a sales drive in the United States of America. In 1959 together they sold 65,000 cars there. But last year British Ford sold only a total of 4,200 and Vauxhall had no significant car exports to the USA (53 to be precise). In both cases these companies are the instruments of international production and marketing policies. [53]

Such criticisms were perhaps natural when the weakness of sterling against the dollar led to emphasis on dollar export markets; in fact for both Ford and Vauxhall in 1965 a greater percentage of turnover was exported than was the case for BMC (39 per cent and 40 per cent respectively, as against 30 per cent for BMC), and in the case of Ford, the value of exports for 1965 was absolutely higher than BMC's (£152,000 as against £146,000). [54] In addition, Ford opened an assembly plant at Genk in Belgium in October 1964, and announced plans for an Antwerp—Basildon tractor manufacturing link for 1965, both Belgian plants being supplied with British—made components.

The UK motor industry contributed a large proportion of total UK exports, but its share of world exports showed a decline, indicating that it was becoming less competitive internationally:

Table 5.7
Export performance of the UK motor industry, 1964—69

	Value of exports (£ million)*	Percentage of total UK exports*	Percentage of world exports†
1964	743	16·8	22·4
1965	783	16·6	20·6
1966	802	15·9	18·7
1967	736	14·6	17·1
1968	896	14·5	13·0
1969	1,073	15·3	N.A.

* Includes ancillary equipment and spare parts
† By volume
Source: Ministry of Technology, SMMT, Motor Manufacturing EDC

Nevertheless the export performance of the motor companies was impressive; in the rankings of top companies compiled annually by *The Times*, they regularly featured among the top ten exporting companies. (See Table 5.8).

Since the publication of sales figures was not made compulsory until the introduction of the 1967 Companies Act, the first year for which a direct comparison of the export performance of the individual motor companies is possible was the 1968—69 financial year. In that year export sales as a percentage of total sales were 43 per cent for Ford, 34 per cent for Vauxhall, 30 per cent for British Leyland, and 19 per cent for Chrysler (formerly Rootes). The total value of their export sales in 1968—69 was £593 million, about 9 per cent of total UK exports for the same period. [55] One estimate of the import content of UK vehicle production rated imports as making up about 10 per cent of output cost, [56] and therefore the motor industry's positive contribution to the trade balance is quite considerable. This was frequently stressed by Labour Ministers when they were criticised for not controlling the foreign-owned motor companies strictly enough; the Minister of Technology, Mr Anthony Wedgwood Benn, said in a 1968 speech:

> International companies own about 10 per cent of our industry and do about 20 per cent of our exports. Ford has had an £850 million net balance in exports in the last few years, and £200 million this year. We have done quite well out of the exports of these big international companies. [57]

5.6.2 The failure to find an alternative to the Chrysler take-over of Rootes

Shortly after Chrysler acquired its stake in Rootes (almost half the voting shares and two-thirds of the non-voting shares) in 1964, three Chrysler nominees joined the Rootes board. Control of the company still rested with the Rootes family, who held almost all the rest of the voting shares, but the company's disappointing profits record (a profit of £5 million in 1964—65 followed two years of losses) made it seem inevitable that Chrysler would seek to rationalise Rootes. *The Economist* commented the 'the crunch will come when (and it is unlikely to be if) Chrysler suggests any major changes in Rootes' pattern of operations in England.' [58] The company's major problem was a declining share of the vehicle market (largely caused by its obsolescent model range) which the introduction of a new rear-engined mini-car, the Imp — to compete with the phenom-

Table 5.8

Export sales and capital employed by motor firms in comparison with other leading UK companies (Ranking of all UK companies by value of export turnover and capital employed)

	1966–67		1967–68		1968–69		1969–70	
	Exports	Capital	Exports	Capital	Exports	Capital	Exports	Capital
Ford	1	12	2	24	3	22	3	23
BMH	3	23	3	28	1	9	1	11
Leyland	7	39	5	34				
Vauxhall	9	41	9	43	11	45	11	51
Chrysler UK (formerly Rootes)					15	85	16	92

Note: Rootes export figures for the period 1966–68 not available
Source: *The Times Leading Companies in Britain* 1967,1968,1969

enally successful BMC Mini – had failed to halt. After Lord Rootes, the Chairman of the company, died in December 1964, Chrysler publicly denied that it was seeking a further stake in Rootes 'at this stage.' [59] Nevertheless, Chrysler began to integrate Rootes into its international marketing structure, and from September 1965 all Rootes cars were blazoned with the Chrysler pentastar. [60] Three months later, in a move which was widely regarded as the penultimate step in a complete take-over of the Rootes Group, Chrysler took over sales, marketing and servicing of all Rootes Group vehicles in the US, leading *The Times* to comment that 'Rootes' protestations of continuing independence sound pretty unrealistic.' [61]

In December 1966, when it was quite clear that Rootes would be making a record loss of almost £2 million in the 1966–67 financial year, Chrysler announced that it was seeking to purchase a controlling share of the Rootes equity in order to protect its investment. [62] The Labour Government was faced with a political problem, since Prime Minister Wilson had strongly opposed the initial Chrysler stake in 1964 when Leader of the Opposition, and attempted to find an alternative to a complete Chrysler take-over. Rootes needed an immediate injection of capital and management, and improved access to world markets, but did not represent an attractive take-over prospect to the other British-owned companies, since it had few technical or managerial resources independent of the Chrysler link and the other British car companies already had excess production capacity. Although nationalisation by the government would have provided Rootes with capital and access to fresh management, it no longer had a world distribution network independent of Chrysler. Chrysler in talks with the Treasury was adamant that it would only provide more capital if it could control Rootes. [63]

In January 1967 the government agreed to the immediate acquisition by Chrysler of enough shares in Rootes to give the American company effective control, and decided that the public interest did not require the merger to be referred to the Monopolies Commission. In announcing this to Parliament, Mr Wedgwood Benn explained:

> The decision taken in 1964 [to allow Chrysler to acquire a minority stake in Rootes] was effectively the decision that conditioned what action could be taken by us now ... The government consulted the leaders of the principal British-owned motor vehicle firms to see whether a viable solution designed to enable Rootes to continue as a British-controlled company could be devised. No such scheme proved practicable. ... The take-over of Rootes by the British Government –

which, of course, was considered, but would have involved massive sums of public money going into an insolvent private enterprise company without any guarantee that in this way it could remain viable — was not a practicable proposition ... This issue is simple. We did not believe that Rootes by itself was a viable organisation with or without government money, owned or not owned by a British company. The alternative ... would have involved substantial government investment in Rootes and then a merger which would not, however, have resulted in government control of the consequential company. This solution was not practical because of the degree of ... entanglements arising out of the previous arrangements. [64]

Essentially the government accepted that the Chrysler take-over was the only alternative to bankruptcy of Rootes, which would have increased unemployment in the motor industry, already suffering extensive lay-offs and short-time working in the depressed market which had followed the severely deflationary July 1966 Budget. Some years later Mr Wedgwood Benn admitted that until that time the Labour Government had done very little thinking about international companies, and that the conditions imposed by Chancellor Lloyd in the 1960 Ford deal strongly influenced the way in which the Labour Government responded to the Chrysler bid in 1967. [65] Indeed, in 1967 he couched the argument against the Chrysler take-over in largely domestic terms:

Our doubts about this did not arise from anti-American feeling, but from the anxiety that Britain, looking ahead over a period of years, might not be able to sustain three large American corporations and a British corporation when the United States which is three times our size and has a much larger output, can only sustain three corporations. [sic] [66]

In an exchange of letters between Mr Wedgwood Benn and Mr I.J. Minett, Group Vice-President of Chrysler, the conditions which the government attached to consent for the take-over were outlined. They are particularly interesting as an indicator of how the Labour Government's policy differed from that of the Conservative Government in the 1960 Ford deal:

(i) Chrysler will not initiate any action to impair either the home or overseas operations or the management and direction of Rootes as a British company in its relations with the Government, labour, its British shareholders, and the public. [67]

This was a reiteration of the general guarantee of best endeavours which the Conservative Government had required from Chrysler in 1964, identically worded.

(ii)   Chrysler undertakes to maintain a majority of British Directors on the Board of Rootes.

Again, this provision was identical to the assurance given by Ford, with the exception that in the Ford case the American company had undertaken to keep on its subsidiary's British chairman, Sir Patrick Hennessey. This omission was an attempt to make the guidelines more flexible, since it was realised that such rigid conditions were valueless 'because in the course of time retirement comes to everybody'. [68]

(iii)   Chrysler confirms the plans of expansion covering development work at various factories, and especially at Linwood in Scotland where the major development will take place and where it is planned to increase employment by several thousands; these plans are essential if Rootes is to remain competitive, achieve its proper share of exports and return to reasonable profitability.

The difference here from the Ford undertakings concerning expansion and employment policies is that the government laid particular stress on one plant (the newest Rootes factory at Linwood) and indicated that Chrysler's major expansion should take place there. Although Ford's expansion programme in 1960 related particularly to its Halewood plant, like Linwood in a development area, it was not mentioned in the Ford undertaking. It should also be noted that, unlike the Ford case, the government did not insist that employment policy should remain in the hands of the Rootes board; instead there was a definite commitment 'to increase employment by several thousands'.

(iv)   Chrysler plans to achieve a progressive increase in the export of Rootes products without restriction to all practicable markets and to continue to make available its full international organisation for this purpose. They note that, in the view of Her Majesty's Government, the test of fulfilment of this undertaking would be that the export percentage of the products of the Rootes Group should be at least as high as the average for the British Motor Vehicle Industry as a whole.

This undertaking was particularly interesting because for the first time the British Government set a concrete performance target for an international company investing in the UK. In the Ford case, Chancellor Lloyd had assumed that the take-over would lead to 'even greater efforts in the export markets'[69] but admitted that he had not discussed export policy with Ford.[70] The test of export performance in the Rootes case, namely 'the average for the British Motor Vehicle Industry as a whole', amounted in 1967 to export of just over one-third of production by volume, or two-fifths by value,[71] although Mr Wedgwood Benn did not make clear which criterion was to be applied. In terms of volume of exports, Rootes' 1968 export performance of 34 per cent of output was slightly below the industrial average of 37 per cent, while its 1969 export allocation of 50 per cent was higher than the average of 44 per cent for the whole vehicle industry. If the criterion was to be value of exports as a percentage of total turnover, the Rootes performance in 1968–9 was markedly below the other major manufacturers, being about 19 per cent as against the average of 32 per cent.[72] In fact Chrysler was never questioned by the Labour Government in subsequent years as to whether it had lived up to its assurances, simply because the government did not have the resources for policing the agreement,[73] and also because, as Mr Wedgwood Benn put it 'that sort of thing wasn't good enough, and interrogating them about whether they'd kept their conditions was much less creative than ... keeping in touch.'[74] To a great extent, therefore, the export performance test was exhortatory rather than mandatory.

The fifth undertaking was interesting because it indicated the Government's recognition that British representation on the Rootes board alone was not sufficient to ensure that the interests of Rootes would be safeguarded:

(v)   Chrysler will nominate a Rootes Director (British) to each of the Boards of Simca SA and Chrysler International SA, and it is understood that a Simca Director (French) will be nominated to the Board of Rootes.

Again, the utility of such a provision came to be doubted in subsequent years, both as a safeguard for British interests and as an efficient method of management; as a senior Ministry of Technology official said, 'British people should be involved in its operations on grounds of ability, not nationality.'[75]

The following three conditions, which may be summarised here, represented a new departure for the government. Chrysler undertook to leave at least 15 per cent of the Rootes equity in the hands of shareholders other than Chrysler, and the government requested its newly created agency, the Industrial Reorganisation Corporation, to take up this 15 per cent shareholding.[76] Chrysler agreed to accept one IRC nominee on the Rootes board as long as it owned the equity. The IRC complied with the government's request, and nominated one of its members,

207

Mr B. Boxall, to the Rootes board; there was a feeling, however, among IRC executives that the government's view of their function in this instance was political rather than managerial: 'It did no harm to Chrysler and the presence of the IRC didn't inhibit it ... IRC was there as an instrument of government policy in the first real attempt by the government to impose serious undertakings on a foreign company acquiring a British asset.' [77] Nevertheless, the IRC director on the Rootes board made it clear to Mr Wedgwood Benn that this job was to help the company succeed, and that he did not wish to discuss company affairs with the Ministry of Technology; for this reason Mr Wedgwood Benn later considered that government-nominated directors on the boards of foreign companies were 'not very relevant' to the problems of communication and control, and 'therefore this did not play as big a part as candidly at the beginning I thought it might play.' [78] At the time of the Chrysler take-over the participation of the IRC was seen by Mr Wedgwood Benn as reinforcing the assurances given by Chrysler:

> When one is considering the future of an industry and the possibility of rationalisation and a take-over by a big international company, it might follow, as a result of market changes, that decisions may be taken which might adversely affect the British element of the corporation. We have seen a vivid example in the case of the French computer industry. We felt that the British public should be represented through the IRC ... The assurances by the Chrysler Corporation are based entirely on best endeavours and lay down some criteria on which they can be judged. The participation of the IRC provides better security in this case than we had under the previous arrangements made with the Ford Motor Company. [79]

It is interesting to note that two of the assurances Ford gave in 1960 were not asked for in 1967 in the Chrysler deal; Ford had pledged to continue its policy of reinvesting a large proportion of its UK profits for future development (since the prospect of any profits in the Rootes case were exiguous, this omission is not surprising); Ford had also undertaken to obtain almost 100 per cent of its components in the UK, a provision which Mr Wedgwood Benn acknowledged as making a nonsense of European integration of production, and which therefore was not demanded of Chrysler.

Essentially the Labour Government was bowing to the inevitable when it consented take-over of Rootes; Rootes was already so enmeshed in Chrysler's world-wide marketing and technical development programmes that, if severed from them, it would not have been an attractive partner for a merger with one of the existing British-owned motor companies. For Chrysler the chief advantage af acquiring Rootes lay in the opportunity to challenge Ford and General Motors in the European vehicle market, which was expanding faster than the US home market; together with Simca, the acquisition of Rootes gave Chrysler 6 per cent of the European market. [80] For the British Government, Chrysler's ability to finance its re-equipment and losses with capital brought into the UK from outside saved Rootes from otherwise inevitable bankruptcy and maintained employment in the adverse conditions then being faced by the UK motor industry; and additional bonus was the access of Rootes products to Chrysler's world distribution network, which boosted exports from the UK. In general the balance of advantage lay decisively on the side of the British economy – it is somewhat difficult to discern any great benefits accruing to Chrysler as a result of its take-over of Rootes. One automotive expert commented in 1970:

> It will be interesting to see whether Chrysler in Europe can survive. Perhaps one of these days some offer will be more attractive to Chrysler management than the prospects of spending hundreds of millions each year for the privilege of staying where it is and not making any money.[81]

Certainly the Chrysler take-over of Rootes was welcomed by the financial press, which noted that it would provide Rootes with access to world markets and that Simca, Chrysler's French subsidiary, had the best export record among French motor manufacturers. *The Economist* considered that the assurances demanded of Chrysler by the government were 'ineffectual window-dressing ... a means of decently releasing Mr Wilson from his rash words opposing the original bid in June 1964.' [82] Indeed, it does seem that the policy of requiring public assurances from foreign companies acquiring British companies was recognised by the Labour Government as being of doubtful validity; after the Chrysler deal in January 1967 public assurances were requested on only one occasion, when the Dutch Philips group took over the Pye electronics company, later in January 1967.

5.6.3   Creation of a major British motor manufacturer

When the Labour Government came to power in 1964 there were four major vehicle manufacturing groups which were entirely British owned; by 1968 these had all been merged to form the British Leyland Motor Corporation (BLMC). While this was mainly the product of economic forces, the necessity of achieving maximum economies of scale in development, production and marketing, it was also actively encouraged by the government. When BMC took over the body manufacturer Pressed Steel Ltd in 1965, the government gave its approval and this was endorsed by the Monopolies Commisssion. [83] BMC had a high reputation for technical innovation, as well as being the largest single employer in the UK motor industry and a leading exporter; when it merged with Jaguar in 1966 to form British Motors (Holdings) it was widely regarded as the only British motor manufacturer with a good chance of survival, and as the obvious nucleus of a giant British-owned motor company:

> The new holding company looks very much as if it is designed to accommodate not only Jaguar, but anyone else disposed to think that 'united we stand' is not a bad motto for those of less than giant size in the British motor industry ... One hopes that this is merely the start of a snowballing series of rationalisations around a wholly British-owned group. [84]

The merger made BMH the fifth largest motor manufacturer in Europe (after Volkswagen, Ford, Fiat and General Motors), [85] and the largest in the UK; when Leyland took over Rover in December 1966, to form the third largest UK group (after BMH and Ford), the Labour Government began to initiate discussions through the IRC between BMH and Leyland to develop closer links with each other.

This initiative was a direct result of the Chrysler take-over of Rootes; the Labour Government considered that the presence of the three main American motor companies in the UK required the creation of a countervailing British-owned company in order to maintain a viable motor industry. In a sense the inability to extricate Rootes from the Chrysler network was the major stimulus to action, and Mr Wedgwood Benn made it clear when he approved the Chrysler take-over that unless the British-owned sector rationalised itself it would suffer the same fate as Rootes:

> I should like to announce a more general decision taken, arising from the full and detailed examination made into this matter. The government are convinced that the British-controlled firms would gain greatly if they could co-operate much more fully in overseas marketing arrangements. The Industrial Reorganisation Corporation has, therefore, also agreed to discuss with the British-controlled motor manufacturing firms the possibility of close co-ordination and co-operation between them in their efforts overseas ... We greatly welcome overseas investment in general, but we are bound to look at it

210

also in the light of the development of certain key industries in this country. [86]

Preliminary merger talks between BMH and Leyland began in the summer of 1967, with the Minister of Technology Mr Wedgwood Benn and Sir Frank Kearton of the IRC being involved from the beginning. The two companies had complementary qualities, since BMH was particularly strong in cars and light commercial vehicles, while Leyland was predominantly a heavy commercial vehicle producer. The major difficulty was that the government favoured a merger with what it considered to be the superior management of Leyland playing the major role, whereas BMC considered that its current poor market record (its UK market penetration had fallen from 44 per cent in 1966 to 29 per cent in 1967, and it made only a minute profit in 1967) was only temporary and the merger should be on equal terms. Sir Donald Stokes, Chairman of Leyland, threatened to make a take-over bid for BMH if it refused to consent to a merger, and the Government indicated that it would give him financial help to do so. [87] Eventually, in January 1968, a merger was agreed upon, and the British Leyland Motor Corporation was formed under the chairmanship of Sir Donald Stokes and with a £25 million loan (for seven years at $7\frac{1}{2}$ per cent) from the IRC 'to proceed with rationalisation and development as rapidly as both the national interest and the interest of the new company demand.' [88]

The effect of the merger was to create the seventh largest company in the UK (in terms of turnover 1968–9), and the UK's most important single exporter, with over 42 per cent of the UK market and assembly plants in over thirty countries. With a UK production of over one million vehicles in 1969, it was the largest producer in the UK (Ford came next with 850,000), and fourth largest in Europe. [89] *The Economist* commented:

> The group has the chance now to become a European General Motors; it does not stand out in terms of sheer turnover, but the range it offers is complete ... It will make the European subsidiaries of the big American companies think hard about their tactics. [90]

The government's interest in bringing about an integrated British-owned group, which could develop, produce and market vehicles on a world-wide scale, was a crucial factor in the creation of BLMC. Sir Donald Stokes considered that the Labour Government's intervention accelerated the deal by twelve months:

They offered helpful suggestions, from the Prime Minister downwards, and the IRC offered us a loan of £25 million at commercial rates provided we made a profit, which we accepted. It all acted as a sort of catalyst, getting it off the ground a bit quicker. [91]

For its part, the Labour Government was satisfied that the creation of BLMC would ensure a viable British-owned company which would act as a countervailing force against the presence of the three major American motor companies in the UK vehicle industry. Mr Wedgwood Benn made this clear:

Whereas there is a strong overlap of interests with national companies operating entirely or principally on a United Kingdom basis, this is not exactly the same in the case of international companies, only part of whose activities are based here ... It was for exactly this reason that the government, with the help of the Industrial Reorganisation Corporation, played a very significant part in bringing about the merger between Leyland and BMH. [92]

5.6.4   Creation of a favourable investment climate

Although the British Government had long been conscious of the ability of international motor companies to divert investment from the UK to other countries (indeed, one of the purposes behind the 1960 consent to the Ford deal was to prevent Ford's expansion programme being diverted to Germany from the UK), the increasing integration of production on a European scale by Ford, General Motors, and Chrysler widened their potential flexibility in considering where new investment was to be located. For this reason the Labour Government became more sensitive to the way in which the American car companies reached their investment decisions, and made positive attempts to improve the UK investment climate.

While Ford and General Motors had long co-ordinated the activities of their British and German subsidiaries (Vauxhall, for example, exported mainly to the Commonwealth and Opel to Europe and the USA), this co-ordination became more structured in the late 1960s. Ford had opened its first Belgian plants in 1964, intending them to participate in an exchange of components with both their British and German plants, and expressed great dissatisfaction when the Labour Government imposed a 15 per cent surcharge on all imports in November 1964 which seriously upset the economies of cross-frontier production. [93] In 1967 it established Ford of Europe, based in Warley near its main British plant, to co-ordinate development, production and marketing on a European basis — a decision

212

which was warmly welcomed by the British Government. Mrs Gwyneth Dunwoody, Parliamentary Secretary to the Board of Trade, spoke of it as a further indication of Ford's commitment to its UK operations, and as an attempt to increase British exports to Europe:

> The establishment of Ford of Europe means that the company is thinking in terms of Europe as a single market, and seeks to organise its activities in Europe as efficiently as possible. We should welcome this outlook and development. [94]

However, the Ford strategy would not inevitably benefit the UK; in part, it was designed to insulate the company from labour disputes, political disturbances or over-rapid wage-inflation in any one country. From 1967 onward models were standardised on a European basis (although all medium and heavy trucks were built in the UK), giving Ford considerable production and marketing flexibility; from 1969, with the introduction of the Capri (a car which was inspired by the success of the Mustang in the US, but shared no components with it), Ford was able to supply most export markets from either British, Belgian or German plants, subject only to the overall balancing of capacity. [95]

Although Britain was traditionally the site of Ford's major European production operations, the growth of the EEC markets and the establishment of Ford of Europe led to a declining dependence on Britain. In 1968−70, Ford's car production in Belgium rose rapidly from 381,000 to 681,000, while output in Britain remained at about 650,000. [96] The balance of investment also shifted to Europe, with Ford investing £42 million in Europe in 1969, as against £36 million in the UK. [97] The reason for this switch was not entirely the sluggish nature of the UK domestic market; the growing number of strikes in the UK motor industry, which caused Ford UK to lose almost 10 per cent of its output in the period 1968−70, was a major factor.

The rising number of strikes in the motor industry had for some time been a major concern Government; in 1965 the Minister of Labour, Mr Gunter, said:

> If there is one industry in the country at the present time that we want to see moving as efficiently, quietly and responsibly as any other it is the automobile industry, because it means so much to the economy. It is an industry which has been bedevilled by unofficial strikes. [98]

As a result the government set up a Royal Commission under Lord Donovan to examine the whole problem of industrial relations, and in January

1969 published a White Paper, 'In Place of Strife' [99] which recommended a compulsory 28-day conciliation period during which the Department of Employment and Productivity could order workers back to their jobs while negotiations proceeded. The major problem was that nearly three-quarters of all working days lost were the result of unofficial (and therefore unpredictable) strikes, and these were particularly serious in the motor industry because of its integrated structure. [100]

Perhaps the most striking examples of the damaging effect of unofficial strikes occurred in February 1969, when a strike of ten men in Vauxhall's plating works at Ellesmere Port (a new plant which GM had set up in a development area as a result of the Labour Government's investment incentive scheme) eventually halted almost all Vauxhall production. Several weeks later, in March 1969, a strike at Ford's Halewood plant (also a new plant in a development area) forced Ford to lay off all its workers and halt production in the UK for the first time in its history. Prime Minister Wilson strongly attacked the strikers:

> I must ask whether those responsible really care about the danger that in the Ford factories of Europe there may be a growing determination not to be dependent in future on British components whose delivery can be so frivolously imperilled. The danger is that companies will start hedging their bets against these unofficial and official strikes, hedging their bets by ensuring that future development will be concentrated abroad. [101]

Since the Labour Party's chief source of political and financial support derived from the trade unions, the concern which inspired this attack was very great indeed. The effects of the strike on Ford's European production were considerable; two thousand workers in Belgium were laid off after a week of the strike because of a shortage of British-made vehicle components, and Ford's UK management took the unprecedented step of attempting to obtain a High Court injunction to prevent the unions from continuing the strike in defiance of a wage agreement which had been negotiated and agreed upon by their representatives. [102] This attempt failed, but under strong government pressure the strike was settled on 19 March 1969, having lasted for three weeks. Ford had lost £30 million worth of production in the UK and £7 million worth in Germany and Belgium as a result of the strike, and the Chairman of Ford Europe, Mr Stanley Gillen, announced that Ford's long-term policy was to make its continental plants self-sufficient. [103] As a conciliatory gesture to Ford, the government announced that it would permit Ford to build a £20 million extension to its Dagenham plant, despite the fact that in the past Ford had only been permitted to expand in areas of high unemployment such as Merseyside and South Wales. [104]

Since attaining full ownership of the UK company in 1961, Ford had made substantial investment in its British plants for improvement and expansion, amounting to almost £300 million in the period 1961–70. (Its after-tax profits during the same period were £122 million, of which £53 million was repatriated). [105] Its return on capital employed took a sharp fall in 1965–6 (from 14 per cent the previous year to 5·4 per cent), but in 1966 the Labour Government had instituted a system of cash grants for capital investment, ranging from 20 per cent of expenditure in industrial areas to 40 per cent in 'development areas' which had high unemployment. This replaced a previous scheme of tax allowances, under which 20 per cent of the cost of new investment in plant machinery could be deducted from a firm's taxable income, which had begun in 1954. [106] Since the cash investment grant scheme provided immediate benefits without the need to generate sufficient profits against which to set off the investment, it had great attraction for companies which were suffering from declining profitability. In the case of Ford it ensured that its rate of investment was maintained in the UK, until the big strike of 1969.

After the 1969 strike, Ford not only began to divert more of its investment to the continent, but also began to sell off some of its equipment in the UK to Ford-Werke, its German subsidiary. The Parliamentary Select Committee on Public Accounts discovered that in 1969 Ford sold equipment to its German subsidiary for which it had received a government cash grant of £347,725 because it had been purchased for use in a UK development area. The sale was discovered by the Board of Trade when Ford UK claimed a further grant of £139,118 in respect of the equipment, and it was found that it had already been moved to Germany. [107] A Ford spokesman later commented: 'It was a misunderstanding which is now a matter of history. Repayment of the grant was made within the same financial year – 1969–70.' [108] Such misunderstandings perhaps illustrate the increased flexibility of Ford's investment plans, and the declining confidence of Ford in the UK investment climate, particularly after the proposed Industrial Relations Bill based on the 'In Place of Strife' White Paper was abandoned in June 1969 after strong pressure from the trade unions on the Labour Government.

The Minister of Technology, Mr Wedgwood Benn, repeatedly stressed that the major issue was not (as left-wing Labour MPs frequently alleged) a Machiavellian uprooting of UK production and transfer elsewhere, but the future prospects for expansion in the UK by Ford and other companies:

215

The rationalisation of design, engine and components supply and even export effort takes place across national frontiers — in some cases, as if they did not exist. This means that what happens here in terms of industrial relations and return on capital is taken into account by these companies in planning where and when their next capacity expansion should take place ... It means, for example, that continual unofficial stoppages could have a significant effect on the prospects for future job opportunity and living standards which may not be apparent to those concerned with a narrow issue on a short-term basis. [109]

The government went to great lengths to persuade the international companies that the UK investment climate was favourable; in February 1970, when Henry Ford II visited his UK plants (and was sharply questioned by shop stewards on rumours that Ford was to transfer all export production for the US to Germany), [110] he saw Mr Wedgwood Benn for an hour to discuss his UK investment plans, in what the Minister of Technology described as 'a sort of super summit meeting.' [111] At the meeting Mr Ford told the Minister that Ford US considered that its German-built cars were better for the US market because (although of identical design) both deliveries and quality of assembly were better than their British counterparts. [112] Although it was later announced that Ford UK would supply half the engines for the new Ford compact car in the US, the new Dagenham plant which was to supply them had already been started in 1969 (at a cost of £18 million — Ford's last big expansion scheme in the UK and the decision did not represent a renewed commitment by Ford to invest in the UK. [113] In October 1970 Ford flew out to Germany a die recovered from one of its strike-bound British suppliers in order to maintain production of components, [114] and in February 1971, during a prolonged strike at Ford UK which lost over £60 million worth of production, the Managing Director of Ford UK announced that the UK subsidiary had advised against the siting of a new £30 million engine plant in the UK, because of industrial unrest: 'The sad and simple fact is that there is no point in expansion until we can make use of the investments that we already have.' [115] When Henry Ford visited London in March 1971, he told Prime Minister Heath that unless labour relations and production quality and continuity improved, Ford would make no new investments in the UK. [116]

In this context it is interesting to examine Ford's internal strike record in comparison with that of the vehicle industry as a whole (although it should be remembered that strikes in component suppliers, such as those

216

in 1970, would also disrupt Ford production). This would seem to indicate that Ford's record of industrial disputes was double the average for the industry, although the wages agreement strike in 1969 (which lost over 560,000 working days) severely inflates the total and was predictable in the sense that it came when a wages agreement expired. Although strikes had only a marginal effect on Ford's exports (which were 60 per cent higher in 1970 than in 1968), because overtime working after the strikes made up for lost production, at somewhat greater cost, the disruption to other Ford plants abroad which depended on UK-manufactured components was considerable. During a visit to Manila in March 1971, Mr Ford told his Asian plant managers that 'what we have got to do is dissociate completely from the British source' because of labour disputes and rising costs. [117]

Table 5.9

Comparison of strikes in Ford and the UK motor industry, 1968–70
(Working days lost per 1000 employees)

	Ford	All UK vehicle industry
1968	2,134	1,800
1969	11,220	3,100
1970	988	2,150
Annual average 1968–70	4,781	2,350

Source: *Ministry of Labour Gazette*; *Employment and Productivity Gazette*

Although Ford's unhappy strike record in the UK was worse than average, Ford allegations that its British labour force were 25 per cent less productive than its German workers seem only partly justified. The key figures in assessing production efficiency are the assets employed per worker and the resulting value added by the company to the vehicle. On this test Ford UK obtained only three-quarters of the Ford Germany value-added figure, but employed under two-thirds the capital per worker, although productivity in Ford UK was higher than any other British vehicle manufacturer. [118]

Nevertheless, the sluggish UK domestic market and the rising number of industrial disputes did not make the UK investment climate in the period 1964–70 very attractive, and the Labour Government's investment incentives were not adequate compensation for these adverse factors.

Faced with the problem of deflating the economy and correcting the balance of payments deficit, the Labour Government was unable to make the investment climate more attractive, and relied in the motor industry on the American companies being trapped by their past involvement into devoting further capital to improve their deteriorating position. [119]

The Ford pattern was followed by both General Motors and Chrysler; increasing integration of European operations and faster expansion of production on the continent than in the UK, resulting in much greater flexibility in production and marketing. For some reason these developments did not attract as much attention in Parliament or the British press as did the Ford operation, perhaps because of the smaller size of GM and Chrysler's UK operations. General Motors' 1969 decision to site its new transmission plant in Strasbourg to supply both Vauxhall in Britain and Opel in Germany was scarcely noticed, and the *Financial Times* commented that 'there are few people who would argue that Britain was the ideal place to build cars.' [120]

5.6.5 *Establishing a dialogue between the government and the motor companies*

When the Ministry of Technology took over sponsorship of the British motor industry from the Board of Trade in 1966, there were only nine members of the Board of Trade engaged on problems concerned with the motor industry; [121] the staff were increased to seventeen, but there was a strong feeling in the industry that the government did not take sufficient notice of its problems. The result of this was the establishment in July 1967 of the Motor Manufacturing Economic Development Committee, one of twenty such industry committees under the aegis of the National Economic Development Office, which included representatives of government, management, and trade unions. [122] All three American-owned companies were represented by their managing directors or chairmen, and one of the first reports issued by the EDC was strongly critical of the way in which government economic policies used the UK vehicle market as an economic regulator, depressing domestic demand so that productive capacity was under-utilised and return on investment was uneconomic. [123] The government's reception of this was not effusive; a Ministry of Technology spokesman telling Parliament: 'None of us doubts that the motor industry requires a large and stable home market, but what we would want to argue about is how large is large and what is the degree of stability required.'[124] Although the trade union representatives on the EDC suggested in 1969 that the activities of the foreign-owned motor companies

218

should be investigated, this was not taken up. When the investment plans of the motor manufacturers were examined in 1969 for a three-year economic forecast for the industry, the three American-owned companies insisted that they be disclosed only to an independent accountant and aggregated before being placed before the committee. [125]

Because Ministry of Technology officials felt that the method of obtaining public assurances from foreign-owned motor companies (as in the Ford and Chrysler cases) was too rigid and prone to obsolescence, it was decided in 1969 to institute a series of dialogues with prominent international companies, including the American motor companies, in order to improve communications:

> We are beginning to establish a direct dialogue with international and multinational corporations that operate within the engineering industry in Britain ... Though there is a common interest here ... , the potential conflicts between the commercial interests of transnational corporations and British national interests cannot be overlooked. We have to see that, through a continuing dialogue, the British national interest is kept in the forefront and that consultation takes place over a whole range of issues that are of concern to us as well as to them. [126]

These dialogues (which took place with about a dozen companies, including all three American motor companies) took the form of a preliminary questionnaire sent to the company on its investment policy, expansion plans, export policy, degree of management devolution, transfer-pricing policy, balance of payments policy, employment practices, profits remission policy, and similar fields. This would be followed by a visit to the company's British headquarters by a team composed of the Minister of Technology and some of his junior ministers and senior civil servants, together with representatives of the Treasury and Board of Trade. The company concerned would make a presentation to them of their plans, and also ask questions of the government delegation if they wished. After such visits official contact would be maintained; 'Just as you have summit meetings between foreign ministers, and after that your ambassadors maintain daily contact', as Mr Wedgwood Benn put it. [127]

Although such dialogues were only commenced in 1969, and (on a formal level) were not continued after the defeat of the Labour Government in the June 1970 General Election, they did provide the Ministry of Technology with a great deal of useful information about the future plans of the motor companies in particular, and enabled the companies to appreciate the government's problems. In talks with Ford (and a summit meeting between Mr Wedgwood Benn and Mr Ford in February 1970), for example, the company's transfer-pricing policy in components was discussed, and its policy of balancing trade in components was criticised by Ministry of Technology officials. [128] In many respects these dialogues led to a change in attitude among government officials as to the motives of multinational companies, replacing a suspicion of malefaction with a conviction that purely negative restraints would not enable the UK to derive maximum benefit from the development of multinational companies:

> The ability to derive maximum benefit from a world dominated by multinational corporations depends on the kind of environment a government can create, not the restraints a government can place on multinational corporations. [129]

5.7 Conclusion

In essence, the Labour Government's policy toward the multinational companies in the UK motor industry manifested a constellation of xenophilic and xenopobic attitudes, which may be expressed thus:

(a) XENOPHILIC

(i) *Efficiency*: American motor companies provide their UK subsidiaries with access to financial, technical and managerial resources superior to, or more abundant than, those available to British-owned companies, and thus improve the efficiency of the motor industry.

(ii) *Employment*: They increase employment in the industry, and are willing to locate new plant in areas of high unemployment, because they are used to controlling geographically decentralised operations.

(iii) *Exports*: Because of their access to a world-wide marketing network, they can export at a lower cost than their British-owned competitors, who have to bear the entire cost of their overseas marketing alone, not as a member of a global group.

(b) XENOPHOBIC

(i) *Control*: Britain has three foreign-controlled motor companies which account for more than half of UK vehicle production, and therefore operates in a more international environment than any other major vehicle-producing country, with the exception of Canada. As these companies increasingly develop their products across national frontiers, they may rationalise their production in a manner inconsistent with British interests, by diverting investment or export business elsewhere, or producing only low-profit (and therefore low-tax) items in the UK.

(ii) *Competition*: It is essential to maintain a British company large enough to be internationally competitive and with a dominant share of the UK market, (so that its interest in a healthy British motor industry is firmly established by virtue of its leading position). The alternative to a viable British-owned unit would be acquisition of the most efficient sectors of the industry by the foreign-controlled companies, and elimination of the rest through competition. A viable British-owned motor company provides sufficient competition for the American companies to ensure that they act broadly in the national interest. This is particularly important in the motor industry, which is a key British industry in terms of employment, capital, and domestic and export sales.

On balance, the Labour government's attitude was broadly xenophilic with regard to the multinational motor companies, particularly after it appeared that the British Leyland merger was going to succeed. The multinationals during the period brought in more investment capital than they repatriated profits (in the case of Chrysler, it covered its subsidiary's operating losses as well), improved efficiency, created employment, and boosted exports; the Labour Government's preoccupation with the balance of payments enabled it to emphasise these factors more than any considerations of loss of economic sovereignty. Ford and Vauxhall were already fully owned by their American parent companies, and hence any investment by them was a bonus, especially in view of the effects of the government's deflationary economic policies; they needed to be seduced rather than cajoled. Chrysler was somewhat of a different case, since it did not have a track record in the UK, but it had improved the performance of Simca in France, and if it had not taken over Rootes, the British company would have gone bankrupt. The rest of the British motor industry was not moribund, but would not have been able to survive the American competition unless it rationalised itself; therefore the Labour Government gave it encouragement, moral and financial, to merge into one major company, the second-largest non-American vehicle producer in the world. [130]

Because the investment climate in the UK motor industry was not an attractive one during the Labour Government's term of office, the shift of emphasis from treaties of good behaviour and best endeavours (of which the 1967 Chrysler undertakings were the last example) to more constructive dialogues with the multinational car companies was perhaps not surprising, but it did represent a very real change in the government's attitude. If the roles of benefactor and suppliant were not completely reversed, the Labour Government did make a real attempt to establish better communications with the American car companies and to clarify their respective problems and objectives. The manner in which the dialogues of 1969–70 were conducted, reminiscent of diplomatic negotiations, is indicative of this change in attitude; the multinational motor manufacturers were being recognised as entities somewhat different from normal commercial concerns (and, indeed, their annual production figures were larger than those of many sovereign states). Although Mr Wedgwood Benn's fear that 'national governments, including our own, will be reduced to the status of parish councils in dealing with the large corporations which will span the world'[131] was somewhat of a millenic vision, the experience of the Labour Government in dealing with the UK motor industry did convince it that multinational companies were worthy of serious consideration, and that the problems and benefits engendered by their operations merited a more sophisticated approach than had hitherto been employed.

Notes

[1] Board of Trade *Report on the Census of Production 1963* HMSO 1969 Vol. 131, Table 1
[2] Society of Motor Manufacturers and Traders *The Motor Industry of Great Britain, 1970*, SMMT, London 1970 pp. 26, 150; Motor Manufacturing EDC *Economic Assessment to 1972* NEDO, London 1970 p. 4.
[3] William Plowden *The Motor Car and Politics* Bodley Head, London 1971, p. 173
[4] Motor Manufacturing EDC *The Effect of Government Economic Policy on the Motor Industry* NEDO, London 1968 p. 18
[5] Graham Turner *The Car Makers* Eyre & Spottiswoode, London 1963 p. 27
[6] George Maxcy and Aubrey Silberston *The Motor Industry* Allen & Unwin, London 1959 pp. 14–15
[7] ibid. p. 107
[8] Society of Motor Manufacturers and Traders Ltd *The Motor Industry of Great Britain 1970* SMMT, London 1970, p. 151
[9] Turner, op. cit., p. 31
[10] ibid., p. 77
[11] Maxcy and Silberston, op. cit., p. 33

[12]   SMMT, op. cit., p. 26

[13]   Turner, op. cit., p. 77

[14]   Quoted in Michael Z. Brooke and H. Lee Remmers *The Strategy of Multinational Enterprise* Longman London, 1970, p. 269

[15]   Quoted in *The Economist* 19 November 1960, p. 803

[16]   Section 9 of the Exchange Control Act 1947 provides that the Treasury must approve any sale of equity in a British company to a non-resident purchaser. In fact the Ford offer price was 50 per cent higher than in the pre-bid market quotation of the shares

[17]   *H.C. Deb*, vol. 630 (17 November 1960) col. 541

[18]   ibid., (21 November 1960) col. 768

[19]   ibid., cols. 769—70

[20]   Interview with the Rt Hon Douglas Jay, MP, 11 January 1971

[21]   *H.C. Deb.* vol. 630 (21 November 1960) col. 769

[22]   ibid., col. 770

[23]   ibid.

[24]   ibid., col. 827

[25]   ibid., col. 840

[26]   ibid., col. 891

[27]   ibid., cols. 893-901

[28]   *United Kingdom Balance of Payments 1970*: HMSO 1970, Table 4, p. 7

[29]   *The Economist* (London) 19 November 1960, pp. 803—4

[30]   Turner, op. cit., pp. 42—7

[31]   *The Times* 5 June 1964, p. 12

[32]   ibid., 8 June 1964, p. 5

[33]   ibid., 6 June 1964, p. 10

[34]   ibid., 8 June 1964, p. 5

[35]   *H.C, Deb.* vol. 696 (8 June 1964) col. 37

[36]   ibid., cols. 37—8, 41

[37]   ibid., vol. 699 (29 July 1964) col. 343

[38]   *UK Balance of Payments 1970* Table 4; *The Times 300 Leading Companies* London 1965

[39]   *The Times* London 1965

[40]   *The Economist* 1 August 1964, p. 488

[41]   see, for example, *The Times* 30 July 1964, p. 16

[42]   Maxcy and Silberston, op. cit. p. 200

[43]   ibid., p. 192

[44]   *UK Balance of Payments 1970* loc. cit.

[45]   John H. Dunning *Studies in International Investment* Allen & Unwin, London 1970, p. 272. Dunning's study shows that between 1957 and

1966 capital investment by US firms rose by two and a half times in the UK and by eight times in the EEC a complete reversal of pre-1957 trends

46   *The Motor Industry of Great Britain 1970*, p. 12
47   Motor Manufacturing EDC *The Effect of Government Economic Policy on the Motor Industry* NEDO 1968, p. 19
48   *H.C.Deb.* vol 795 (11 February 1970) col. 1274
49   Motor Manufacturing EDC op. cit., p. 19
50   *The National Plan* Cmnd. 2764 (1965) p. 107; *H.C. Deb.* vol. 795 (11 February 1970) col. 1275
51   Motor Manufacturing EDC op. cit., p. 18
52   *H.C. Deb.* vol. 720 (9 November 1965) Cols. 82–8
53   *The Times* London 31 August 1965, p. 13
54   Figures computed from company annual reports for 1965–66
55   Figures derived from company accounts and *The United Kingdom Balance of Payments 1970* p. 7
56   Motor Manufacturing EDC, op. cit., p. 30
57   *H.C. Deb.* vol. 774 (27 November 1968) col. 491
58   *The Economist* 3 October 1964, p. 67
59   *The Times* 16 December 1965, p. 16
60   *The Economist* 11 September 1965, p. 1026
61   *The Times* 13 December 1965, p. 13
62   *The Economist* 10 December 1966, p. 1165
63   Interview with the Rt Hon A.N. Wedgwood Benn, MP 2 December 1970
64   *H.C. Deb.* vol. 739 (17 January 1967) cols. 35–9
65   Interview with the Rt Hon A.N. Wedgwood Benn, MP
66   *H.C. Deb.* vol. 739 (17 January 1967) col. 40
67   ibid., cols. 45–6
68   Wedgwood Benn interview, loc. cit.
69   *H.C. Deb.* vol. 630 (22 November 1960) col. 769
70   ibid., col. 771
71   *The Motor Industry of Great Britain 1970* pp. 19, 26
72   sec section (i) above
73   Interview with a Department of Trade and Industry official, 12 January 1971
74   Wedgwood Benn interview, loc. cit.
75   Interview with a senior Ministry of Technology official 22 December 1970
76   Industrial Reorganisation Corporation *Report and Accounts 1967–8* p. 19

[77] Interview with an IRC executive 28 October 1970
[78] Wedgwood Benn interview, loc. cit.
[79] *H.C. Deb.* vol. 739 (17 January 1967) cols. 42–3
[80] George H. Wierzynski 'The battle for the european auto market' *Fortune* September 1968
[81] J. Wilner Sundelson 'U.S. automotive investments abroad', in Charles P. Kindleberger (ed.) *The International Corporation* M.I.T. Press, Cambridge, Mass 1970, p. 271
[82] *The Economist* 21 January 1967, pp. 239–40
[83] ibid., 31 July 1965, p. 458
[84] ibid., 16 July 1966, p. 277
[85] *The Times* 12 July 1966, p. 1
[86] *H.C. Deb.* vol. 739 (17 January 1967) cols. 36, 41
[87] Interview with an IRC executive, 25 November 1970
[88] IRC *Report and Accounts* 1967–8, p. 21
[89] SMMT, op. cit., pp. 29–31
[90] *The Economist* 20 January 1968, p. 60
[91] Quoted in William Davis *Merger Mania* Constable, London 1970 p. 99. The Prime Minister had in fact invited the chairmen of both companies to dinner in September 1967
[92] *H.C. Deb.* vol. 798 (23 March 1970) cols. 1289–90
[93] *The Economist* 14 November 1964, p. 742
[94] *H.C. Deb.* vol. 757 (29 January 1968) col. 1059
[95] *Financial Times* 27 July 1970, p. 17
[96] SMMT, op. cit., pp. 29–31
[97] *Financial Times* 25 February 1971, p. 20
[98] *H.C. Deb.* vol. 720 (9 November 1965) col. 305
[99] Cmnd. 3888
[100] *H.C. Deb.* vol. 779 (3 March 1969) col. 49
[101] *The Times* 15 March 1969, p. 10
[102] ibid., 7 March 1969, p. 1
[103] ibid., 17 March 1969, p. 17
[104] *H.C. Deb.* vol. 780 (27 March 1969) col. 356
[105] Address by Mr William Batty, Managing Director of Ford UK to the American Chamber of Commerce in London, 23 June 1970
[106] Board of Trade *Investment Grants*, 1968, p. 8
[107] Select Committee on Public Accounts *Third Report* (1969–70 Session) para. 24
[108] *The Times* 17 March 1971, p. 19
[109] *H.C. Deb.* vol. 798 (23 March 1970) col. 1289
[110] *The Times* 27 February 1970, p. 17

[111] Wedgwood Benn interview, loc. cit.

[112] *The Times* 16 March 1971, p. 1

[113] ibid.

[114] *Christian Science Monitor* 10 October 1970, p. 10

[115] *The Times* 23 February 1971, p. 13

[116] ibid., 16 March 1971, p. 1

[117] ibid., 3 March 1971, p. 15

[118] *The Sunday Times* 28 February 1971, p. 45

[119] Louis Turner *Invisible Empires* Hamish Hamilton, London 1970, p. 91

[120] *Financial Times* 27 July 1970, p. 17

[121] *H.C. Deb.* vol. 736 (22 November 1966) col. 1120

[122] National Economic Development Office *EDC Activity Report 1969* p. 13

[123] Motor Manufacturing EDC *The Effect of Government Economic Policy on the Motor Industry* NEDO, London 1968, p. 18

[124] *H.C. Deb.* vol. 786 (9 July 1969) col. 1342 (Mr Gerald Fowler)

[125] Interview with a NEDO official, 8 December 1970

[126] A.N. Wedgwood Benn 'A message from the Minister to the staff' *Mintech Review* September 1969, pp. 3—4

[127] Wedgwood Benn interview, loc. cit.

[128] Interview with a senior Ministry of Technology official, 5 December 1970

[129] ibid.

[130] 'The Fortune Directory of the 200 largest industrials outside the US' *Fortune* August 1970, p. 143

[131] *H.C. Deb.* vol. 774 (27 November 1968) col. 493

6 The Labour Government and the UK Computer Industry

'There is no problem in the computer business which could not be solved by the demise of IBM.'
    – Mr Arthur Humphreys, Managing Director ICL, 4 February 1970

'To fail to produce an indigenous industry would expose the country to the possibilities that industrial, commercial, strategic or political decisions made in America could heavily influence our ability to manufacture, to trade, to govern or to defend.'
    – Ministry of Technology memorandum on the UK Computer Industry, March 1970.

6.1   Introduction

Almost all the politicians and civil servants interviewed for this study cited the computer industry as a key industry in which the national interest required a viable British-owned component; indeed, the government-sponsored amalgamation of the three major British-owned computer manufacturers into one company, International Computers (ICL), was stressed as one of the Labour Government's greatest successes in the 1970 General Election campaign.[1] The Labour Party had in its 1964 election campaign stressed the need to harness 'the white heat of the Technological revolution' to achieve increased efficiency in the British economy, and the computer industry was singled out as one of the key sponsorship functions of the new Ministry of Technology when it was created in November 1964.[2] In its policy of bringing advanced technology and new processes into British industry, the computer industry was something of a talisman for the Labour Government; it represented a new, dynamic industry whose products would in the future have a profound effect on every aspect of economic and social activity in Britain.[3]

For this reason the Labour Government considered the computer industry to be one of the 'commanding heights' industries, not by reason of its present size, but because of its future growth potential in a field which epitomised the industrial application of advanced technology. It was also an industry in which over half the UK market was controlled by American-owned companies, predominantly IBM with 40 per cent of the market (by value) in 1964, with the four British-owned computer companies together accounting for 41 per cent.[4] Because of IBM's dominance of the world computer market (with a market share of over 60 per cent since the mid fifties) and its self-proclaimed status as a multinational company operating in the field of advanced technology, the UK computer industry provides an ideal subject for a case-study of the Labour Government's attitudes toward multinational companies. If the computer industry was considered the epitome of a key industry in terms of its political, strategic, economic and social implications, then IBM, with plants in thirteen countries around the world (all controlled by the American parent) was the paradigm of a multinational company, conducting its operations on a global scale which could not accord individual national interests first priority.[5] The ambivalence of the Labour Government toward multinational companies (and IBM in particular) may be seen in these two extracts from speeches by Prime Minister Wilson, who during his term of office made advanced technology something of a leitmotiv. In a speech to the English-Speaking Union in 1966 he said:

> Americans, because they are friends, should understand that however much new American investment is welcomed when it brings a wider market and benefits of new techniques, no one on either side of the channel wants to see capital investment in Europe involve domination.[6]

Later, in his celebrated Guildhall speech proposing a European Technological Community, he said:

> There is no future for Europe, or for Britain, if we allow American Business ... so to dominate the strategic growth industries of our individual countries, that they, and not we, are able to determine the pace and direction of Europe's industrial advance, that we are left in industrial terms as the hewers of wood and drawers of water while they, because of the scale of research, development and production which they deploy, based on the vast size of their single market, come to enjoy a growing monopoly in the production of the technological instruments of industrial advance ... This is the road not to partnership but to an industrial helotry, which, as night follows day, will mean a declining influence in world affairs, for all of us in Europe.[7]

Essentially, this agreement, applied to the UK computer industry, ran as follows: IBM dominates the world computer industry, and can, because of its oligopolistic position in computer technology, choose whether or not to develop, produce and/or market its computers in the UK unless it is confronted with sufficient competition from the British-owned computer companies that it is forced to maintain an adequate level of transfer of technology from its American headquarters to its UK subsidiary in order to preserve its market position. In order to provide credible competition to IBM, the British computer companies had to have firstly an adequate market for their computers, and secondly, government aid for their research and development programmes in order to offset the advantage accruing to IBM and other American computer firms from their large home markets and federally-founded research contracts. In computer production the costs of developing third generation computers (i.e. using solid-state electronics, including microcircuits) were very high – IBM spent almost five billion dollars between 1964 and 1967 on developing and marketing its 360 range of computers, approximately ten times the total value of the largest British computer producer ICT's gross sales for the period[8] – and the penalties for not being in the technological forefront were equally high. Christopher Layton has commented:

> The company which is first or at least close second in the field makes the highest monopoly profits. Those which follow, say by buying the technology, only come into the market in time to see competition bring down prices and cut profit margins; by the time the market has stabilised, a new product may be ousting the old ... Time thus places a premium on internal innovation in a company, and on carrying out that innovation fast.[9]

The Labour Government therefore had three main objectives: firstly, to secure an adequate market for the British-owned computer companies by encouraging or requiring the purchase of British-made computers; secondly, to provide sufficient funds for research and development programmes by those companies to enable them to keep abreast of technological developments; and thirdly, to encourage further rationalisation in the British-owned sector of the computer industry in order to ensure its long-term viability and international competitiveness. This case study will examine each of these objectives in order to assess the degree to which they were achieved.

6.2 Purchase of British computers

Although the previous Conservative Government had implicitly followed a 'Buy British' policy in purchasing computers for use in government departments (only nine of the eighty-two computers in use in government departments as of July 1964 were American),[10] the Labour Government was the first to explicitly encourage the purchase of British-made computers not only by central government, but also by local government, and the private sector. There were two reasons for this; firstly, the need to reduce the UK's trade deficit in computers (over £11 million in 1965),[11] which caused Mr George Brown, the First Secretary of State to 'call for immediate action to improve the present balance of trade in electronics. Improvement here must be a first consideration.'[12]; secondly, to protect the British-owned computer industry and enable it to have a sufficiently large home market to enable it to export competitively and finance research and development from sales as far as possible.

On 1 March 1965 the then Minister of Technology, Mr Frank Cousins, outlined the Labour Government's computer policy, saying that 'a flourishing British computer industry is vital to the economic well-being of this country', and announcing a four-point plan to create a healthy British computer industry and promote the rapid increase of computer techniques in British industry and commerce. The plan included a review of the computer requirements of central government (including the universities), a total of £7 million for various research programmes, a possible national computer programme library and, most significant in this context, a Computer Advisory Service to be run by the Ministry of Technology to advise on requirements throughout the public sector.[13] The predecessor of the Computer advisory Service, the Treasury's Technical Support Unit, had only advised government, and the rest of the public sector had been free to make its own choice between available equipment, with the result that about 40 per cent of the computer installations in the rest of the public sector were foreign in 1964.[14] In particular the universities, which hitherto had been attracted by the substantial educational discounts offered by IBM, were told by the Ministry of Technology that finance would only be forthcoming after 1965 if the computers ordered were British.[15]

The government's chief difficulty lay in deciding what constituted a 'British' computer: Mr Cousins told the House of Commons in December 1965 that: 'I regard an independent British computer industry as consisting of firms whose policies in respect of production, research and development are determined in this country.[16] He named as major constituents of the independent British computer industry International Computers

230

and Tabulators (ICT), English Electric—Leo—Marconi (EELM), Elliott—Automation, and Ferranti; but in fact none of these firms was independent of foreign technology — ICT and EELM produced several computers under licence from RCA, Ferranti had developed much of its technology in conjunction with Hewlett Packard, and Elliott—Automation produced NCR-designed computors.[17] In addition, four major American computer firms (IBM, Honeywell, Burroughs and NCR) had production facilities in the UK for producing part of their computers, and a substantial part of the development of IBM's 360 range of computers was carried out in its UK research laboratory.[18] In February 1965, IBM announced that it would centre all production of its smallest computer, the 1130, for non-US markets in its plant at Greenock in Scotland, which would increase its exports by £9 million a year, and pointed out that it had been a net exporter since it had begun operations in the UK in 1955.[19]

Essentially the Labour Government had to resolve how to gain maximum advantage of international developments in the computer field, and yet maintain a viable British-owned computer industry: Mr Cousins told a meeting of British computer experts in November 1965: 'The government are not prepared to see British industry dependent technologically on foreign industry, subject to techniques suitable to foreign conditions and perhaps made available to Britain a stage later.'[20] The Flowers Committee, which had been set up to report to the government on the use of computers in research, advised in its January 1966 report that British-made machines should be used 'wherever possible'.[21] The new Minister of Technology, Mr Anthony Wedgwood Benn, outlined the Labour Government's purchasing policy:

> Machines made in Britain by subsidiaries of foreign firms are regarded in this context as British. Of the 44 computers [ordered by the government since October 1964], 33 have been British; 31 of these were purchased because, taking all considerations into account, they were the most competitive, and two were given a measure of preference.[22]

The criteria for purchase of British computers were developed by the Ministry of Technology during 1966, and although not made public until 1968, were as follows:

1   Suitability for application
2   Price (see below)
3   Performance
4   Delivery date and success in achieving prompt delivery

5   Efficient performance on previous contracts
6   Compatibility with existing equipment

Provided British-made computers satisfied these requirements in relation to their foreign competitors, they would be given preference in public sector contracts. [23] On the question of price, however, several American companies, in particular IBM, alleged that British-owned companies were given computer orders provided that the price for the equipment was no more than 25 per cent dearer than the equivalent foreign product. [24] The Labour Government never commented on these allegations, but they were repeated by the Chairmen of both IBM and Honeywell's UK subsidiaries early in 1970. [25] The existence of such price discrimination was, however, confirmed by the Conservative Government in 1971, when the Minister for Industry, Sir John Eden, told a Parliamentary Select Committee on Science and Technology that the policy was being discontinued:

> We feel it is unnecessary to continue for computers made in Britain a price preference which in fact played no part in practice in enabling British firms to win government contracts. Because the prices of British made machines have proved to be fully comparative we see no point in continuing that. [26]

The statement that the price preference had never worked to the advantage of British computer firms was not strictly correct; in 1969, to cite one example, ICL was awarded a contract for the London Airport Cargo Scheme (LACES), although the equipment it offered was based on RCA designs, with over 50 per cent imported components, and considerably more expensive than the equivalent IBM installation.[27]

Although attempts were made to define what constituted a 'British' computer, by using criteria such as the ownership of the company, the country in which it was designed, and the proportion of components and value added to the hardware accounted for by UK production, the Ministry of Technology found that it was unable to distinguish between British and non-British companies, but only between British and non-British computers. Mr Ieuan Maddock, Controller of Industrial Technology at the Ministry of Technology, stated in April 1970:

> There are American companies which make a very considerable part of the totality of computers in this country and there are British computer companies which import a large proportion of their components. Therefore, it is very difficult to say what is a British computer company ... This is a matter of judgment. We look not only at the company, but the particular products of the company. In some

cases the company imports the products entirely, although they may have other products which are made almost entirely in this country. Therefore, we classify by products as well as by company. [28]

These classifications were circulated to relevant bodies in the public sector, and if any such body wished to purchase a computer which was not classified as British, it would have to apply to the Ministry of Technology for authorisation. [29] The confidential nature of this classification, and the vague character of the published criteria meant that frequently American computer companies tendered for government contracts with no clear idea as to whether or not they had any chance of success when the 'British computer' criteria were applied, causing the managing director of IBM's UK subsidiary to complain of a 'waste of manpower and resources' in cases where 'we have been invited to tender when the issue has been prejudged.' [30] The chairman of Honeywell UK Mr L.R. Price, considered that this company's failure to gain more than a quarter of their share of the public sector market (related to their share of the private market) in competitive tender, despite the fact that three-quarters of the cost of its computers was accounted for by UK production, seriously damaged Honeywell's chances of gaining export orders in public sector markets in Europe. [31]

To counter such dissatisfaction, the Labour Government announced in 1968, in the White Paper on the Computers Merger Project (which merged the major British-owned computer companies to form ICL) that it intended to place orders for large computer systems with ICL by single tender, i.e. other companies would not be invited to submit tenders. [32] The result of this was that between April 1968 and March 1970, of the £27 million worth of computers ordered by the central government, 68 per cent were ordered from ICL, and over two-thirds of these were by single tender. [33] Since the central government (including the public corporations and universities whose computer purchasing it ultimately controlled) was the largest single purchaser of computers in the UK market, accounting for over 30 per cent of the market in the period 1964–8, [34] this support of the indigenous computer industry was very significant. Table 6.1 indicates the disparity between the British-owned computer companies' share of the public sector market and of the private sector, and compares this with the performance of the foreign-controlled computer companies.

The comparison of private and public sector market shares controlled by the various companies is very interesting because it indicates the success of the Labour Government's operation of a 'Buy British' policy in the

Table 6.1

Manufacturers' shares of UK computer market by value, 1964–69

Manufacturer	Sector	Market share per cent					
		1964	1965	1966	1967	1968	1969
ICL (including ICT, English Electric)	Central government	69·2	37·9	41·6	39·5	51·2	69·2
	Local government	51·2	50·4	50·4	52·2	55·5	81·1
	Public corps	35·7	35·5	53·5	34·6	59·4	75·6
	Total public	53·8	39·0	47·0	40·2	55·2	73·2
	Private	34·6	29·1	28·4	28·5	33·6	39·9
	Total market	41·4	32·0	34·4	32·4	41·0	49·4
Other British	Central government	0·7	7·4	1·7	2·5	1·4	5·7
	Local government	0	0	0·5	0	0	0·7
	Public corps	3·6	7·5	1·4	0·2	2·1	7·4
	Total public	1·7	6·2	1·3	1·2	1·7	5·6
	Private	0·8	1·2	0·9	0·4	0·6	1·9
	Total market	1·1	2·5	1·1	0·7	0·9	2·9

Table 6.1 continued

IBM						
Central government	21·1	19·3	31·6	25·4	12·7	12·1
Local government	17·5	12·7	36·7	21·6	24·5	3·3
Public corps	47·9	30·9	29·6	51·3	1·5	7·9
Total public	31·1	23·1	32·6	34·0	9·6	9·4
Private	44·5	39·9	48·5	46·8	30·6	35·0
Total Market	40·0	35·1	43·2	42·5	23·4	27·7
Other US						
Central government	9·1	34·2	25·2	32·6	34·5	13·0
Local government	31·1	35·0	12·0	26·2	20·0	14·6
Public corps	11·7	25·0	15·4	14·0	37·2	9·2
Total public	13·0	30·4	19·1	24·6	33·5	11·8
Private	18·4	26·7	21·2	21·0	33·5	22·6
Total market	16·3	27·7	20·7	22·3	33·5	19·5

Source: Percentages calculated from Ministry of Technology figures in *U.K. Computer Industry* vol. II pp. 6–8; Select Committee on Science and Technology (Sub-Committee A) *Minutes of Evidence* (Session 1970–71) pp. 26–9

public sector. Although the central government's control over capital expenditure by local government and public corporations (included with central government in the public sector portion of the Table) was not as complete as its control over expenditure by the various departments of central government, being limited to persuasion and the possibility of reduced financial aid in the future, it did seem to be increasingly effective in favouring ICL and its two antecedent companies, ICT and EELM (which merged in 1968 to form ICL). From 1965 onwards, ICL's share of the public sector market showed a marked increase (from 39 per cent in 1965 to 73 per cent in 1969), much greater than the increase in its share of the private sector market, which rose from 29 per cent in 1965 to 40 per cent in 1969. This increase was at the expense of the American-owned computer companies (whose share of the public sector market fell from almost 54 per cent in 1965 to 21 per cent in 1969), and in particular it marked a swing away from IBM, whose share of the public sector market fell from 23 per cent in 1965 to 9 per cent in 1969. With the exception of 1969, the year in which the Government's policy of obtaining computers from ICL by single tender took full effect, the other US-owned companies (excluding IBM) had a share of the public sector market which was similar to their market share in the private sector, whereas IBM's share of the public sector market during the period was only half its share of the private sector market.

The difference may be partially explained by the more specialised character of the non-IBM American computers (Burroughs, for example, specialised in financial accounting computer systems, and Control Data marketed high-capacity computers for scientific uses, while IBM's main strength lay in general data processing, which was also ICL's chief objective), but the figures do seem to bear out IBM's allegations that the Labour Government consistently discriminated against it. Out of 160 computer installations ordered in the public sector from October 1964 to June 1970, IBM provided seven, largely where no British machine was available. [35] The result of this policy of favouring British-owned computer firms was that the UK was by 1969 the only major European market in which IBM accounted for less than 50 per cent of the numbers of computers installed; in Germany its share was 57 per cent, in France 66 per cent, In Benelux 52 per cent, and in the UK 30 per cent. [36]

As the largest single purchaser of computers in the UK, the government was therefore able to provide to some degree a protected market for British-owned computer firms, and its policy of favouring British-made computers was successful in boosting the British-owned computers firms' market share. It was able to do this because the UK market for computers was sufficiently large and possessed a high growth rate, making it an attractive market for foreign-owned computer firms. In 1964 the UK had less computers per head of the working population than the US and all of Western Europe (except Austria),[37] and during the period 1964–69 the UK market grew at an average rate of 30 per cent a year, in comparison with a growth rate of 25 per cent for the US during the same period.[38] Consequently the UK market was potentially profitable for American-owned computer firms, even discounting the pro-British bias in the public sector, and contained sufficient British-controlled competition to ensure that the latest and most sophisticated American computer systems were marketed there at competitive prices. The government was therefore able to protect the British-owned computer firms without cutting the UK off from access to advanced computer technology.

Nevertheless, the policy of favouring British-made computer for public sector purchase was not completely successful. Firstly, it was never very explicit; the 1965 declaration by the Labour Government that it would support the British computer industry seemed to indicate that public sector purchases would be made from British-owned computer firms; in 1966 the definition of a 'British' computer was widened to include computers made in the UK by subsidiaries of foreign firms, but the list of computer models which were regarded as 'British' was never made public, and in practice foreign-controlled computer firms were not awarded contracts unless the British-controlled computer firms were unable to provide a suitable installation, even if such an installation was developed from American licences, and contained more than 50 per cent imported components. This reinforced the suspicion on the part of the American-owned computer firms that there was prejudice against them when they were invited to tender for contracts in the public sector: the chairman of Honeywell UK stated in March 1970:

> We think that the government's procurement policy is that it will give an equal opportunity to companies that are manufacturing computers in this country. We think that this is a stated policy of the government. What we do not see is the implementation of the policy.[39]

This frustration experienced by the American-controlled computer firms may have prompted the Labour Government to abandon the practice of competitive tenders for public sector computer contracts and replace it with a single-tender policy which openly favoured British-controlled ICL, but it never attained the formality of the US Government's 'Buy American' regulations. The rationale for an informal government procurement policy was that it was more flexible than published specific criteria could be; as Dr Jeremy Bray told the House of Commons, 'this is not a simple matter ... a precise formula is not appropriate.' [40] The reason why a precise formula would not be appropriate may be seen in the difficulty of favouring British-owned computer firms when their computers contained perhaps more imported technology and components than those of some American-owned computer firms, and their advantages in terms of price, performance or delivery were by no means decisive. The possibility of obtaining public sector contracts if the computer model was regarded as 'British' was an incentive for the American firms to increase the British content in their computers, which would no longer have existed if the Labour Government had explicitly stated that it would only purchase computers from British-controlled firms; the tensions engendered by an implicit preference for the British firms were considered to be outweighed by the advantages of such a flexible computer procurement policy.

The second aim of the Labour Government's computer procurement policy, to prevent deterioriation in the balance of trade in computers, was not so successful, as the following table indicates.

Table 6.2

UK trade in computers, 1965–70

(including peripheral equipment, parts and accessories), £ million

	1965	1966	1967	1968	1969	1970*
Imports	18·6	35·9	56·5	74·8	97·5	110·0
Exports and re-exports	7·2	15·0	37·8	47·6	56·8	51·8
Visible trade balance	−11·4	−20·9	−18·7	−27·2	−40·7	−− 58·2

* 9 months to 30 September 1970

Source: *U.K. Computer Industry* vol. I, p. 355; Subcommittee A *Minutes of evidence* (Session 1970–71) p. 30

Although the Labour Government's computer procurement policy may have prevented imports on computers from rising as much as they might have it had purchased more American computers for the public sector, it seems that its procurement policy had little effect on purchases by the private sector, which accounted for the six-fold increase in computer imports during the period 1965–70. Indeed, some MP's criticised the government's procurement policy as a means of cushioning the British computer firms from the consequences of their inefficiency and backwardness, and being more concerned with the origin of hardware rather than the benefits it could confer. Peter Hordern, a Conservative MP, stated in 1966:

> By insisting, where they can, on forcing organisations to buy British, the government are running the risk of depriving the research establishments, the nationalised industries and the rest of industry of the opportunity of applying new techniques efficiently ... It is the benefits that flow from the computers, not the labels they bear, that matter. [41]

The Labour Government's computer procurement policy was in some respects preoccupied with hardware, rather than the software (programming) element of data processing, which constitutes about 50 per cent of the cost of installation of a complete computer system. [42] In the case of the 1969 London Airport Cargo project (LACES), for example, the Post Office awarded the hardware contract to ICL, and the software contract to an American company, without inviting British software houses to tender for the software portion of the contract. [43] Since software production is dependent more on brain-power than massive capital investment, it is perhaps surprising that the Labour Government did not extend its support to an area where British-owned firms had a better chance of competing against much larger American firms; the Conservative Government announced in 1971 that it would remedy this by contracting software projects out to British software firms. [44]

6.3 Government support for research and development in the UK computer industry

The Labour Government was quick to recognise that a 'Buy British' policy was not by itself sufficient to ensure a viable independent British computer industry; in March 1965 Mr Frank Cousins, the Minister of Technology, announced that the government was to spend £2 million on research by universities and other bodies into advanced computer technology, and that the National Research Development Corporation would grant ICT £5 million to develop its 1900 series of computers. [45] The research grant to ICT was particularly important, since it was the first major government grant to a computer manufacturer; hitherto grants had been made largely to non-commercial bodies for pure research, rather than commercial development. The reason for this change was the research-intensive nature of the computer industry (where the ratio of research and development expenditure to capital investment was $2:1$ as against $1:2\frac{1}{2}$ for manufacturing industry as a whole),[46] and the problem faced by the British computer firms in attempting to remain technologically competitive *vis-à-vis* their American rivals, while having to amortise their R and D costs over an increasingly short model life from sales which were much smaller than their American competitors. The government's Central Advisory Council for Science and Technology expressed the problem succinctly in its 1968 report:

> If the R and D expenditure is maintained at the level necessary for them to be able to compete technologically with the world at large, it is then too great to be recouped from sales unless export markets far larger than the domestic market can be secured. On the other hand, if it is held down to the level where it could be recouped from domestic sales, the technological competitiveness is then insufficient to prevent foreign imports from taking over much of the domestic market.[47]

In the absence of a domestic market as large as that available to the American computer firms, the British computer firms were in urgent need of capital to develop their ranges of third-generation computers. As was noted above, IBM spent almost $5 billion between 1964 and 1967 on developing and marketing its 360 range of computers, almost ten times the value of ICT's gross sales for the period. An OECD report[48] estimated that in 1965 R and D expenditure in the UK computer industry represented about 18 per cent of the value of UK production, compared with 15 per cent for the US and Japan, 12·per cent for France and 10 per cent for Germany. The large and unified American home market (which was worth £730 million in 1965, compared to £60 million for the UK)[49] meant that American companies were able to devote over ten times as much R and D as their British competitors, even though their expenditure represented a lower percentage of their gross sales than was the case for the UK industry.

Although there had been some government aid to the UK computer industry since 1963 (under the Advanced Computer Technology Project — ACTP — which paid half the cost of contracts for work on promising developments, in return for a levy on sales of successful end products[50] the £5 million development contract for ICT which the Labour Government announced in March 1965 was at that time the largest single government grant to the UK computer industry ever made.[51] Whereas in 1965 the US Government spent $300 million on computer R and D, half of it in industry, the total UK Government expenditure on computer R and D up to June 1968 from the early forties was only £11·6 million, of which one third had been made available since 1964. The US Government in 1965 accounted for nearly a third of the US computer industry's total R and D on computers ($500 million), and of this $100 million went to IBM. [52] In contrast, the UK Government's expenditure on computer R and D in 1965 was £120,000, about 1 per cent of the total R and D expenditure of the UK computer industry for that year. [53]

Until the formation of ICL in 1968, the bulk of government R and D grants went not to the computer firms themselves, but to government-sponsored research bodies, which contracted out some work to the computer firms; as a result of the Minister of Technology's statement of policy on the computer industry in March 1965, four bodies were set up to handle research in computers, in addition to the existing ACTP programme: the Science Research Council sponsored university computer projects; the National Computing Centre carried out education and training in the use of computers and promoted standardisation of programmes; the Aldermaston Project for the Application to Computers to Engineering sponsored process-control computer applications; and the Computer Aided Design Centre sponsored development of computer aided design techniques in industry. [54] However, all these projects were peripheral to the major problem of the UK computer firms, which faced the problem of financing increasingly costly research programmes from a turnover which was far smaller than most of the American companies (in 1965, £55 million for ICT and £12 million for EELM, compared with £3·5 billion for IBM).[55]

The 1968 report of the Central Advisory Council for Science and Technology stressed the importance of market awareness in successful technological innovation, and criticised the tendency for most government R and D finance going into government research establishments which 'leaves the R and D man outside the control of dynamic and commercially motivated management.' [56] The problem for the Labour Government was that aid for R and D could not be separated from the question of rationalising the British-controlled sector of the computer industry in order to provide that dynamic and commercially motivated management; as *The Economist* commented:

> If we want a native computer industry, and since it is at the heart of the current industrial revolution, it is reasonable to assume we do, then it is the efficiency of the companies that needs sponsoring, even

more than their designs. How many separate companies will the British market support? [57]

In granting £5 million (spread over four years) to ICT in 1965, the Labour Government had implicitly recognised ICT as the nucleus of the British-controlled computer industry, and it did not make any further large grants until ICL was formed in 1968 out of ICT and EELM (see the following section on rationalisation of the UK computer industry). The table indicates the trend of government expenditure on R and D in the computer industry.

The increase in government R and D funds for the UK industry after the formation of ICL in 1968 was designed to enable the new company to overcome the technical incompatibilities arising from the merger, rather than to underwrite the whole of the new company's R and D programme; Mr Wedgwood Benn made this clear when he told the Select Committee on Science and Technology that 'broadly speaking we gave support in the form of research and development. But it was conceived as the requirement necessary to bring [ICL] into being.' [58] There was no attempt to emulate the US Government's massive R and D aid to the computer industry, and even the grant to ICL was limited to £13·5 million spread over four years, with no commitment to further grants after 1972. [59] In the view of the Labour Government, the R and D problem could best be solved by rationalising the UK computer industry into one large and more efficient unit, providing it with a large home market by utilising the position of the public sector as the largest single purchaser of computers, and encouraging links with foreign (particularly European) computer firms to engage in large development programmes, rather than by underwriting the industry's R and D programme.

6.4 Government support for rationalisation in the UK computer industry

During the 1964 General Election campaign, the Labour Party had expressed concern over the erosion of British capabilities in high technology, and one of the main functions of the Ministry of Technology when it was created in October 1964 was the sponsorship of the UK computer industry. [60] At that time Britain was the only advanced industrial country apart from Japan where IBM controlled less than half of the computer market; in France the computer consortium CITEC (which had been formed after GE took over Machines Bull in 1964) had less than 20 per

Table 6.3

Government R and D expenditure on computers, 1964–70 (£'000)

	1964–65	1965–66	1966–67	1967–68	1968–69	1969–70
Total	84	120	676	2,022	6,648	5,915
Of which:						
Government research establishments	–	–	324	1,481	1,805	1,076
Computer firms	84	120	352	541	4,843	4,839

Source: Select Committee on Science and Technology *Minutes of Evidence* (Session 1970–71) 19 May 1971

cent of the French market, and in Germany Siemens and AEG—Telefunken had a similar share of the German computer market. [61] In terms of both size and independent technological capability, the British-controlled computer industry was the most significant in Europe, but it was fragmented; according to Mr Ieuan Maddock, Controller of Industrial Technology at Mintech:

> [Our] main preoccupation at that time was to do whatever was thought sensible to make sure that there was, indeed, such a thing as a computer industry in the United Kingdom. We were facing the situation of almost the complete extinction of an indigenous industry. [62]

Although by 1964 rationalisation had reduced the number of major British computer firms from ten (in 1959) to four, none of them were large enough to provide effective competition for the American computer firms or to finance independent R and D programmes to ensure long-term viability in the computer field. ICT, whose predecessors had marketed IBM equipment in the UK until 1949, (and which was therefore able to use an existing list of customers to build up a 30 per cent share of the UK computer market by 1965) had a turnover of £55 million in 1965, and was the largest British-owned computer firm, but its 1900 range of computers (announced in September 1964) had cost over £50 million to develop, and were being sold at prices 10—15 per cent lower than their IBM 360 equivalents in order to capture part of IBM's share of the UK market. [63] EELM, a subsidiary of English Electric, was much smaller (turnover £12 million in 1965) and its System 4 range of computers, directly competing with IBM and ICT, was derived from the RCA Spectra 70 computers so that development costs were only £5 million; again, its computer range was priced to undercut those of its competitors. [64] The two other two British computer firms were much smaller — Elliott—Automation (turnover £47 million in 1965) was mainly concerned with industrial process control equipment rather than data-processing computers, which it produced and marketed in partnership with NCR; AEI, which manufactured GE computers under licence, had a turnover of just over £1 million in 1965 in its computer business, and sold out to Elliott-Automation in early 1967. [65]

All the British-owned computer firms were therefore handicapped by their small size, relative to their American competitors, and by their inability to finance R and D without extensive borrowing of capital (in the case of ICT) or technology (in the case of EELM, Elliott—Automation, and AEI). In order to compete against IBM's strong-market position

244

(40 per cent in the UK and over 65 per cent world-wide)[66] the British firms were caught in a vicious circle of undercutting the prices of each other and IBM, while striving to match IBM's technological achievements in producing third generation (solid-state) computers and its marketing resources. The result of this was a dramatic decline in their profits (ICT's return on capital employed for 1965 was 2 per cent),[67] and consequently a fall in share prices and increasing difficulty in borrowing capital on the open market. In March 1965, when the value of ICT's stock was only one-third of its value in 1962, the Minister of Technology announced that the government was giving ICT a £5 million grant to develop its 1900 series computers, and stressed that 'there should be a flourishing British computer industry' which would be protected as a matter of policy.[68] The Labour Government had decided that the only alternative to 'technological colonialism' was to rationalise the UK industry around ICT, and 'rushed in, with more haste than logic' to support ICT with a cash grant.[69]

The reasons for this determination to preserve a British-controlled sector of the computer industry were partly techno-economic and partly political:

> Computers are a growth field in which the UK ought to have a capability without a dominant partner. Unless you have such a capability, you lag technologically and therefore your costs are higher than the prime source and you don't have any say in development. This applies over the whole field from defence to education; computers influence the whole spectrum of social activity.[70]

The US Government's ban on the sale of giant Control Data 6600 computers to the French nuclear programme in 1964 had reinforced the Labour Government's conviction that technological dependence on American-controlled computer firms was undesirable; Sir Maurice Dean, Permanent Secretary of Mintech, told an audience of civil servants in 1965 that 'there are certain points in the economy which must be held ... The government has decided that the computer industry is one such point.'[71] In the long term subsidising the individual companies' R and D programmes would not solve the basic problem that the UK computer market alone was not large enough to support even one British firm, let alone four, but to expand into Europe required large resources which the British companies did not possess. (ICT was forced to withdraw from the lucrative Italian market in 1966 because of lack of resources).[72] Mergers between the British companies and American companies would be politically unacceptable, and joint ventures with other European companies were not welcomed by European governments for much the same reason; a proposal made by Mr Wilson to General de Gaulle in 1965 that there should be a joint ICT—EELM—CITEC computer project was rejected by the French Government on the ground that the British companies would dominate the project technologically while the French Government would not gain an adequate technological return for its financial contribution. [73]

The only possible solution was, therefore, to merge the British companies into one unit in order that they might devote their resources to competing against the American firms rather than with each other. The research grant made to ICT and the 'Buy British' policy for the public sector were designed to keep the British-controlled computers firms going while rationalisation was taking place. Early in 1967 the IRC initiated talks between English Electric, which owned EELM, and Elliott—Automatation; on 22 June 1967 the merger of the two companies was announced, with the IRC supporting the merger by the provision of £15 million of new finance. [74] With AEI's withdrawal from the computer field earlier in 1967, this left ICT and EELM as the only major British-controlled computer firms, and in the autumn of 1967 the Ministry of Technology brought them together for merger talks, which for some time were bogged down by the incompatibility of their respective computer ranges. [75] Eventually, in March 1968, the merger of the two companies to form ICL was announced, with government financial aid provided under a new measure, the Industrial Expansion Act 1968, in the form of a purchase of £3½ million of shares in the company and the payment of grants totalling £13½ million over four years towards the new company's R and D expenditure. [76]

The Minister of Technology, Mr Wedgwood Benn, told the House of Commons: 'We have now succeeded — and this is a product of work done over many years — in ensuring that this country remains in the computer industry.' [77] He made it clear that the government's shareholding in the company was not a commercially-motivated one, but rather a further source of R and D finance, and that the merger would not be referred by the Board of Trade to the Monopolies Commission. In a written answer a few days later, Mr Wedgwood Benn stated that the government would continue to purchase computers from ICL 'wherever reasonably possible. Other public authorities have been invited to take into account the desirability of supporting the British industry.' [78] The new company, which was the largest in Europe and fifth largest in the world (after IBM, Univac, Honeywell and Control Data, and before RCA, GE, Burroughs and NCR), was well received by the financial press, although The Economist urged the

246

new company to specialise rather than attempt to compete across the board with the American firms:

> If the British merger is being pushed through solely with the object of attempting to erode a little of the unbreakable American hold on the world business market, then we are probably wasting our time, our money, and our talent. [79]

In the House of Commons, criticism of the Labour Government's sponsorship of ICL by the Conservatives and Liberals was limited to the possible danger of cutting Britain off from access to American technology and a failure to seek out European linkages when the European market was only large enough to support one major European company (indeed, Mr Wilson himself advocated the creation of such a company in April 1968, one month after the creation of ICL). [80] Mr Benn's reply to these criticisms revealed an interesting distinction in Labour policy between mergers (which might mean control passing out of British hands), and joint ventures with foreign companies:

> I must make clear that the use of computers ... is so fundamental to our future industrial structure and competitive power that we cannot as a nation afford to depend wholly on foreign or foreign-controlled manufactures ... We do not intend to pursue a narrow nationalistic policy, and the company has made it clear that it is willing and anxious to collaborate in joint projects with firms in other countries for the mutual benefit of both parties ... When we were considering our computer policy, we had to ask ourselves whether it would be right to go for the international linkage, based on two British companies, or to go for the British companies as the first stage in our thinking about international groupings. We concluded that to leave two British companies pursuing different technologies, separate from one another, and by themselves very small firms by American standards, would have been a great mistake. [81]

The difficulty which ICL was later to face in seeking international links with other European companies arose from its size, the very quality which Mr Benn singled out as necessary for the continued viability of the British-controlled computer industry; as a director of ICL, Mr Basil de Ferranti, remarked in 1970: 'In a sense, ICL is too big. The problem is that we have been almost too successful and this makes it difficult for us to make mergers like that we have made in the United Kingdom come off in the wider European context.' [82]

The reason for this difficulty lay in the fact that each of the major

European computer markets had one indigenous computer manufacturer (two in the case of Germany, but one, Siemens, was largely dependent upon RCA technology) — Philips in Benelux, CII in France, Olivetti in Italy, and Siemens and AEG—Telefunken in Germany. In every case (except Olivetti) these companies were receiving substantial financial support and/or preference in government procurement policies: in France the 1966 'Plan Calcul' allotted £40 million over five years to CII, and a special government department was set up to administer a 'Buy French' computer policy; in Germany the government granted £30 million in R and D funds during 1969—70, with a pledge of a further £400 million for 1971—75, and instituted a preference for German-made computers for public sector contracts; in Belgium the government announced in 1969 that it would buy at least 50 per cent of its computers from Philips or Siemens, and the Netherlands Government similarly pledged that 25 per cent of its orders would be placed with Philips. [83]

ICL was therefore faced with a situation where, because it was the largest single computer firm in Europe, mergers with other European firms were impracticable, either because the firms were the only indigenous computer capability in their home country (and a merger was therefore politically impossible) or because they were part of much larger companies (Philips, Olivetti, Siemens) which were unwilling to relinquish their interest in a growth market. The obvious solution was a series of joint ventures, but by 1970 these had not been conspicuously successful. The Aigrain Group set up by the EEC Council of Ministers proposed in March 1968 that the five European computer firms should collaborate in marketing a giant computer by 1980, but despite an enthusiastic response from ICL, which had cancelled its 1908A giant computer project in 1969 because of lack of a large enough market, the other companies did not respond favourably. [84] The German government preferred a national solution, and promised £60 million to Siemens and AEG—Telefunken to develop a giant computer; a consortium of ICL, CII, AEG—Telefunken and Olivetti did co-operate in 1969 to bid for a £10 million system for the European Space Research Organisation, but since most of the business would have gone to ICL, and Britain had just withdrawn from ESRO, the order was given to IBM. [85] The only concrete results of international collaboration were an EEC-sponsored project costing $400,000 between the European manufacturers to develop common standards and standard interfaces for computers, and the formation of a joint study company, Multinational Data, in November 1970 (by ICL, CII, and the US company Control Data) to explore the possibility of common R and D and marketing. [86]

248

The disappointing response to ICL's initiatives for European co-operation after its formation in 1968 provides some justification for the Labour Government's decision to encourage a merger between the major British-controlled computer firms before exploring the possibility of international links. Dr Jeremy Bray, Joint Parliamentary Secretary to the Ministry of Technology, told the House of Commons in 1968:

> To have formed a merger between separate British companies and separate European companies would, in effect, have made the United Kingdom the cockpit in which the major computer companies of the world would have fought it out. [87]

He did agree that the necessity for wider markets and access to advanced technology made it essential for ICL to form links with other manufacturers in Europe and the US, but it was clear that the Labour Government's policy had not evolved very much beyond the initial decision to preserve a British-controlled sector when ICL was formed in 1968, and that considerations of international linkages were only seriously entertained when it was certain that ICL had at least medium-term viability. Mr Wedgwood Benn explained:

> I think in the case of ICL, it was clear to us that as between an American purchase of ICT, and English Electric Computers going out of business, there is no doubt that the proper thing to do was to build the home one first ... We began with the [British] control idea, and as we went further forward and thought this through more carefully, we saw the merit of the international linkage and recognised that this linkage would sometimes include a majority of the foreign partner in the firm; in which case it would then move into the area of non-British controlled companies which one would deal with as we were dealing with Ford, Chrysler, or Philips ... I don't think that by the end [of the Labour Government] British control, in the sense of majority control, was any longer thought of as a requirement. [88]

This change in attitude was not put to the test during the Labour Government's period of office, but the disappointing progress in European computer collaboration would seem to indicate that it was not a sentiment shared by any other European government.

The result of the creation of ICL is difficult to assess, given the relatively short period in which it has been in existence. From the table of market shares given in the preceding section of this study it can be seen that 1968 and 1969 showed marked rises in ICL's shares of both the public and private sectors (from 52 per cent of the public sector in 1967 to 81 per cent in 1969, and from 29 per cent of the private sector in 1967 to 40 per cent in 1969), but the improvement in the public sector may be attributed to the government's policy since 1968 of obtaining computers from ICL by non-competitive single tenders. The rise in ICL's share of the private sector may be more significant, especially since ICL's 1900 range of computers were nearing the end of their model life in 1969, having been introduced in 1964; the greater marketing resources available to ICL might account for this rise. The improvement in the performance of ICL was especially remarkable when it is remembered that it faced massive reorganisation problems caused by the merger of two companies which marketed incompatible but similar ranges of computers, but these problems did mean that ICL was the only major computer firm not to announce a new range of computers in 1970, causing a rapid fall in its share price and a statement by the Conservative Government in July 1971 that it would continue to support ICL. [89]

6.5 The Labour Government's relations with the American computer companies

Government support for the British-controlled sector of the UK computer industry, by means of preferential public sector purchasing, R and D grants, and sponsorship of mergers, was not seen by the Labour Government as inimical to the interests of American computer firms operating in the UK. Mr Wedgwood Benn assured the House of Commons in 1968 that:

> There is no intention of pursuing a policy of cybernetic autarchy. We do not want to cut Britain off from the many benefits we obtain from access to foreign technology ... What we are doing ... is investing in success. We are identifying success and trying to help it along ... No other country in the world has succeeded in establishing and maintaining a computer industry without government support, direct or indirect. [90]

Mr Wedgwood Benn gave three reasons for the preservation of a British-controlled computer industry: firstly, that it was a key industry whose advanced technology would improve the country's economic efficiency and spin off to other technologies; secondly, that it was a high value-added industry which would help the balance of payments by reducing imports and increasing exports; and thirdly, that it would promote competition while being strong enough to withstand its foreign competitors.

250

This rationale is interesting because it can be inverted to suggest the Labour Government's attitude to the American computer firms: firstly, that they have the capability to deny the UK access to foreign technology; secondly, that they do not make a substantial contribution to the balance of payments; and thirdly, that they do not act competitively in the absence of a countervailing domestic firm. Each of these propositions will be examined in turn.

6.5.1 Access to technology

Broadly speaking there are four main groups which benefit from technology; the scientists and engineers who produce it, the companies which exploit it by incorporating it in their products, the factors of production whose productivity is increased through a technological advance, and consumers who are able to purchase a superior product.[91] As far as basic R and D programmes are concerned, only ICL and IBM had significant R and D programmes operating in the UK during the period 1964–70. According to a Ministry of Technology survey of R and D expenditure in the UK computer industry during the 1969–70 financial year, the total (including expenditure by American-controlled firms) was £23 million, of which ICL accounted for £15·4 million.[92] No figures for IBM's R and D expenditure in the UK are available, but it is known that its research laboratory at Hursley, the largest of seven IBM research establishments outside the US, earned £12 million from overseas royalty transactions between 1965 and 1968.[93]

Although Dr Jeremy Bray told the House of Commons that the proportion of a computer system designed in the UK was a relevant criterion for determining whether or not a certain model was to be regarded as a British computer for public sector purchase,[94] the Labour Government was more concerned with access to technology developed by the American computer firms world-wide, rather than having them conduct self-sufficient R and D programmes in the UK. This was particularly the case after the formation of ICL, and Mr Wedgwood Benn summed up this shift of emphasis:

> Our thinking developed on technology ... as things went on, we became less and less interested in technology and more and more interested in industrial performance ... I don't think that the R and D question is anything like as important as it is supposed to be. Clearly, if you were to find that you were just the helots of an international company manufacturing what had been designed abroad, this would

be both politically unacceptable and bad management. But fighting to see that you have a set proportion of scientists and engineers working in this area is not really rational. You have got to go across frontiers for this purpose. [95]

This realisation that R and D programmes in multinational companies had to be integrated and centrally directed if they were to be effective was reinforced by the hard fact that UK industry as a whole was seriously undermanned in respect of technically-qualified personnel, [96] and that scientists and engineers employed by the American computer firms in the UK effectively reduced the pool of qualified personnel available to their British-controlled competitors. Sir John Wall, Chairman of ICL, said in May 1970 that 'our particular problem in ICL is not money but manpower. We are desparately short — as all Europe is — of manpower capable of doing this kind of work for us.' [97] Steuer's study of the technology problem concluded:

> But from the sole point of view of the implications for technology, working for a foreign subsidiary is like working for its parent. Either way foreign interests are buying domestic ability to produce ideas. If it is bad for British technology when a scientist emigrates, it is bad when foreign subsidiaries hire, or retain, British scientists. [98]

Although it may be argued that scientists employed by foreign-owned companies in the UK are more likely to be available for subsequent employment by British firms than British scientists who emigrate, the products of their work remain the property of the foreign companies employing them, and despite the fact that the British research programmes may earn foreign exchange through royalty transactions, the value of UK-based R and D programmes by the American computer firms probably lies more in their symbolic significance (a further commitment to operations in the UK) rather than any measurable economic gain. Indeed, in the case of IBM, there would seem to be a definite link between the performance of the local manufacturing and sales affiliates and the location of new research programmes; the bulk of the European-based research for the 360 computers was done in Germany and France, where IBM has a 65–70 per cent share of the market. [99] The symbolic political value of R and D programmes may be seen from IBM's decision to build up one of its biggest European research facilities at La Gaude in France during the mid-1960s, when French official hostility to foreign companies was at its height, and the establishment of a research centre at Peterlee in the north of England 1968 as a *quid pro quo* for obtaining government permission

252

to expand their manufacturing plant in the industrially congested south of England. [100] Certainly no IBM research laboratory is self-sufficient, with each laboratory competing with the others for development projects, and usually a US and an overseas laboratory collaborating on projects to ensure that IBM is never entirely dependent on foreigners; although the laboratories are controlled administratively by their local IBM subsidiary, the finance for their work and the results of it are channelled through the American parent company, which also allocates the research projects, according to the available skills and effectiveness of the various laboratories. [101]

The integration of IBM's world-wide research programme, and the consequent interdependence of the laboratories, which depend on a free exchange of information for their effectiveness, is paralleled by the integration of its computer production; in the UK only one IBM computer, the 1130 (its smallest) is wholly assembled in its Scottish factory — the rest of IBM's production in the UK consists of components and peripheral equipment for incorporation into computers assembled in France, Germany and elsewhere. A typical 360 computer installed in the UK might have a central processing unit assembled in Germany containing components manufactured in France, Italy, and the UK, with ancillary equipment coming from the UK (punches and verifiers), Sweden (printers), Latin America (sorters) and Italy (readers). [102] Consequently IBM's UK production capability is not self-sufficient, and depends on an extensive cross-trade in components (see next section below). Although IBM has a deliberate policy of purchasing 30 per cent of its components for UK production from UK suppliers, and in 1965 sent a travelling exhibition around the country advertising its requirements in an attempt to encourage local manufacturers, [103] the extent to which its UK production provides the rest of the UK economy with access to technology is small, apart from the technological spin-off arising from its purchase of locally-manufactured components. From the UK Governemnt's point of view, IBM's UK production provides employment for 2,500 people (over half of them in Greenock, a high unemployment area of Scotland) and contributes to the balance of payments by substituting for otherwise inevitable imports, but only ensures access to technology in the negative sense of producing important components for IBM's European computer production — components whose production could be shifted elsewhere as a result of a decision by the American parent.

Just as with location of research programmes, location of IBM production facilities has been closely matched to its sales revenue in the countries in which it operates; the largest manufacturing plants are in France and

Germany, where IBM has been operating longer than the UK, and where its market share is twice as large. Mr Edward Nixon, the managing director of IBM (UK) explained in February 1970:

> I think we had to earn our spurs in a sense within the Corporation. We have earned our spurs in the Corporation and as time goes on I am quite confident that we are going to get more and more of the manufacture of our product lines in the United Kingdom. [104]

Considerations other than those of efficiency do play a role in IBM's location policy; the establishment of a second manufacturing facility at Havant in the UK in 1967 (in preference to an alternative site in Belgium) was a conscious political decision, [105] and its expansion in 1969 was prompted, according to Jacques Maisonrouge (President of IBM World Trade Corporation), not only by the availability of labour and good communications, but also by Britain's balance of payments needs. [106] Both decisions may not have been unrelated to the Labour Government's 1965 policy of buying computers which were largely manufactured in the UK, although IBM's declining share of the public sector market during the period 1964–1969 would indicate that they did not secure any government preference for IBM equipment.

Three other American computer firms have production facilities in the UK, all of them sited in development areas; Honeywell manufactures its H200 general purpose range at Newhouse, Scotland, and serves all its markets (apart from Japan and the US) from its UK production, except for its largest computers, which are made in the US; NCR produces some of its 'Century' series in Dundee; Burroughs makes some peripherals, but none of the main range of processors, at Cumbernauld. [107] As with IBM, Burroughs makes its decision on location of manuacturing plants in accordance with the results of its marketing within a given country, and its relatively small manufacturing capability in the UK is in line with its 3 per cent share of the UK market. [108] The major exception to this pattern is Honeywell, which began manufacture of computers in its Scottish plant in 1964, and is the only American computer firm to have chosen the UK as its major world-wide manufacturing centre for export business; nevertheless its labour force is smaller than that of IBM (2000 as against 2500 for IBM), and it carried out no R and D activity in the UK until 1969. Honeywell have pursued a policy of obtaining at least 70 per cent of their component supplies for UK production from British firms, involving over 800 suppliers, and claim that the British content of their UK manufactured computers is 'as high or higher than in any competitive product.' [109]

254

As far as access to technology is concerned, it would seem that the location of R and D programmes in the UK by American computer firms do not provide the UK with direct access to technological innovation; the proprietary interest in such innovations accrues to the American parent, and with it the benefits of exploiting it. The economic and social benefits of having a foreign-controlled R and D facility located in the UK (since R and D is a high value-added activity, and may give British scientists an alternative to emigration) would also seem to be outweighed by the withdrawal of scarce scientific talent from the labour pool available to British computer firms. In the same way, location of manufacturing facilities in the UK by American computer firms does not of itself guarantee the UK access to their technology, although it might have what James Quinn calls an 'indirect technological multiplier effect' on their component suppliers to provide more sophisticated components at higher quality or lower cost, [110] but this would depend on the extent to which the American computer firms purchased components from UK suppliers, and whether or not these included the more sophisticated items. Both R and D and manufacturing facilities established in the UK by American computer firms benefit the UK by providing employment, increasing production and taxable revenue, and possibly reducing imports or expending exports, but they do not of themselves guarantee the UK access to advanced technology, which can only be brought by the parent company deciding to market its products in the UK directly, or to licence another manufacturer to produce computers embodying that technology. The existence of R and D laboratories and/or manufacturing plant does seem to represent a commitment by the American computer firms to the UK market, (since the decision to locate plants in the UK is usually predicated on success in marketing computers there) and hence has a symbolic value; a guarantee that the American computer firms will continue to market their products in the UK – although not necessarily that these will embody the most advanced technology.

In a sense, the decision of an American firms to market computers directly in the UK reduces the degree of access to foreign technology which British computer firms might otherwise enjoy; both ICT and EELM used RCA technology in their computer ranges (the EELM System 4 computers were derived from RCA designs, and at the time of their introduction in 1965 were the only computers using all integrated circuits), and this was possible because RCA did not market any of its own computers in the UK until 1967, and was therefore willing to grant licences on terms advantageous to the British computer firms. [111] The main beneficiaries in the UK of the advanced computer technology developed by the

American computer firms are their customers, who are able to make cost savings or quality improvements which would not otherwise be possible; IBM has claimed that eighteen of the top twenty British exporting companies in 1968 were users of IBM equipment. [112] Although Mr Frank Cousins, the Minister of Technology, expressed in 1965 the government's concern that British industry might become 'dependent technologically on foreign industry, subject to techniques suitable to foreign conditions and perhaps made available to Britain a stage later,' [113] there is no evidence to indicate that the marketing (as distinct from the production) policies of the American computer firms denied customers in the UK access to their most advanced products. By 1969 thirteen American computer firms were selling in the UK market, which was the second largest market (after Germany) in Europe, and the only one in which there was a strong indigenous computer industry. [114] With such competitive forces, the main inhibiting factor was the lack of sophistication in computer usage on the part of British industry, which was the reason for the extensive education programmes carried out by all the major computer firms.

Far from being denied access to advanced foreign technology, John Dunning has indicated that British consumers might be enjoying lower prices for the products of American-controlled subsidiaries, because the parent company may charge its subsidiary less than the market price for the technology it transmits. [115] In addition, technological innovations by the American computer firms increased the pressure on the British computer firms to rationalise in order to lower their costs and develop more advanced computers; hence the formation of ICL in 1968 and the creation of the joint British, French and American Multinational Data Consortium in 1970.[116] The American computer firms' chief contribution to the diffusion of advanced technology in the UK therefore lay in their marketing operations and the stimulus these provided for their British competitors to improve their own products, rather than in their location of manufacturing and R and D in the UK.

As far as direct access to advanced technology is concerned, the presence of a viable British-controlled computer industry is undoubtedly important. In a study of the electronics industry published in 1965, it was found that an independent research capability was essential if a firm was to be able to obtain know-how and licences from other firms on favourable terms, and that there were no examples of firms achieving commercial success through licensing arrangements without some independent development work. [117] For this reason the Labour Government's R and D support for the British computer firms was especially important as a means not only of developing an independent technological capability, but also of ensuring access to foreign technology; as Sir John Wall, chairman of ICL, commented in 1970, 'if we have independent technology we buy [American equipment and technology] on our terms and not on their terms.' There is some evidence to suggest that the UK industry did not in fact take as much advantage of licencing agreements as some of its competitors in other European countries; in 1964 the 'electrical engineering' sector of UK industry (which includes computers) spent £6 million on overseas royalty transactions (less than 10 per cent of its own R and D expenditure) and received £7·3 million, representing a surplus of £1·3 million of receipts over expenditure. This may be contrasted with the position of French and German industry, which at that time spent on foreign royalties nearly three times as much as they earned from receipts on their own. [118] The R and D activity of the American computer firms in the UK, which Freeman found to be much lower in intensity than in the US, [119] was certainly not a major agent of technological diffusion in the UK computer industry as a whole, although it could be argued that it enabled British scientists and engineers to raise their skill levels whilst allowing them to continue to live in the UK (and therefore be available for future employment by British computer firms). Diffusion of technology through computer manufacture in the UK by American firms is probably only significant to the extent that components are purchased from UK firms, which would therefore have a greater incentive to improve their products (and a larger sales revenue from which to finance R and D).

Diffusion of technology by marketing advanced computer systems, the most important contribution by the American computer firms, depends on the degree of competition in the UK market and the degree of sophistication in computer applications existing among UK customers. There is no recorded example of the sale of an American computer system to the UK being forbidden by the US Government (as happened in the case of the French nuclear programme in 1964), and in view of the close co-operation between the British and American Governments in the defence field, this was not likely to be an inhibiting factor. The size of the UK market for computers and the existence of an indigenous computer industry would seem to provide sufficient incentive for the American computer firms to market their most advanced computers in the UK, rather than obsolescent systems which could be surpassed by products of the British computer firms.

6.5.2 Contribution to the balance of payments

The location of computer manufacturing facilities in the UK by the Ame-

257

rican computer firms is much more significant in terms of balance of payments effects than it is for the diffusion of technology. The alternatives to local manufacture of American computer systems would be either direct imports from the US or manufacture by British firms under licence from the American firms; both have adverse effects on the balance of payments, with direct imports doing the greatest damage, and manufacture under licence involving a flow of royalty payments amounting to about 5 per cent of sales and, in most cases, a restriction on markets (sometimes EFTA and the Commonwealth, sometimes Britain alone). [120] The balance of payments consequences of manufacture in the UK by American computer firms are more complex, since they vary in their manufacturing policy and export performance. IBM supplies 85 per cent of its European computer sales from European-based production, but its European production facilities are highly integrated and components and sub-assemblies destined for computers sold in the UK may cross national frontiers several times in the course of production. Thus although IBM exports 85 per cent of its UK production, it imports an equivalent amount into the UK, with its declared policy being to balance its exports and imports, 'taking one year with another.' [121] None of the computer firms issues separate export or total turnover figures for computers (as distinct from any other office machinery etc. which it manufactures), so it is not possible to make an accurate comparison of their performance; the following table gives aggregate figures for 1969.

The Table indicates that ICL made by far the largest net contribution to the computer balance of payments in 1969; when it is remembered that the trade figures do not take account of profits remitted by the American-controlled computer firms to their parent companies, ICL's contribution is even more impressive. IBM, for example, remitted £27·5 million to its US parent in 1969, turning its £4·5 million visible trade surplus into a £23 million overall deficit, and during 1967 and 1968 had in fact been a net importer on the visible trade balance. [122] Table 6.5 indicates the large increase in imports of computers and their components, largely attributable to a substantial volume of parts and sub-assemblies for manufacture into computers in Britain by the American computer firms (although the Table indicates that in 1969 ICL was responsible for some 7 per cent of total UK computer imports). While the overall trade deficit in computers increased rapidly (from £7·9 million in 1964 to £58 million in the first nine months of 1970), there was actually a trade surplus in complete computer systems in 1968 and 1969, with the deficit being accounted for by net imports of peripheral equipment and parts and accessories. This extensive cross-trade in accessories and component makes it especially

Table 6.4

Export and import performance of computer firms in the UK, 1969 (£ million)

	Turnover	Exports	Imports	As percentage of turnover		Visible trade balance
				Exports	Imports	
ICL	115·4	23·5	8·5	20	7	+15·0
IBM	124·9	38·6	35·0	31	28	+ 3·6
Honeywell	41·1	16·3	11·8	40	29	+ 4·5
Burroughs	35·8	9·2	N.A.	26	N.A.	N.A.
NCR	50·8	9·6	N.A.	19	N.A.	N.A.

Notes: Above figures are for total sales, including products other than computers
Source: Company reports, personal interviews

259

Table 6.5

(a) Overseas trade in electronic computers, 1964—70 (£ million)

	1964[†]	1965[†]	1966[†]	1967	1968	1969	1970[‡]
Exports*	7·2	7·2	15·0	37·8	47·6	56·8	51·8
Imports	15·1	18·6	35·9	56·5	74·8	97·5	110·0
Visible trade balance	−7·9	−11·4	−20·9	−18·7	−27·2	−40·7	−58·2

Notes: *Includes re-exports
      †Excludes parts and accessories
      ‡9 months to 30 September
Sources: *H.C. Deb.* vol. 747 (6 June 1967) cols. 179—80; Subcommittee A: *Minutes of Evidence* (1970—71) p. 30

(b) Overseas trade in computers (by product class), 1967—69 (£ million)

	1967	1968	1969
Computers:			
Exports*	18·5	25·6	27·7
Imports	24·9	24·9	17·8
Visible trade balance	−6·4	+0·7	+9·9
Peripherals:			
Exports*	3·4	4·3	7·9
Imports	14·7	26·7	34·0
Visible trade balance	−11·3	−22·4	−26·1
Parts and accessories:			
Exports*	15·5	17·2	20·5
Imports	16·6	22·9	44·3
Visible trade balance	−1·1	−5·7	−23·8

Note: *Includes re-exports
Source: Sub-committee A op. cit. p. 29

difficult to assess the contribution of the American computer firms' production in the UK to the balance of payments; from the fragmentary evidence available it seems that those firms exporting a high proportion of output are also responsible for importing a substantial amount of components, sub-assemblies and other lines of manufacture.

Nevertheless, it must be recognised that in the absence of production in the UK by the American computer firms, the level of imports (and consequently the overall visible trade deficit) would be much higher, and the incentive for the British computer firms to export would be reduced; Dunning found a definite relationship between the industrial concentration of American investment (between 1957 and 1964) and those industries which recorded the most impressive increase in exports. [123] Moreover, production in the UK by the American computer firms represented an import of technological capital which, in the absence of other forms of technological borrowing, represented a net addition to capital stock, quite apart from the employment and taxable revenue which it created. The experience of the American firms in developing, manufacturing and marketing computers at home permitted them to produce at least as efficiently as their British competitors, and thus make computers available at a cost which was probably lower than if they had been wholly imported from abroad. For this reason manufacture in the UK by the American companies is far more preferable than direct imports of computers, particularly since assembly of computers is a high value-added activity, even if the American firms made no significant contribution to the balance of payments. [124] In fact both Honeywell and NCR won the Queen's Award for export performance in 1968, and the table of comparative export performance indicates that all the American computer firms (except NCR) exported a higher percentage of their total turnover in 1969 than ICL, although ICL's net contribution was much greater (exporting 40 per cent of the UK total in 1969 and importing 6 per cent of the UK total).

The Labour Government did recognise that American computer firms with manufacturing facilities in the UK did not have the same incentive to increase exports as ICL had, and consequently the Minister of Technology, Mr Wedgwood Benn had talks with the major firms to explore methods of increasing their contribution to the balance of payments.[125] Dr Jeremy Bray, Joint Parliamentary Secretary at Mintech, indicated when he opened the new Burroughs factory in Scotland in 1968 that 'while the government has a "buy British where all other things are equal" policy, American manufacturers who are net exporters generally stand an equal chance with ICL.' [126] Such statements evoked complaints from Honeywell, in particular, which stated that although it exported two-thirds of its UK production and was a net exporter, it had received no orders from central Government at all. [127]

It is difficult to foresee any circumstances in which the American computer firms would in fact become significant net exporters, given that their production in the UK was only commenced at a point where the size of their UK market share made direct investment more profitable than direct importing; the size of the UK market was only 10 per cent of the

US market in 1969, and was 30 per cent smaller that the West German market, [128] and could not by itself provide an adequate base for export production, especially in view of ICL's entrenched position. The alternative (which was chosen by IBM) would be to integrate production on a European basis, with an extensive cross-trade in components and a policy of balancing trade for each country in which it operates. Such a strategy insulates the company from possible complaints by host governments that it contributed nothing to the balance of payments, but at the same time prevents it from favouring one country more than another lest it disturb the balance and provoke complaints. 'The formula of local production in proportion to local market share makes economic and political sense for the computer firms, even though it does not satisfy the desires of host governments.' [129]

Table 6.6 shows the growth of the UK computer market and of computer manufacture in the UK by both British and American firms. The percentage of the UK market supplied from UK production was 51 per cent in 1966, 67 per cent in 1967, 60 per cent in 1968, and 62 per cent in 1969; of this, production by American firms accounted for 36 per cent in 1966 and 1967, 31 per cent in 1968, and 16 per cent in 1969. Because export figures by nationality of ownership are unobtainable, it is impossible to assess whether or not the value of production in the UK by the

Table 6.6

Growth of the UK computer market and manufacture (£ million))

	1966	1967	1968	1969
Value of UK market	81·3	89·9	124·4	144·9
Value of hardware of UK manufacture delivered to UK market	46·7	60·5	74·3	89·2
Of which:				
Produced by British-owned firms in UK	29·7	39·3	50·4	74·8
Produced by US-owned firms in UK	17·0	21·2	23·9	14·4
Value of foreign-made hardware	34·6	29·4	50·1	55·7
Value of UK-made hardware exported	31·7	35·6	40·0	62·0

Source: Ministry of Technology Data Bank; *U.K. Computer Industry* vol. I p. 356

American computer firms corresponds to the level of their total sales in the UK; however, it is quite clear that the proportion of their sales in the UK supplied from UK production is lower than their share of the UK market. For the period 1966–69 the four American firms with UK production facilities controlled 52 per cent of the UK market, but supplied only 32 per cent of their sales from UK production. [130]

Table 6.7 shows that the UK during the period 1967–69 has consistently accounted for a higher level of trade in computers than either France or Germany, and was a greater net importer (£86·6 million, as compared to £6·4 million for France and £44·6 million for Germany).

Table 6.7

UK, French, and German overseas trade in computers

	1967		1968		1969	
	Exports	Imports	Exports	Imports	Exports	Imports
UK	37·8	56·5	47·6	74·8	56·8	97·5
France	31·8	37·5	32·5	40·4	43·0	35·8
Germany	27·8	45·6	33·7	55·0	57·0	62·5

Source: Sub-committee A: *Minutes of Evidence* (1970–71) p. 29

This is particularly interesting in view of the fact that Germany is a much larger market for computers than the UK (£200 million in 1969, compared to £145 million for the UK) and German-controlled computer firms accounted for only 25 per cent of the market in 1969, whereas ICL in the UK had 43 per cent of its home market. In France, a marginally smaller market than the UK in 1969 (£143 million), the only major French firm, CII, had less than 20 per cent of the market. [131] This would seem to indicate that the strength of domestically-controlled computer firms, in terms of home market share, is inversely related to the level of net imports, probably because the American computer firms are able to capture a large enough share of the market to justify substantial local production in order to serve it. There does, however, seem to be a correlation between level of exports and the strength of domestically-controlled firms; during the period 1967–69 the UK exported £142·2 million worth of computers, compared with £118·5 million for Germany and £107·3 million for France. This may be partly explained by the wider export markets open to domestic computer firms; ICL, for example, makes about 20 per cent of its export sales in Eastern Europe, a market which is closed to the American computer firms. [132]

In general, therefore, it would seem that production in the UK by American computer firms benefits the UK balance of payments in terms of import substitution, and the UK economy in general in terms of increased employment (particularly in development areas), increased efficiency (through import of financial and technological capital) and increased income (since computer manufacture is a high value-added activity). It must be recognised, however, that such production may not bring about a net increase in exports, simply because the greater relative value of the German and French, and to a lesser extent the Italian, computer markets for American firms makes it more profitable for them to concentrate their European production within the tariff barriers of the EEC. Where production facilities have been established in the UK by American firms, these have either been integrated with production in the rest of Europe (as in the case of IBM) or with US production (in the case of Honeywell, Burroughs and NCR), so that imports of components and sub-assemblies have equalled or surpassed exports. The Labour Government's sponsorship of the mergers which created ICL was in part a recognition that the limited size of the UK market, which discouraged export production by the American computer firms, would have the reverse effect on ICL; in order to survive it would have to finance research and development programmes from sales revenue, and the only way to increase sales substantially was by increasing its exports. In 1969 and 1970 ICL was a net exporter (£15 million and £20 million respectively), while its American competitors were net importers (£56 million and £90 million). [133] The available evidence therefore justifies the Labour Government's conclusion that the American computer firms do not have the same interest in promoting exports that a British computer firm must have in order to widen its market.

6.5.3 *Competitiveness of the American computer firms*

The dominant position of IBM in the European computer market, with over 50 per cent of total European computer sales, has been noted above; the UK is the only European market in which IBM's share is less than half, and the only one in which an indigenous computer firm has more than 20 per cent of the market. By 1969 there were seventeen computer firms selling their products in the UK market, thirteen of them foreign owned.[134] Although IBM's position in the UK market is relatively weaker than anywhere else in the world (except possibly in Japan, where it has 34 per cent of the market), [135] its dominant position in the world market tends to be self-reinforcing; quite apart from the fact that customers using its equipment are reluctant to change when upgrading or adding to their systems, because of the expense of re-writing programmes and re-training staff, IBM's long production runs enable it to produce its computers more efficiently than most of its competitors. Above all, it must be remembered that the success of a computer system is more important from the customer's viewpoint than its price, and IBM is able to capitalise on its marketing experience and dominant position which has created what one writer has called 'the IBM mystique': 'An atmosphere of experience, competence, and knowledge that its salesmen exploit when dealing with nervous executives hesitating to invest in what still looks to many like an arcane art.' [136]

The response by IBM's competitors has either been to undercut the price/performance ratio of IBM equipment, or to offer guaranteed performance levels to safeguard customers against incompatibility problems. This was not necessarily effective; ICL's two computer ranges, the 1900 and the System 4, were both priced to be between 10 and 25 per cent cheaper than IBM equipment of the same performance capability, but in fact ICL's share of the private sector of the UK market remained static at around 30 per cent between 1964 and 1968, and the System 4 range, which had the greatest price differential vis-à-vis IBM computers, had a very disappointing sales record. [137] Because of its oligopolistic position, IBM's pricing policy was the subject of close scrutiny by the Labour Government; when IBM announced in December 1967, shortly after the 14 per cent devaluation of sterling, that it was increasing its computer selling and rental prices by 10 per cent, the Minister of Technology referred the matter to the National Board for Prices and Incomes, which had partial responsibility for enforcing the price and wage restraint policies instituted by the Labour Government in 1966. [138]

Mr Wedgwood Benn saw this as a test case in the Labour Government's attempt to control the activities of the multinational companies:

IBM we referred to the Prices and Incomes Board because after devaluation they adjusted their prices to ensure a British devaluation didn't affect the pattern of their world pricing, which was not perhaps immensely significant in terms of the amount of money involved, but one could foresee a situation where, if people devalued, it made absolutely no difference whatsoever to the balance of payments if the key international companies repriced to deny that particular country the advantages that flow from devaluation. [139]

In fact the report of the Prices and Incomes Board was confined to the question of rental charges, and the increase in selling prices was allowed to take effect. The report did reveal that IBM had increased its selling prices early in 1967 by 5 per cent for every country except the UK, perhaps a reflection of the greater competition it faced in the UK market, as well as the government's prices and incomes policy. [140] The report admitted that the major difficulty in determining whether or not the price increases were justified lay in the international character of IBM, which prevented consideration of the affairs of any one national subsidiary in isolation:

> Without access to the parent's books, an informed judgment cannot be made about the level of prices being charged, either from the point of view of the return on capital achieved or to ascertain whether research and development costs are appropriately reflected. [141]

The Prices and Incomes Board recommended that future rental contracts by IBM should be allowed to be increased by 10 per cent, since there was a direct link between rental and selling prices, and selling prices were internally determined in a manner which prevented investigation for the reasons given above. For existing rental contracts, however, the Board recommended that the increase should be limited to 7 per cent for post-1964 equipment, and 5 per cent for earlier computers, on the ground that capital cost of the equipment was incurred before the valuation of sterling, and had been at least partly repaid. [142] It did criticise IBM's inflexibility in its retal agreements, but concluded that:

> If IBM had been a monopoly supplier in the UK we would have considered the lack of flexibility in their rental agreements to be rather disquieting and would have made specific proposals to change the position. However, we found that the terms of the agreement being offered by competitors provided a sufficiently wide range of options to protect users' interests. [143]

The report, which was accepted by IBM, was interesting in that it indicated that IBM's pricing policy, although internationally determined, was not uniform on a global basis, and that the degree of competition it faced in the UK market forced it to keep its prices lower there than in the rest of the world. The report's recommendations were not very controversial, and the whole exercise was described by one IBM executive as 'a

266

political decision ... an expression of the government's suppressed hostility toward IBM.' [144] Nevertheless, it is significant that IBM did not offer the government access to its group accounts, unlike Burroughs, whose president (Mr Macdonald) made a point of calling on the Minister of Technology whenever he visited London and providing him with copies of Burroughs' world accounts. [145] The relationship between IBM and the Labour Government is difficult to characterise, because of the different perspectives offered by both sides; a senior civil servant at Mintech stressed that his department 'had very friendly relations with IBM', and a junior minister at Mintech considered that 'IBM make a valuable contribution and has several impressive men who are sensitive to government policy', while an IBM executive complained that 'there was a severe credibility gap ... we could not get in to see the Labour Government and consultation was on a complaint and pressure basis.' [146] Part of this credibility gap may be ascribed to the absence of a clear definition on the part of IBM of the degree of autonomy it permitted its UK subsidiary in marketing; by contrast to its research and production activities, which were controlled by the parent company directly, IBM claimed that it treated every country as a separate and independent geographic market, with responsibility for selling in that market lying with the local IBM management, 'subject only to overall policy control.' [147] The extent of this control was never particularly clear, however, as can be seen from this statement by Mr Edward Nixon, the chief executive of IBM UK:

> Each national company operates according to the local environment in which it operates, so there may be some specific marketing practices which operate in one country which are different from another, but essentially we have one internationally based price for our products and then there may be some local variations according to local needs. [148]

Since the 'local variations' were quite marked in the case of IBM's pricing policy for the UK market (its 10 per cent price increase in January 1968 was less than might have been expected in view of IBM's 5 per cent price increase in its other markets in 1967, and the 14 per cent sterling devaluation), it could be argued that IBM should have been less ambiguous in explaining its policies to the Labour Government, particularly in view of the latter's sensitivity to the computer industry.

Because it is not possible to determine how far the price levels determined by the American computer firms adequately reflected R and D costs, an examination of the profitability of their UK operations is not a valid measure of their competitiveness. However, as Table 6.8 indicates,

Table 6.8

Profitability of leading computer firms in UK, 1969

	IBM	ICL	Honeywell	Burroughs	NCR
Turnover (£m)	124·9	115·4	41·1	35·8	50·8
Capital employed (£m)	79·2	120·7	40·9	40·6	47·6
Profits before tax (£m)	34·9	9·1	6·1	9·7	7·7
Profit as percentage of capital	56·8	8·5	21·9	38·2	24·6
Profit as percentage of turnover	27·9	7·9	14·7	27·2	15·1

Note: Figures relate to all products, including computers
Source: Company reports

the American computer firms achieved a much higher level of profitability, both in terms of return on capital employed and return on turnover, than ICL was able to produce. If efficiency is measured by the value of sales per employee, IBM was over four times as productive as ICL, although it was more than twice as capital-intensive (in terms of assets per employee) as ICL. In fact, all the American computer firms were more capital-intensive, and more productive, than ICL, as well as being more profitable. It should be noted, however, that these figures do not reveal the extent to which this greater efficiency and profitability was obtained at the expense of imports, which were higher for the American firms than for ICL, the majority of whose output was manufactured entirely in the UK. The above average profitability of the American computer firms (the average for the 500 largest UK companies in 1969 was 7·5 per cent to turnover and 16·5 per cent to capital employed, compared with an average of 21·2 per cent to turnover and 35·4 per cent to capital employed for the four major American computer firms) [149] was almost certainly due to the low marginal cost of marketing computers abroad after recouping capital expenditure from sales in the US market. It does, however, support the conclusion of most of the politicians and civil servants interviewed that manipulation of transfer prices by international companies is not a serious problem; considering the extensive cross-trade in computers and their components (IBM exports over 85 per cent of its UK production, and aims to balance its trade) it is significant that the firms did not take advantage of it to shift their profits out of the UK to an area of lower taxation, or even to transfer more of their profits as royalty or service payments in order to avoid taxation on profits.

Given that the Labour Government did not have access to the world accounts of most of the American computer firms, and thus could not determine whether or not they were acting competitively in the UK market, its support for the creation of ICL as a viable countervailing force is quite comprehensible. There is evidence that the entrenched position of ICL in the UK market forced IBM to maintain a lower level of prices than it did elsewhere, and it is unlikely that the other American computer firms were able to charge higher prices than elsewhere, since together they accounted for less than 30 per cent of the UK market and were thus forced to follow ICL and IBM if they wished to increase their sales. The only exception to this pattern may be in the field of giant computers and specialised software and peripheral equipment, where ICL did not have a significant capability, but there is no evidence to indicate any abuse in this area, which in any case was not dominated by any one firm. The main problem for ICL was that its American competitors could generate suffi-

Table 6.9

Productivity of leading UK computer firms, 1969

	IBM	ICL	Honeywell	Burroughs	NCR
Employees ('000)	9·0	34·0	8·6	6·7	12·6
Sales per man (£'000)	13·9	3·4	4·8	5·3	4·0
Profits per man (£'000)	3·9	0·3	0·7	1·5	0·6
Assets per man (£'000)	8·8	3·6	4·7	6·1	3·8

Note: Figures relate to all products, including computers
Source: Company reports

cient profits from their UK sales to finance expansion from retained earnings (and still remit sufficient profits to satisfy their parent companies' stockholders), while ICL had to maintain market confidence by distributing reasonable dividends, and finance expansion and innovation from a turnover which was much smaller than that of its major competitors. In 1969, for example, ICL's total profits were £9·1 million before tax, only £2 million more than IBM's distributed profits, and only a quarter of IBM's total UK profits. This was one of the main reasons for the Labour Government's support for ICL's attempts to establish joint ventures with European and American computer firms in 1968—70, as Dr Jeremy Bray made clear to the House of Commons when ICL was created in 1968:

> I think that we are all completely agreed that the future market does not lie solely in this country; and that if we are to market more widely we must also form wider associations of some kind between manufacturers ... in Europe and in the United States. [150]

There are, however, some grounds for doubting whether the Labour Government's attempt to create a British manufacturer of computer systems to act as a countervailing force will be sufficient in the future to maintain a high level of competition in the UK market. The increasingly adverse balance of trade in both peripheral equipment and components referred to in the previous section points to a weakness among UK manufacturers in these sectors, and in view of the increasing use of integrated microcircuits in computers the absence of a strong British-owned manufacturer of microcircuits could lead to the dependence of ICL on foreign component manufacturers. In 1970, 60 per cent of the UK market for semiconductors was controlled by four American firms, 25 per cent by four European firms, and 15 per cent by four British firms (whose total turnover of £11 million prevented them from emulating the £40 million annual R and D expenditure of Texas Instruments, the largest manufacturer). [151] A government-sponsored study of the microcircuit industry which appeared in 1971 (but was initiated by the Labour Government before its defeat in 1970) concluded that neither Britain nor any single European country has a big enough market to support even one locally-owned company in the industry, because of the dominance of US manufacturers in Europe, and that even a unified European market would not be sufficiently innovative to support an indigenous microcircuit manufacturer, forcing it to enter the American market which is both large and innovative. [152]

The result of dependence on American component suppliers for ICL would be to negate many of the advantages accruing to the UK from the existence of an independent British computer firm, and this would indicate that the Labour Government framed its computer policy somewhat too narrowly; although it did make a £5 million R and D grant to three of the British microcircuit manufacturers in 1969, it did not (as it had done to form ICL) put any pressure on them to merge. [153] Similarly, the Labour Government was more concerned with computer hardware than it was with software, which is of crucial importance in maintaining an advanced computer capability; in the case of the London Airport Cargo Scheme (LACES), for example, ICL was awarded the contract for the hardware while the software contract was given to an American firm. [154] The consequence was that in ICL, the Labour Government had created the largest non-American manufacturer of central processing units, but had not created a similar capability in software, peripherals, or microcircuits, so that the future independence of the British computer industry, and hence its role as a countervailing competitive force, could not be assured.

6.6 Conclusion

The Labour Government's computer policy rested on two basic assumptions: firstly, that computers represented a powerful and pervasive technology which would rapidly become decisive in most of the nation's activities; and secondly, that a failure to produce and maintain an indigenous capability in that technology would entail a surrender of decision-making power to the American computer firms (and therefore ultimately to the American Government). The sheer size of the American market for computers, and the extensive federal aid for R and D programmes, had enabled the American computer firms to achieve a dominant position, supplying over 90 per cent of world demand (with IBM alone controlling 65 per cent of the world market) in 1969. [155] Table 6·10 indicates the importance of the American market in terms of annual demand.

The higher growth rates for the non-American markets indicate their increasing importance for the American computer firms as a source of revenue; the high return on capital employed by them in their UK operations, (outlined in an earlier section of this study), is evidence of the great advantage they had over their competitors, in that the cost of R and D and risk-taking had already been largely covered by sales in the American market. In the absence of such a large and innovative domestic market for computers, the British-controlled computer firms were unable to achieve such large production runs and sales revenue to finance development of

Table 6.10

World computer demand, 1965–70 (£ million)

	1965	1967	1970	percentage growth p.a.
USA	730	1,625	2,300	18
UK	60	100	180	19
Industrial Europe*	190	400	545	22
World total	1,200	2,400	3,800	20

*Sweden, France, Germany, Italy, Benelux
Source: *U.K. Computer Industry* vol. I p. 12

competitive products; hence government R and D grants and support for rationalisation of the British firms and subsequent joint ventures with foreign computer firms.

The Labour Government had to maintain a fine balance between protection of an infant computer industry and ensuring continued access to the products of American advanced technology. Its task was made easier by the size of the UK market (about 25 per cent of European demand and 5 per cent of world demand) which made it attractive to the American computer firms, and the fact that the UK was the only country apart from the US which had a significant indigenous computer industry, capable of developing into a world class international enterprise. The formation of ICL in 1968 created the fifth largest computer firm in the world, with no other non-American company appearing in the top ten, as Table 6.11 indicates.

The non-American computer firms were either subsidiaries of large companies in the electrical engineering or office equipment fields, or else (in the case of ICL and CII) were the product of government-sponsored merger schemes. All the European computer firms (except Olivetti) received some form of support from their home governments, either in the form of development grants or preference in government contracts; ICL received £25·5 million in grants and loans for the four years after its formation in 1968, and a 25 per cent price preference in public sector contracts; CII received £40 million over the five years from 1966, and also enjoyed government preference; Siemens and AEG-Telefunken similarly received £40 million in grants and low-interest loans 1966–71, and were supported by the German Government in its purchasing policies; Philips

Table 6.11

Estimated turnover in data processing, 1968–69

	Company	Country of origin	Turnover in D.P. ($ million)
1	IBM	US	5,000
2	Honeywell	US	630
3	Univac	US	400
4	Burroughs	US	300
5	ICL	UK	270
6	Control Data	US	255
7	RCA	US	230
8	NCR	US	190
9	GE	US	160
10	Xerox	US	70
11	Digital Equipment	US	60
12	Siemens	Germany	60
13	Olivetti	Italy	40
14	AEG-Telefunken	Germany	25
15	CII	France	20
16	Philips	Netherlands	10

Note: Figures for Japanese computer firms not available
Source: *U.K. Computer Industry* vol. II, p. 251; *The Financial Times* 8 February 1971, p. 8

received some measure of public sector preference in the Benelux countries. [156] In comparison with the amount of development aid given by the US Government to the American firms ($150 million in 1965, 30 per cent of their total R and D expenditure) and the degree of price preference for American computer contracts in the public sector (50 per cent in defence, 6 per cent in civilian contracts, with a 9 per cent tariff on computer imports), this level of government assistance was not particularly high, especially when the advantages of the large domestic sales base available to the American firms are taken into account. [157]

The base of immense scale available to the American computer firms gave them a head-start in their European operations, and in 1964 the Labour Government had been faced with the possibility of the extinction of the British computer firms through competition and take-overs by the

274

American giants. The creation and survival of ICL represented a considerable achievement for the Labour Government's computer policy, but it was recognised that ICL could not achieve long-term viability without an international link, and could not acquire such a link unless it had something to offer in terms of expertise and credibility. While Mr Wedgwood Benn spoke of 'investing in success', the prime objective of the Labour Government's aid for ICL was to invest it with credibility — to show that it was capable of development into a world-class international enterprise. As with the British nuclear deterrent, possession of an indigenous computer capability gave the UK influence out of all proportion to its actual power, at least in the Labour Government's view. If ICL could keep abreast of technological developments, it would provide sufficient competition to ensure that the American companies marketed their most advanced computer systems in the UK; if such access to foreign technology were ever denied (as had happened with the French nuclear programme), then ICL would be able to develop an alternative. In a very real sense, the chief benefit of ICL for the Labour Government was the bargaining power accruing from its continued existence, rather than the actual equipment which ICL produced.

The research laboratories and manufacturing facilities established in the UK by the American computer firms were viewed with approval by the Labour Government not so much because of any contribution they made to employment (although most were located in development areas, attracted by the 40 per cent capital investment grants offered by the Government from 1966), or even their contribution to the balance of payments (only Honeywell among the American computer firms was a significant net exporter), but rather because the establishment of research and production facilities represented a commitment by the companies to the UK market. Such facilities of themselves did not provide the UK with access to technology (which remained the proprietary interest of the parent companies, except in so far as they contracted out work), and indeed the Labour Government recognised that R and D activities had to be global if they were to be efficient. They did, however, represent a recognition by the American companies that their position in the UK market was a viable one, and justified some measure of local production. It is interesting in this context to note that all the American computer firms manufacturing in the UK stressed in evidence to the Select Committee on Science and Technology that their UK subsidiaries were almost exclusively staffed by British nationals (IBM pointed out that it had only one American in its senior UK management, and that the President of IBM World Trade Corporation was French), while their operations were run on a global basis for maximum efficiency and access to technology. [158]

Location of production and research facilities and nationality of staff both represented a symbolic commitment by the American computer firms to the UK market, and one which the Labour Government actively encouraged when for public sector purchases it defined 'British' computers as ones which were predominantly manufactured and/or designed in the UK by British or foreign companies. The fact that the government did not adhere to this definition when purchasing computers (frequently by non-competitive tender after 1968) from ICL may have evoked complaints from the American computer firms, particularly Honeywell, but it did encourage the American computer firms to expand their production facilities in the UK; IBM opened a second plant in 1967, Burroughs in 1968, Honeywell doubled its production between 1965 and 1970, NCR began computer production in the UK in 1968, and Univac commenced some manufacture in 1970. Such expansion was, of course, partly dictated by the growth of the UK market, but it was also prompted by the attitude of the government, particularly since the public sector accounted for over 30 per cent of the total UK market and the government itself was the largest single customer for computers.

Although hard evidence is practically non-existent, it does seem that where ICL was unable to supply equipment for public sector contracts, preference was given to American firms which manufactured some of their computers in the UK. While IBM and Control Data both produced a range of high-capacity computers (neither manufactured in the UK), IBM received over £15 million worth of orders from the government in the period 1965–69, most of them for large computers where British firms had no capability, while Control Data reveived only £1·8 million worth of orders in the same period; it is not possible to determine how much this was due to the fact that IBM had the largest manufacturing operation in the UK of any of the American firms, while Control Data did no manufacturing in the UK at all, but it is significant that Control Data's share of the UK market was lower than its share in both the French and German computer markets. [159]

In essence, the Labour Government's policy toward the UK computer industry was a manifestation of a complex of attitudes, which may be summarised thus:

(a) XENOPHILIC
   (i) *Access to technology*: The marketing of computers in the UK by American firms provides the UK with access to advanced technology which it might not be able to develop itself.

276

(ii) *Employment*: The American computer firms employ over 30,000 people in the UK, a large number of them in areas of high unemployment.

(iii) *Efficiency*: In so far as they manufacture in the UK and purchase components from UK sources, they increase the productivity of the UK electronics industry.

(iv) *Balance of payments*: Some American computer firms are net exporters, and all those manufacturing in the UK are substituting for imports to the degree that manufacture in the UK accounts for added value.

(b) XENOPHOBIC

(i) *Control*: All the American computer firms are centrally controlled in respect of R and D and production, and (to a lesser extent) in marketing. They thus have the power to withold technology from the UK, either as a result of a company decision or under pressure of their home government.

(ii) *Competition*: By virtue of their large domestic market, the American computer firms can spread out their fixed costs over large production runs, and can thus retain larger amounts of earnings to finance future expansion than their British competitors. There is probably no world industry so subject to the power of a dominant single producer as the computer industry, where IBM determines the pattern of technical standards and pricing, and this makes it vital to build up strong alternative enterprises. Since Britain has the largest indigenous computer industry outside the US, this must be defended in order to create the nucleus of a non-American competitor to IBM and to prevent it being eliminated by American competition or take-over.

(iii) *Exports*: Britain is a large and growing net importer of computers and accessories; American companies do not have the same interest in increasing exports as ICL does, because they produce in the UK only when their market share justifies it, and follow the same practice in other countries. Consequently net exporting by American computer firms is rare, and when it occurs may be outweighed by remission of profits, royalties, or service charges to the parent company. In addition, some export markets (such as Eastern Europe and the US itself) are closed to the American subsidiaries because of parent company or home government policy.

(c) GEOCENTRIC

(i) *Technology*: Technology can only be developed and exploited efficiently on a global basis, since (apart from the US) no single market is large enough to enable companies to finance R and D programmes from local sales, and any insistence on autonomous research efforts would have deleterious effects.

(ii) *Marketing*: For the same reason, computer firms must be international if they are to achieve maximum economies of scale, particularly in view of IBM's dominant position in world computer markets.

On balance the Labour Government's attitudes were xenophobic in so far as the activities of the American computer firms affected the chances of creating and maintaining a Britain-controlled capability in what it considered to be a key industry, but these were muted in the interest of maintaining access to American technology, the chief benefit conferred by the presence of American-controlled computer firms. This was a delicate balance, fully appreciated by the Ministry of Technology:

> We need to provide a 'sensible' amount of help for the indigenous company, but to avoid injury to help the 'good neighbour' policy towards American industry or alienation of the sources of advanced technology. This is no easy course to follow: there are no clear rights and wrongs, judgements must be qualified, adjustments will have to be made. [160]

In general it must be said that the Labour Government was remarkably successful in maintaining this delicate balance, since the UK continued to benefit from American technology and an indigenous computer capability continued to exist. The long-term problem, that ICL would only be viable as part of an international consortium, and that such participation would dilute British control over a key industry, was not one which the Labour Government had to face, although their strategy of creating a sound British computer firm before seeking international links would seem to have been justified by the meagre success of such international ventures as the Aigrain project. Although the creation of ICL was not a certain defence against the advent of the 'industrial helotry' Prime Minister Wilson feared would be the result of dependence on American technology and investment, it was well suited to its role as a countervailing force to ensure that the American computer firms lived up to their neighbourly assurances.

Notes

[1] Labour Party *Notes for Speakers: The Economy — Government Machinery* Labour Party, London 1970, p. 10

[2] Statement by Prime Minister Wilson *H.C. Deb.* vol. 702 (26 November 1964) col. 217

[3] Interview with Dr Jeremy Bay (former Joint Parliamentary Secretary, Ministry of Technology 1967–69) 15 February 1971

[4] Select Committee on Science and Technology (Session 1969–70), *U.K. Computer Industry*, vol. II, p. 4 (Hereinafter referred to as *U.K. Computer Industry*)

[5] See Christopher Tugendhat *The Multinationals* Eyre & Spottiswoode, London 1971, Chap. 9; Louis Turner *Invisible Empires* Hamish Hamilton, London 1970, p. 19

[6] *The Times* 1 December 1966, p. 12

[7] Ibid., 14 November 1967, p. 4

[8] T. A. Wise 'IBM's $5,000,000,000 Gamble' *Fortune* September 1966, p. 118

[9] Christopher Layton *European Advanced Technology* PEP and Allen & Unwin, London 1969, p. 19

[10] *The Times* 1 January 1965, p. 14

[11] *U.K. Computer Industry* vol. 1, p. 355

[12] *The Times* 31 December 1964, p. 10

[13] *H.C. Deb.* vol. 707 (1 March 1965) cols. 925–6

[14] *The Economist* 3 October 1964, p. 68

[15] Interview with a director of a University Computer Unit, 4 June 1971

[16] *H.C. Deb.* vol. 722 (7 December 1965) col. 226

[17] *The Times* 1 August 1964, p. 11

[18] *The Times* 1 January 1965, p. 14; *U.K. Computer Industry* vol. I, p. 354

[19] *The Times* 11 February 1965, p. 17

[20] ibid., 9 November 1965, p. 5

[21] *The Flowers Report* Cmnd. 2883

[22] *H.C. Deb.* vol. 731 (15 July 1966) cols. 283–4

[23] Statement by Dr Jeremy Bray, Parliamentary Secretary to the Ministry of Technology, *H.C. Deb.* vol. 761 (21 March 1968) col. 1534

[24] *The Times* 27 August 1966, p. 13

[25] *U.K. Computer Industry*, vol. I, pp. 73, 100

[26] Subcommittee A (session 1970–71) Minutes of Evidence, 24 February 1971, p. 90

[27]   Interview with a senior Ministry of Technology official, 5 December 1970

[28]   *U.K. Computer Industry* vol. I, p. 381

[29]   Statement by Mr E.F. Newley, UK Atomic Energy Authority, 11 February 1970 in *U.K. Computer Industry* vol. I, p. 55

[30]   ibid., vol. I, p. 73

[31]   ibid., vol. I, pp. 97, 100

[32]   Ministry of Technology *The Computers Merger Project* 1968 Cmnd. 3660, p. 2

[33]   *U.K. Computer Industry* vol. I, p. 447

[34]   ibid., vol. II, p. 9

[35]   Interview with Mr John Hargreaves, Director of Public Affairs, IBM (UK) Ltd, 15 July 1970

[36]   *Fortune* 15 August 1969, p. 88

[37]   *The Times* 4 March 1965, p. 18

[38]   *U.K. Computer Industry* vol. I, pp. 6–7

[39]   ibid., p. 100

[40]   *H.C. Deb.* vol. 761 (21 March 1968) col. 1534

[41]   *The Times* 19 September 1966, p. 13

[42]   *U.K. Computer Industry* vol. I, p. 356

[43]   ibid., pp. 216, 340

[44]   *The Times* 18 February 1971, p. 20

[45]   *H.C. Deb.* vol. 707 (1 March 1965) cols. 925–6

[46]   Electronics EDC *Economic Assessment to 1972* NEDO, London 1970, p. 39

[47]   Central Advisory Council for Science and Technology *Technological Innovation in Britain* HMSO, London 1968, p. 11

[48]   OECD *Gaps in Technology – Electronic Computers* OECD, Paris 1969

[49]   *U.K. Computer Industry* vol. I, p. 12

[50]   ibid., p. 358

[51]   *The Times* 2 March 1965, p. 12

[52]   OECD *op. cit., U.K. Computer Industry*, vol. II, p. 249; Sub-committee A *Minutes of Evidence* (Session 1970–71), p. 108

[53]   Sub-committtee A *Minutes of Evidence* (Session 1970–71), p. 106

[54]   *U.K. Computer Industry* vol. I, pp. 358–63

[55]   *Management Today* July/August 1966, p. 49

[56]   Central Advisory Council for Science and Technology: op. cit., p. 15

[57]   *The Economist* 6 March 1965, p. 1036

[58]   *U.K. Computer Industry* vol. I, p. 404

[59]   *The Computers Merger Project 1968* Cmnd. 3660, p. 4

60 *The Ministry of Technology 1964—69* Ministry of Technology, London 1969, p. 6

61 *Management Today* July-August 1966, p. 48

62 *U.K. Computer Industry* vol. I, p. 370

63 *Management Today* July-August 1966, p. 49; *The Times* 29 September 1964, p. 16

64 *The Times* 23 September 1965, p. 16

65 *The Economist* 25 February 1967, p. 754

66 ibid., 26 September 1964, p. 1252

67 *Exchange Telegraph Statistics*

68 *H.C. Deb.* vol. 707 (1 March 1965) col. 925

69 Interview with a senior Ministry of Technology official 5 December 1970

70 Interview with Dr Jeremy Bray (Joint Parliamentary Secretary, Ministry of Technology 1967—69), 15 February 1971

71 *The Times* 23 November 1965, p. 17

72 ibid., 27 August 1966, p. 13

73 *The Economist* 31 July 1965, p. 461; *The Times* 18 January 1966, p. 13

74 Industrial Reorganisation Corporation *Report and Accounts 1967—68,* p. 19

75 *U.K. Computer Industry* vol. I, p. 404

76 *The Computers Merger Project, 1968* Cmnd. 3660, p. 1

77 *H.C. Deb.* vol. 761 (21 March 1968) col. 612

78 ibid., (27 March 1968) cols. 293—4

79 *The Economist* 16 March 1968, p. 88

80 ibid., 20 April 1968, p. 70

81 *H.C. Deb.* vol. 766 (21 June 1968) cols. 1495, 1505

82 *U.K. Computer Industry* vol. I, p. 31

83 Brian Murphy 'Computing – the future in Europe' *New Scientist and Science Journal* 18 February 1971, pp. 358—60

84 *The Economist* 6 September 1969, p. 67

85 *The Financial Times* 31 July 1970, p. 17

86 *The Times* 13 November 1970, p. 22

87 *H.C. Deb.* vol. 766 (21 June 1968) col. 1539

88 Wedgwood Benn interview, 2 December 1970

89 *The Sunday Times* 1 August 1971, p. 37

90 *H.C. Deb.* vol. 766 (21 June 1968) cols. 1504—6

91 M.D. Steuer *American Capital and Free Trade* Trade Policy Research Centre, London 1968, p. 31

92 Select Committee on Science and Technology (Sub-committee A)

Minutes of Evidence (Session 1970–71) p. 107
93   *U.K. Computer Industry* vol. I, p. 66
94   *H.C. Deb.* vol. 766 (21 June 1968) col. 1534
95   Wedgwood Benn interview, 2 December 1970
96   Merton J. Peck, 'Science and technology' in Richard E. Caves (ed.) *Britain's Economic Prospects* Allen & Unwin, London 1968 pp. 448–84
97   *U.K. Computer Industry* vol. I, p. 417
98   Steuer op. cit., p. 37
99   Tugendhat op. cit., pp. 125–6
100   Interview with a former Junior Minister, Ministry of Technology, 15 February 1971
101   *U.K. Computer Industry* vol. I, pp. 64, 66
102   ibid., p. 65
103   *The Times* 8 January 1970, p. 23
104   *U.K. Computer Industry* vol. I, p. 76
105   Interview with an IBM (UK) executive, 15 July 1970
106   *The Times* 8 January 1970, p. 23
107   *U.K. Computer Industry* vol. I, p. 354
108   Interview with a Forward Economic Planning executive, Burroughs Machines Ltd, 14 January 1971
109   *U.K. Computer Industry* vol. I, pp. 89–91
110   James B. Quinn 'Technology transfer by multinational companies', *Harvard Business Review* (November–December 1969) pp. 147–61
111   *The Sunday Times* 1 August 1971, p. 37
112   *U.K. Computer Industry* vol. I, p. 69
113   *The Times* 9 November 1965, p. 5
114   Philip Siekman 'Now its the Europeans versus IBM' *Fortune*, 15 August 1969, pp. 86–178
115   John H. Dunning 'Technology, United States investment, and European economic growth' in C.P. Kindleberger (ed.) *The International Corporation* MIT Press, Cambridge, Mass. 1970 pp. 141–76
116   *The Financial Times* 8 February 1971, p. 8
117   C. Freeman 'Research and development in electronic capital goods' *National Institute Economic Review* (No. 34) November 1965 pp. 40–98
118   *Board of Trade Journal* 29 July 1966, pp. 276–9; Central Advisory Council for Science and Technology, op. cit., p. 5
119   Freeman, op. cit., p. 77
120   ibid.
121   *U.K. Computer Industry* vol. I, p. 68
122   Interview with an IBM executive, 15 July 1970
123   John H. Dunning 'US foreign investment and the technological gap'

in C.P. Kindleberger and A. Shonfield (eds.) *North American and Western European Economic Policies* Macmillan, London 1971 pp. 364–406

[124]   Interview with a Ministry of Technology official, 23 November 1970

[125]   Wedgwood Benn interview, 2 December 1970

[126]   *The Daily Telegraph* 24 April 1968, p. 18

[127]   *U.K. Computer Industry* vol. I, pp. 90–2

[128]   ibid., p. 353

[129]   Interview with a Burroughs executive, 14 January 1971

[130]   *U.K. Computer Industry* vol. II, p. 4

[131]   ibid., vol. I, p. 6; *Fortune* 15 August 1969, p. 88

[132]   Interview with an ICL executive, 17 March 1971. (Note: the sale of large computers by ICL to Eastern Europe does require NATO permission; in 1969 ICL gained a £6 million order from the Soviet nuclear physics programme, but the US Government did not approve the sale, and NATO permission was not granted. See *The Times* 21 December 1970, p. 13)

[133]   Interview with ICL executive, 17 March 1971

[134]   *U.K. Computer Industry* vol. I, p. 4

[135]   *The Financial Times* 17 November 1970, p. 17

[136]   Siekman, op. cit., p. 90

[137]   *U.K. Computer Industry* vol. I, p. 22

[138]   National Board for Prices and Incomes *Increase in Rental Charges for Equipment Hired from IBM United Kingdom Limited* (Cmnd. 3699) HMSO 1968

[139]   Wedgwood Benn interview, 2 December 1970

[140]   Prices and Incomes Board op. cit., p. 4

[141]   ibid., p. 3

[142]   ibid., p. 8

[143]   ibid., p. 7

[144]   Interview with an IBM executive, 15 July 1970

[145]   Interview with Dr Jeremy Bray (Joint Parliamentary Secretary, Mintech, 1967–69), 15 February 1971

[146]   Interviews, 22 December 1970, 15 February 1971, 15 July 1970

[147]   *U.K. Computer Industry* vol. I, p. 65

[148]   ibid., p. 68

[149]   *The Times 1000 Leading Companies in Britain* (1970–71 edition) Times Newspapers Ltd, London 1970, p. 15

[150]   *H.C. Deb.* vol. 766 (21 June 1968) col. 1540

[151]   Christopher Layton 'Catching up in semiconductors' *New Scientist and Science Journal* 18 February 1971, pp. 361–3

[152] *The Guardian* 4 August 1971, p. 12; *The Economist* 7 August 1971, p. 77

[153] Interview with a member of the Electronics EDC, 23 November 1970

[154] Interview with a senior Ministry of Technology official, 5 December 1970

[155] *The Financial Times* 8 February 1971, p. 8

[156] Murphy op. cit., p. 359

[157] *U.K. Computer Industry* vol. II, p. 250

[158] *U.K. Computer Industry* vol. I, pp. 66, 90; vol. II, pp. 67, 69, 70. (It is perhaps significant that NCR gave office space to the 'I'm Backing Britain' campaign in 1968)

[159] *The Financial Times* 20 July 1970, p. 20

[160] *U.K. Computer Industry* vol. I, pp. 352–3

7 Multinational Corporations and the British Government 1964 – 70 : A Case of Benign Neglect

'Is there any point to which you would wish to draw my attention? '
'To the curious incident of the dog in the night-time.'
'The dog did nothing in the night-time.'
'That was the curious incident,' remarked Sherlock Holmes.
    – Sir Arthur Conan Doyle, *Silver Blaze*

'One law shall be to him that is homeborn, and unto the stranger that sojourneth among you'.
    – Exodus xii, 49

7.1   Foreign investment as a non-issue

One of the major themes of this study has been that in most important respects the Labour Government did not seek to differentiate between foreign-owned and domestic business enterprises in the formulation and execution of its economic policies. When it is recalled that the value of foreign investment in the UK almost doubled between 1964 and 1970 (and that it was concentrated in industrial sectors whose growth rates were above average) this lack of differentiation is surprising. Like the nocturnal silence of the dog in the Sherlock Holmes story, it is curious that the Labour Government did not consider foreign investment to be a salient policy issue, and that it continued the policy of 'qualified welcome' for foreign investment which it had inherited from its Conservative predecessors.

In Chapter 1 it was hypothesised that the emergence of foreign investment as a policy issue was dependent on the degree of economic intervention by the host government in its economy, and the level and industrial distribution of foreign investment in the host country's economy.[1] Although foreign investment in certain sectors, chiefly the motor and computer industries, did arouse the concern of the Labour Government, this concern was limited to those specific industries rather than to more general questions of the costs and benefits of foreign investment for the UK economy, or to the implications of the evolution of multinational corporations for national economic management. The fragmentation of responsibility for governmental control of foreign-owned companies (outlined in Chapter 3), the small number of civil servants directly concerned with foreign investment issues, and the bipartisan consensus in Parliament on the merits of foreign investment, are all indications that foreign investment was not a salient policy issue for the Labour Government. Foreign investment issues were dealt with on an *ad hoc* and relatively informal basis, and there was no attempt to promulgate a general code of conduct for foreign investors, or even any systematic effort to rectify the most serious gaps in the information available to decision-makers on the behaviour of foreign firms operating in the UK. No data on the balance of trade of individual companies was collected, and where undertakings were requested from foreign investors (as in the Ford, Chrysler and Philips cases), no attempt was made to police these assurances.

The lack of differentiation between foreign-owned and domestic firms, so far as the Labour Government's formulation of economic policy is concerned, would therefore suggest that the level of horizontal interaction brought about by foreign investment — and the actual or potential constraints on the Government's decision-making autonomy arising from such horizontal interaction — was not sufficient to make foreign investment in general a salient policy issue. As the two preceding chapters indicated, where policy issues concerning foreign investment did arise, these were limited to specific industries in which the UK had an actual or potential domestic capability, and Government policies were aimed not at control of foreign firms, but rather at maintaining a viable British element wherever possible. A foreign monopoly of the UK production of carbon black (where there was no viable domestic producer and local production represented an alternative to dependence on imports) was not considered to be a threat to UK economic development, while a fifty per cent foreign share of UK computer sales (where there were potentially viable British firms) was a source of concern for the government.

Why, then, was foreign investment in general not a salient policy issue for the Labour Government? There are several plausible explanations; as Chapter 2 made clear, the value of UK overseas investments was double that of foreign investment in the UK, and any attempt to discriminate against foreign-owned firms might have provoked retaliation against UK firms operating abroad. The costs of controlling foreign-owned firms might therefore be greater for the British Government than for host governments of countries which were not net creditors on the direct investment account, such as Canada and Australia. Moreover, well over two-thirds of the total foreign investment in the UK is accounted for by American firms, and the image (if not the reality) of a common Anglo-Saxon culture and a long-standing 'special relationship' between the British and American Governments[2] would tend to assuage fears of alien values being imposed by American firms, or their being used as a tool of home government policy to the detriment of host country objectives. As Chapter 2 indicated, the majority of foreign-owned firms operating in the UK were organised in a polycentric manner, with some emphasis on adapting to the UK environment (the greater resources devoted by foreign firms to personnel management is an example of this emphasis on adaptation), and this in itself would tend to reduce the likelihood of an open conflict between the objectives of the British Government and those of multinational companies with UK subsidiaries. The instability of sterling and the persistent balance of payments deficit of the 1964—68 period made it even less likely that the Labour Government would eschew the short-term benefits of direct investment (in terms of capital, import substitution, and access to overseas export networks) in favour of long-term economic autonomy.

The analysis of attitudes of civil servants and politicians contained in Chapter 4 makes it clear that most foreign investment was perceived to be beneficial to the UK economy, and that few serious problems were considered to have arisen from foreign investment. Indeed, the substantial areas of agreement between the Labour and Conservative parties on the advantages accruing from foreign investment (although back-bench Labour MPs were more dubious about this than their front-bench colleagues) effectively depoliticised foreign investment as an issue-area; foreign investment issues were therefore dealt with as administrative rather than as political problems. A consequence of this was that governmental reactions to foreign investment problems were conditioned by the division of functional responsibilities among various departments, and the attitudes of key decision-makers within those departments.

The survey of governmental control over foreign investment in the UK contained in Chapter 3 demonstrated that the major functional responsibilities of those departments concerned with foreign investment accorded only a peripheral significance to foreign-owned firms as such, with the result that they were dealt with for the most part on the same basis as purely domestic firms. Moreover, because these responsibilities were divided among several departments, for each of which foreign investment was a peripheral issue (and between which there was little communication or co-ordination of foreign investment matters), there were definite organisational barriers which made it unlikely that a general assessment of the implications of foreign investment for the management of the UK economy would be undertaken, or that foreign-owned firms would be differentiated from domestic firms in the formulation of economic policy. The only major legislation which did seek to distinguish between British and foreign-owned firms — the Exchange Control Act, 1947 — was administered by the Treasury, which had no specific industrial responsibilities (let alone an intimate acquaintance with the operations of multinational companies in the UK), and a strong prejudice against impediments to the free flow of capital. Thus the extensive powers conferred on the government by the Act, which enabled the Treasury to block any overseas financial transactions at its discretion, were used in only a very small number of cases; the discretionary element in the administration of exchange control regulations may be seen as an ultimate deterrent against malpractice by multinational companies, but not as a flexible and sensitive means of controlling foreign investment in the UK.

Why, then, did the Labour Government not develop a more comprehensive and effective strategy for controlling the operations of multinational companies in the UK? Some of the factors inhibiting the development of such a strategy have already been discussed, but a more general explanation may be found in the extensive literature on decision-making theory.[3] Decision-making processes involve certain common ingredients, which may be briefly outlined thus:

1 Dissatisfaction with outcomes within an existing goal structure.
2 A search process to discover new goals.
3 The formulation of objectives after search.
4 The selection of alternative strategies to accomplish objectives.
5 The evaluation of outcomes.[4]

For the decision-making process to commence, therefore, there must be an awareness that a problem exists — i.e. there must be dissatisfaction with the results of prior policy objectives. In the case of foreign investment in the UK, it has been shown that the division of responsibility for overseeing foreign investment among various government departments led to foreign investment problems being defined in terms of the functional responsibilities of the departments concerned. A consequence of this division of responsibility on functional lines was that problems arising from the operations of multinational companies in the UK were seen as limited in scope, not substantially different from the types of problems arising from the activities of purely domestic firms, and therefore amenable to the same kinds of governmental control mechanisms.

The general consensus among both politicians and civil servants that foreign investment was on balance beneficial to the British economy reinforced this structural tendency to define foreign investment problems in limited terms, rather than prompting a more general evaluation of the costs and benefits of foreign investment. Such problems were seen as aberrations from the general pattern, and the decision-makers concerned tended to reject or downgrade the significance of undesirable consequences arising from foreign investment because these did not fit in with their previous experience and attitudes. Because such deviant behaviour on the part of foreign investors was considered to be rare, there was no great stimulus to search for new goals with regard to foreign investment; problems were dealt with on an *ad hoc* basis, utilising procedures (such as the request for assurances from the foreign investor) which had been developed in earlier cases.

As Simon has pointed out, the administrator 'satisfices' rather than 'maximizes', and will not search beyond the point at which he is enabled to make a decision that appears satisfactory to him.[5] Given the generally favourable attitudes of British Government decision-makers toward foreign investment, the paucity of information available to them on the UK operations of multinational companies, and the absence of dramatic conflicts between the objectives of such firms and those of the government, one would not expect a radical departure from the established liberal policy toward foreign investment, or any serious attempt in policy formulation to distinguish between foreign and domestic firms. Festinger's theory of cognitive dissonance suggests that decision-makers would tend to reject or minimise the significance of information which is at variance with the belief-system they already hold,[6] and the survey of governmental attitudes to foreign investment contained in Chapter 4 makes it clear that the undesirable effects of foreign investment in the UK were de-emphasised, and that such effects were seen as isolated deviations from the generally beneficial character of foreign investment — and therefore not affecting the validity of the British Government's liberal policy toward foreign investment.

While foreign investment in general was not seen as a problem for which new solutions were necessary, it is clear that in the case of the motor and computer industries there was a substantial foreign-controlled element; the motor industry was one of the most economically important sectors of UK manufacturing (in terms of sales, employment, and assets) and the computer industry was considered to occupy a vital role in future economic development; in both industries there was a British-owned component which was in danger of becoming vulnerable to competition by foreign-owned firms. Moreover, functional responsibility for both industries lay with the Ministry of Technology (from 1964 for computers, and 1966 for motor vehicles), so that the impact on policy-making of the problems caused by foreign investment in these sectors was not diffused by a dispersion of responsibilities among several government departments. It is perhaps significant in this context that preliminary analysis of the general implications of the evolution of multinational corporations for the management of the UK economy did not commence until the Ministry of Technology assumed sponsorship functions for virtually all manufacturing industries in 1969, although this analysis had not progressed to the goal-setting stage by the time of the Labour Government's defeat in the General Election of June 1970.

In the case of the motor industry, as was seen in Chapter 5, the critical point was reached in January 1967, with the Chrysler take-over of Rootes; the American Big Three were now firmly entrenched in the UK motor industry, and neither of the two British-owned motor companies (Leyland and British Motor Holdings) seemed likely to survive competition from the American multinationals. The initial response by the Ministry of Technology to the Chrysler take-over was to follow the precedent set in the Ford case — to request assurances of 'best endeavours' similar to (but more specific than) those which had been given by Ford in 1960 — but it soon became apparent that this would not guarantee the continued existence of a viable British element in the motor industry. Indeed, the creation of an internationally viable UK-owned motor firm appeared the best method of ensuring acceptable behaviour on the part of the American motor firms in their UK operations; the assumption being that competition, rather than governmental regulation, was more effective in guaranteeing continued benefits accruing to the UK economy from investment by the Big Three. The Ministry of Technology therefore gave every encouragement (including financial aid through the IRC) to the Leyland/BMH merger which produced British Leyland — the indigenous countervailing force in the UK motor industry — in 1968.

This strategy was designed to place limitations on the influence of the multinational motor firms, without discouraging them from continued investment in the UK motor industry, but it did not solve the basic problem; this was that the high level of foreign investment in the UK motor industry made the industry especially vulnerable to shifts in existing production or future expansion by the American firms to their plants elsewhere in Europe. These considerations provided the stimulus

290

for the Ministry of Technology to engage in dialogues with the Big Three in 1968—69 in order to achieve mutual understanding of both governmental and corporate objectives. The way in which the Ministry of Technology dealt with the implications of foreign investment in the UK motor industry between 1967 and 1970 demonstrated an increasingly sophisticated approach to the problems caused by the operations of multinational companies — from the rather static type of control mechanism implicit in the Ford/Chrysler type of assurances to a more flexible and constructive dialogue designed to reduce areas of uncertainty without provoking an aura of confrontation.

A similar process can be seen in the evolution of the Ministry of Technology's policy toward the computer industry, described in Chapter 6; official encouragement and financial aid to regroup the indigenous computer firms, culminating in the formulation of ICL in 1968, in order to guarantee access to advanced technology by creating a countervailing British company — as in the case of the motor industry, this was an example of indirect governmental control of multinational companies by encouraging the creation of a viable UK-owned competitor. The viability of ICL was ensured by governmental finance for its R and D, and the utilisation of a 'Buy British' public procurement policy which was sufficiently ambiguous in its definition of what constituted a 'British' computer to encourage the American computer firms to expand UK production (in the hope that their products would qualify) while giving preference to ICL computers. The importance of the public sector in the UK computer market was a key factor in the success of the 'Buy British' policy, but it did lead to some tension in the relationship between the Ministry of Technology and the American computer firms, and (as in the case of the motor industry) a series of dialogues between Mintech and the computer firms in 1969—70 were intended to remove some of the mutual suspicions and misconceptions which permeated their relationships.

In the case of both the motor and computer industries, therefore, the Labour Government's policy toward multinational corporations showed signs of a learning or adjustment process at work. Initial concern provoked by the salience of foreign investment in a 'key industry' was followed by an attempt to create a countervailing British-owned capability in that industry, on the assumption that a British firm would be more likely to conform to the economic objectives formulated by the British Government. It should be noted, however, that although the *intention* might have been to faciliate indirect governmental control over multinational firms, the *procedures* for achieving this were no different from those used to promote rationalisation in industries where foreign investment did not play a major role. (Identical policies were pursued by the Labour Government in the electrical engineering industry, for example). To this extent the creation of a 'countervailing force' was not a radical departure from established modes of economic intervention; the most important development in the Labour Government's policy toward multinational companies occurred after this initial redeployment of indigenous capabilities.

Once such a countervailing power had been created, a reassessment of goals took place, and it was realised that the government had insufficient information on the operations and intentions of foreign companies in the industry concerned; 'constructive dialogues' therefore took place, in order to gain more information on which to base future policy. It was this stage, the commencement of the search process, that the Labour Government had reached by the time of its defeat in the General Election of June 1970; its Conservative successor to some extent rationalised the formulation of industrial policy by merging the Ministry of Technology and the Board of Trade to form the Department of Trade and Industry, in order to avoid 'an unreal dichotomy between the "internal" and "international" aspects of commerce and industry'.[7] At the same time, it dismantled the IRC, which had been one of the Labour Government's principal agencies for the creation of 'countervailing' British firms, and Mr John Davies, the Secretary for Trade and Industry, went so far as to say that: We wouldn't, of course, want one of the cornerstones of the economy passing into foreign hands, but if any of our overseas friends wanted to invest in a lucrative state enterprise in Britain, who am I to stop them? '[8]

The less interventionist stance of Prime Minister Heath's Conservative Government appears to have caused the down-grading of the search for methods of controlling the multinational corporation, with the Minister of Industrial Development, Mr Chataway, arguing in 1973 that:

> If Britain is to continue to secure a good share of international investment, for which there is fierce competition, we should guard against some of the sillier nationalistic attempts to cast the multinational company in the role of universal villain.[9]

While there were indications that the Labour Government's search for fruitful methods of controlling the multinational corporation was in 1970 on the point of spreading from consideration of certain industries to a more general consideration of the effect of multinational companies on traditional methods of economic management, the Conservative Government which succeeded it did not develop this approach. The 1973 White Paper on Company Law Reform devoted only two paragraphs to multinational companies, and stressed that UK disclosure requirements for multinational companies were already more extensive than those of most other advanced countries:

> These enterprises are a strong force for economic growth at both the national and international levels, but they also raise certain issues for national governments which need to be resolved on an international level ... The Government's aim is to secure improvements in both the quality and comparability of information available in all member countries of the EEC and of the OECD about the activities of international enterprises. [10]

The implication is that the British Government is unwilling to unilaterally increase governmental surveillance of multinational companies, and that the policy of a 'qualified welcome' for foreign investment (perhaps even less qualified than it was under the Labour Government) will continue.

7.2 The preliminary hypotheses reconsidered

In conclusion, it is necessary to return to the preliminary hypotheses on multinational corporation – host government relationships in order to assess their validity in the light of this study of the British Government's policy toward multinational corporations. With regard to the first set of propositions, on the salience of foreign investment as a policy issue, [11] it is clear that foreign investment in general was not a particularly salient issue for the Labour Government in the 1964–70 period, although there were specific industries in which it presented obstacles to economic intervention by the Government (the SKF affair, for example), or threatened to undermine the viability of the British-owned element (as in the motor and computer industries). Because most foreign-owned multinational firms in the UK endeavoured to adjust to local conditions, cases of 'Detroit-style' insensitivity to host country objectives were rare, and insufficient to cause a reorientation in the Labour Government's basically favourable attitudes toward inward investment. The fact that the bulk of inward investment was carried out by American firms, whose reputation for harnessing the 'white heat of the scientific revolution' (to use Mr Wilson's famous phrase) to modern industrial development was seen as a laudable example for British industry as a whole, meant that foreign investment in the UK was not seen as a threat to the achievement of the Labour Government's economic objectives, but rather as a means of fulfilling them. In short, foreign investment was perceived by the Labour Government as consistent with its economic objectives, and (with the exception of certain industrial sectors) was not so pervasive or dominant in the overall economy as to arouse misgivings that it would impose significant constraints upon the formulation or achievement of official economic objectives.

With regard to the second set of propositions, concerning host government reactions to foreign investment,[12] it would seem that the likelihood of an adverse host government reaction to further foreign investment in a given industry depends on the existence of an actual or potential host country capability in that industry, and the salience of the industry in the overall economy. No concern was expressed about a near-monopoly of UK carbon black production by foreign firms, since there was no pre-existing UK capability in that field, and UK production provided some measure of import substitution; a dominant foreign element in the production of canned baby-food or foundation garments was, for obvious reasons, not seen as an obstacle to the pursuit of national economic objectives. The economic and political power of the investing firm's home country was not a significant factor in the UK case (although it might well be for less developed countries), because the bulk of foreign investment in the UK originated from the United States, and there was assumed to be a relatively high degree of complementarity between the policy objectives of the UK and US Governments, diminishing the likelihood of the host government suffering from extraterritorial enforcement of unacceptable policies by the home government. Moreover, the majority of foreign-owned firms in the UK were anxious to avoid a confrontation with the British Government, and to this end tended to be more willing to co-operate than their domestic competitors. Such compliance may, of course, have been more apparent than real, since the Labour Government had little hard information on which to base any assessment of the foreign firm's actual performance.

It is also clear that the Labour Government saw inward investment as an important source of capital and skills, as well as a means of alleviating the recurrent balance of payments difficulties which were the major constraint upon its economic policies, and this reinforced the already liberal policy toward inward investment. Because most foreign investment was considered to be beneficial to the UK economy, particularly if it did not involve the take-over of a viable British firm, and because the UK remained a leading creditor nation on the direct investment account, there seemed little reason to adopt a more restrictive policy toward inward investment. The potential costs of such a policy, in terms of a deterioration in the attractiveness of the UK as a location for foreign investment, far outweighed the likely benefits of increased control over multinational corporations, given the rarity of conflicts between corporate and governmental objectives in the UK experience.

Nevertheless, this case-study of the UK Government has confirmed the importance of the third set of propositions, concerning the attitudes of host government decision-makers toward foreign investment. [13] The dispersion of responsibility for overseeing various aspects of foreign investment among several departments meant that very few decision-makers in the Labour Government were able to form a balanced and comprehensive judgement on the costs and benefits of foreign investment. At best, their judgement was limited to those aspects of foreign investment which came within their remit, and even then it was often based on a very selective choice of admittedly imperfect information on the operations of multinational corporations in the UK. A striking example of this can be seen in the case of two Board of Trade officials interviewed for this study, both responsible for industrial location policy, who stressed the contribution made by foreign companies to employment in the Development Areas. They neglected to mention, however, that foreign investors had made less of a contribution to employment in the underdeveloped regions than they had to employment in the industrially congested areas (18 per cent and 33 per cent respectively of the 1945—65 total). [14] Similarly, statements on the contribution of foreign firms to UK exports were almost invariably made without reference to the net balance of trade of those firms; indeed, the fact that information on the imports of foreign firms was never collected in a systematic fashion underlines the somewhat uncritical attitude of many UK Government decision-makers toward foreign investment.

Those decision-makers who did have specific industrial responsibilities, and frequent contact with multinational firms, tended to be more ambivalent in their attitudes toward foreign investment, and their assessments of the costs and benefits of foreign investment were more complex and far-ranging than those of their colleagues who did not have such an intimate acquaintance with the operations of multinational corporations. As was mentioned above, the major legislative weapon for controlling foreign-owned firms (the Exchange Control Act 1947) was administered by Treasury officials who had little or no contact with the world of industry, and made their decisions on the desirability of foreign investment proposals so rapidly that any balanced and comprehensive analysis of the wider implications of such investment was impossible. [15] The vague and unpublicised exchange control criteria, and the extensive discretionary powers afforded to the UK Government by the Exchange Control Act provided reassurance for this liberal approach, since unacceptable behaviour on the part of multinational corporations could (in theory) lead to swift and terrible governmental retribution. This ultimate deterrent, however, could hardly be called a sensitive control mechanism, let alone a substitute for a comprehensive analysis of the consequences of the evolution of multinational corporations for national economic management.

The objective of this study has been to analyse the complex relationship between the activities of multinational corporations and the policy-making of one host government over a relatively short period of time. It has indicated that the response of a host government to the evolution of multinational corporations is conditioned not only by the level and extent of horizontal interaction brought about by transnational economic activity, but also by the way in which responsibility for managing such interaction is allocated within the host governments decision-making system, and by the attitudes of the decision-makers involved. If foreign investment constitutes a salient policy issue, the crucial factor is whether these decision-makers consider their goals to be threatened by such foreign investment; if they do not, then they are unlikely to discriminate between foreign and domestic firms in their policy-making, although the recognition of foreign investment as a salient issue might well lead then to engage in a more intensive monitoring of the activities of multinational corporations, and a continuous assessment of goal vulnerability.

If it is considered that goals are threatened, the host government is likely to follow the kind of learning process outlined in this study; new investors (and possibly some existing ones) will be asked for assurances of best endeavours, and if a viable domestic capability exists, the host government might guarantee its future by preferential purchases and grants, together with officially sponsored or encouraged rationalisation to create an indigenous countervailing force. Should such an indigenous capability be impossible to create, the host government might then seek an alternative transnational grouping, or else engage in 'infant industry' protectionism, unless (as in the case of carbon black production in the UK) there is no alternative to foreign-controlled production. At some point, however, the static type of 'best endeavours' assurance, and the rather crude and indirect 'indigenous countervailing force' strategy will be seen as an ineffective method of ensuring that multinational corporations confer the maximum benefit on the host economy. At that stage, the host government will reassess its foreign investment policies, and will engage in dialogues with the foreign subsidiaries and their parent companies in order to clarify their respective goals. In the event that a balanced relationship is impossible to establish, the host government might extend these dialogues to include the home governments of the multinational corporations involved, and perhaps even attempt some co-operative ventures with other host governments to establish more comprehensive and sensitive methods of surveillance and control.

There are manifest dangers in generalising in this manner on the basis of a unique case study, but it is hoped that the hypotheses utilised in this study will prove useful for others investigating similar areas of this important but relatively unexplored aspect of 'multinational politics'. There are obvious difficulties in attempting such analysis; as with most contemporary policy issues, official archives are not open for inspection, and governmental decision-makers are unwilling to jeopardise the success of their policies in such a sensitive area by revealing the extent of their uncertainty or internal disagreements. As Sir Anthony Part, Permanent Secretary of the Board of Trade, remarked; 'In my view we shall cross a fatal Rubicon if we insist on revealing differences of view between departments or exchanges between Ministers and civil servants';[16] the scholar therefore encounters the danger of belittling the attempts which host governments have made to come to grips with the problems arising from the evolution of the multinational corporation, or of exaggerating the ineffectiveness of policies aimed at controlling transnational business activity. Nevertheless, it is submitted that it is no longer acceptable to treat either national governments or multinational corporations as relatively homogeneous entities when examining the complex relationships between them, and that case-studies of the type attempted here are a necessary step toward a better understanding of an issue which has profound implications for the future development of international relations. To invert Marx's famous dictum, what matters is not to change the world, but rather to interpret it; it is hoped that this study constitutes a modest step toward that end.

Notes

[1]   see Propositions (a)–(d), p. 13

[2]   see B.M. Russett *Community and Contention: Britain and America in the Twentieth Century* MIT Press, Cambridge, Mass. 1963, p. 202

[3]   see F.G. Castles, D.J. Murray and D.C. Potter (eds.) *Decisions, Organizations and Society*, Penguin Books, Harmondsworth 1971; R.G.S. Brown *The Administrative Process in Britain*, Methuen, London 1970

[4]   W.G. Scott 'Decision concepts' in Castles, *et al.* op. cit., p. 19

[5]   see H.A. Simon 'Theories of decision making in economics and behavioural science' in Castles *et al.* op. cit., p. 44

[6] L. Festinger *et al. Conflict, Decision and Dissonance*, Tavistock Publications, London 1964, p. 157

[7] *The Reorganisation of Central Government* (Cmnd. 4506), para. 20

[8] *Fortune* December 1970, p. 45

[9] *The Times* 15 August 1973, p. 17

[10] Department of Trade and Industry *Company Law Reform* (Cmnd. 5391) HMSO, London 1973, p. 8

[11] see Propositions p. 13

[12] ibid., pp. 13–14

[13] ibid., p. 14–15

[14] see Table 3.2, p. 93

[15] Most proposals were approved within a week of the initial application: see p. 79

[16] *The Observer* 28 February 1971, p. 19

Appendix

Interview schedule for politicians and civil servants

General

1 How would define 'multinational corporation'?
2 Can you give me the names of some multinational companies?
3 What are, in your opinion, the principal benefits to the UK economy of investment by foreign companies? What is their relative significance ?
4 What, in your opinion, are the main disadvantages or problems brought about by foreign investment in the UK? What is their relative significance? On balance, what is the effect of foreign investment on the UK economy?
5 How much contact do you have personally with the management of multinational companies operating in the UK?

Contribution of multinational companies to the UK economy

6 In terms of UK economic interests, which form of foreign investment is preferable — the establishment of a new firm or the take-over of an existing UK firm?
7 Are there any UK industries in which foreign firms play a prominent part?
8 Are there any UK industries in which further foreign investment should be prevented or discouraged? If so, for what reasons?
9 Should foreign firms carry out research and development in the UK? If so, for what reasons? What criteria should be used to determine whether or not a foreign firm's R and D programme in the UK is adequate?
10 Should foreign firms be offered the same investment incentives (investment grants, etc.) as UK firms?
11 In your opinion, do foreign firms make a greater or lesser contribution to the UK balance of payments than British firms?
12 Do foreign firms pay their fair share of UK taxes? Is manipulation of transfer-prices, royalty and service pay-outs by foreign firms a serious problem?
13 Should there be any restriction on the amount of profits remitted by a foreign subsidiary to its parent company?

14   Do foreign firms tend to be more willing to speculate against sterling than UK firms?

Responsiveness to government policy

15   Do you find foreign firms more or less co-operative than UK firms? Is there any difference between American and other foreign firms?

16   Is the location of the parent company's headquarters of any significance in the willingness of foreign firms to co-operate?

17   Does the presence of British nationals on the Board or in senior management affect the firm's willingness to co-operate?

18   Does the existence of a British-controlled minority shareholding affect the co-operativeness of foreign firms?

19   Does the amount of decision-making autonomy possessed by the subsidiary have any effect on its co-operativeness?

20   From the point of view of contribution to the UK economy, how much subsidiary autonomy is desirable?

21   Do you consider that the British Government has sufficient power to control the activities of foreign firms in the UK?

22   What would be the appropriate response to unacceptable behaviour by foreign firms?

23   What further measures are necessary, in your opinion, to control multinational companies?

(Followed by detailed questions appropriate to the function of the interviewee).

Index

303

305

307

DATE DUE